In the name of GOD
This book and its cassettes
have been produced
by
Christoph Bangert
and
I should like to thank
my wife **Chiho Bangert**
for unfailing encouragement
and support
Here
I want to express my gratitude to
my mother and father
and
to all my friends
(specially The New York Times)
who helped me
Thank you very much

Christoph Bangert
Photographer

RUMORS OF WAR

CHRISTOPH BANGERT

KEHRER

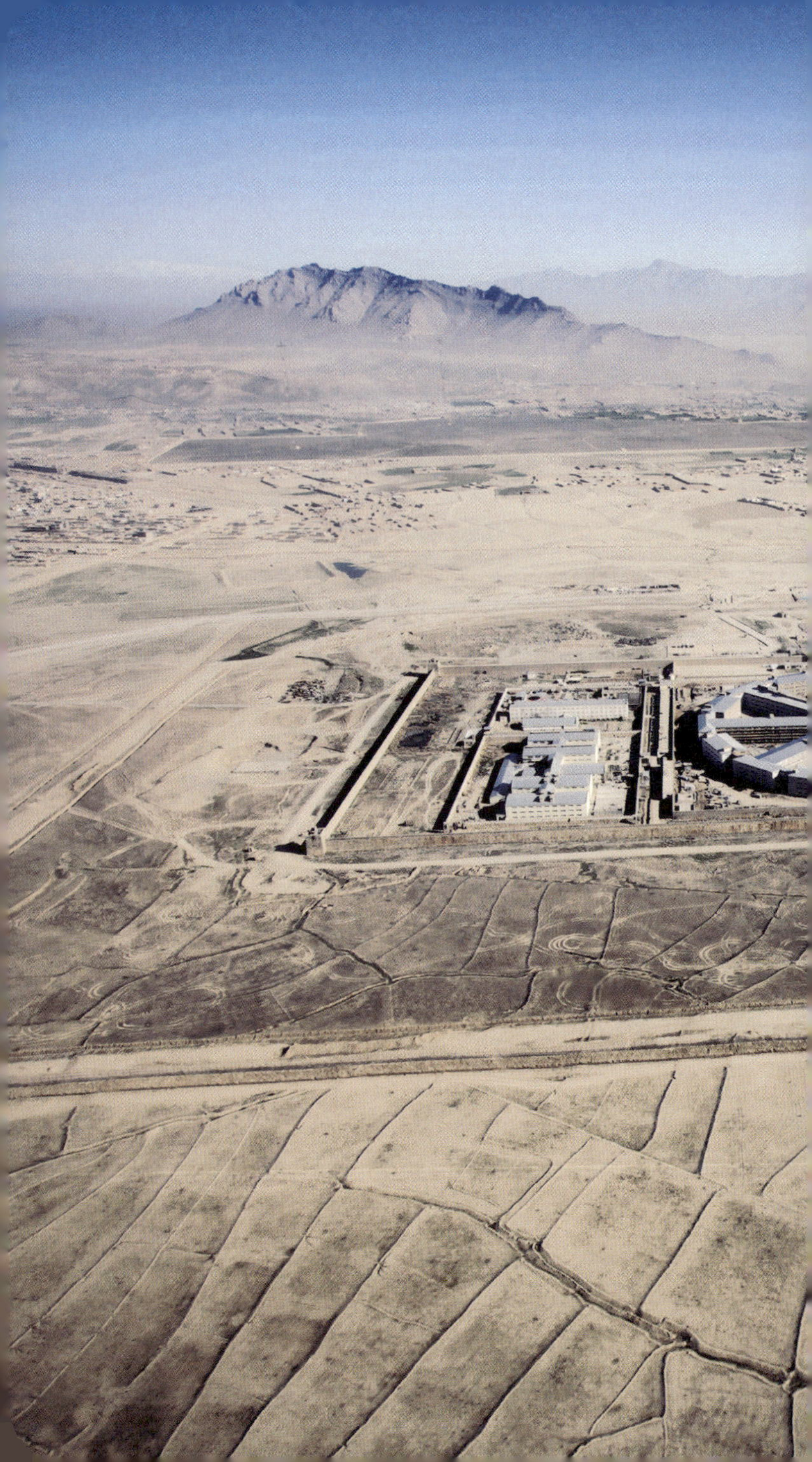

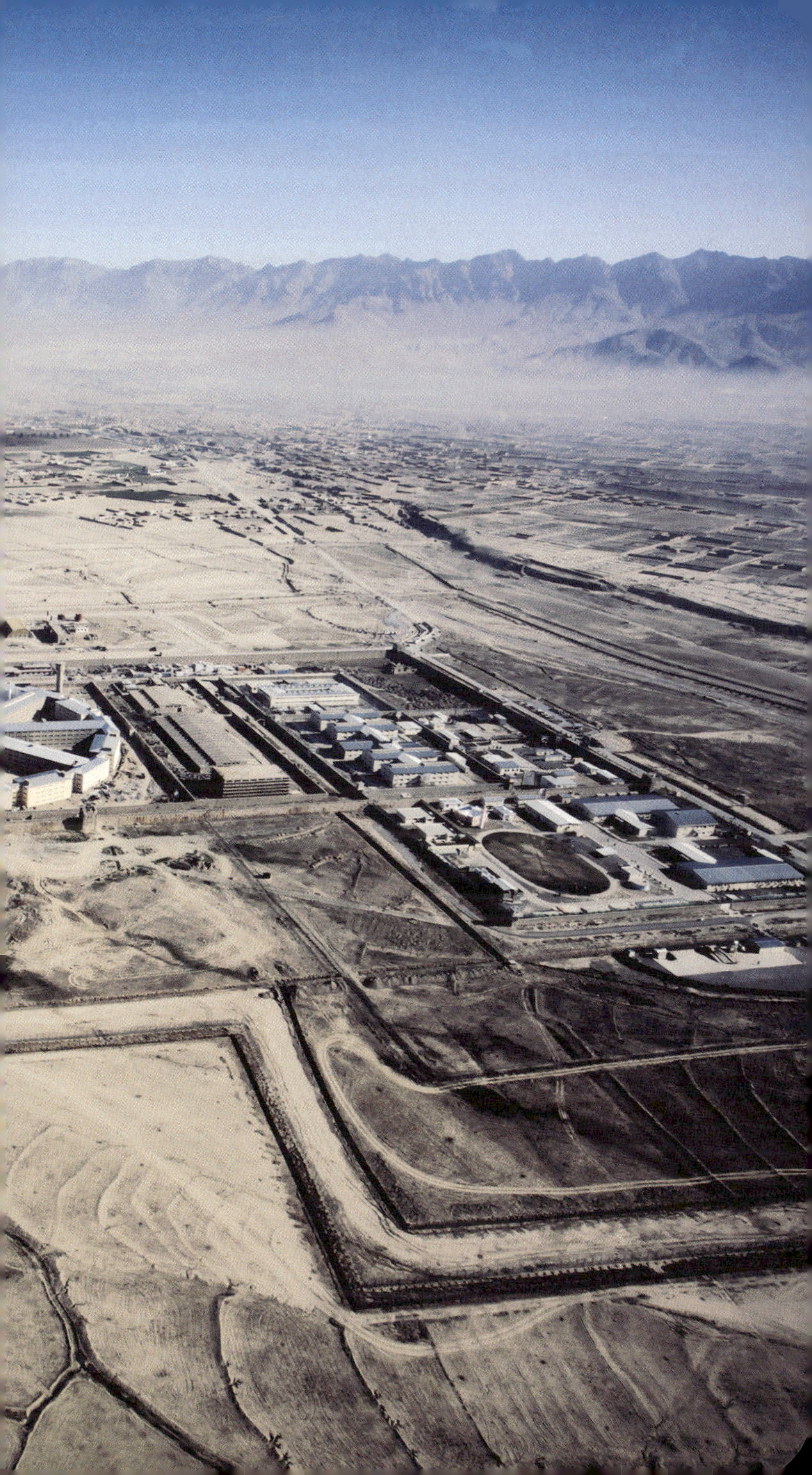

I miss war. Nothing is as raw. Nothing feels as real. I miss doing meaningful work and being able to witness political events with my own eyes. I miss the loyalty and self-sacrifice. Despite the hatred and horror. And yes, I miss the adventure of it, the excitement, the intensity and simplicity of life at war.

War is the greatest human folly on this planet. It is fueled by nationalism, racisms and fear. Since ancient times, generation after generation of soldiers, civilians and journalists who lived through war suffered the same dramatic disillusionment: The myth of war is shattered as soon as the killing starts and war reveals itself as what it really is—organized murder. Only those who witnessed war truly understand the misery, loneliness, trauma and death that it causes.

In his book *War Is a Force That Gives Us Meaning* the *New York Times* war correspondent Chris Hedges describes covering war as a highly addictive drug. But it is not the adrenaline rush and excitement of battle that makes war something we long for and we miss as soon as it is over. It is an overwhelming sense of purpose and meaning that draws us back to war time and again.

War took its toll on me. It wore me down. It fucked me up. But the greatest problem with covering wars was that I forced my family and friends to go through hell. It is crucial for any functioning society to find journalists who volunteer to work in difficult circumstances and report truthfully on relevant issues. But covering war is always also an inherently selfish endeavor.

So I decided to try peace. I'm struggling with the banality of everyday life at home: numbing bureaucracy, consumerism, small mindedness, insecurities, backstabbing and petty problems. Mixed with PTSD and nightmares.

It will probably take the rest of my life to work this out. I'm trying to be a good husband and father. Without my family I'd be completely lost. I also started a photography school on wheels. I'm driving an old blue bus to magical places. I call it teaching, but I'm basically just listening to the students and creating experiences. Maybe even reasons to live. The idea is to use photography as a tool to connect young people from different cultures, classes and backgrounds. So they may find meaning in each other.

It will be a struggle to figure out peace. There will be setbacks. But one thing I'm sure about: I will never go to war again.

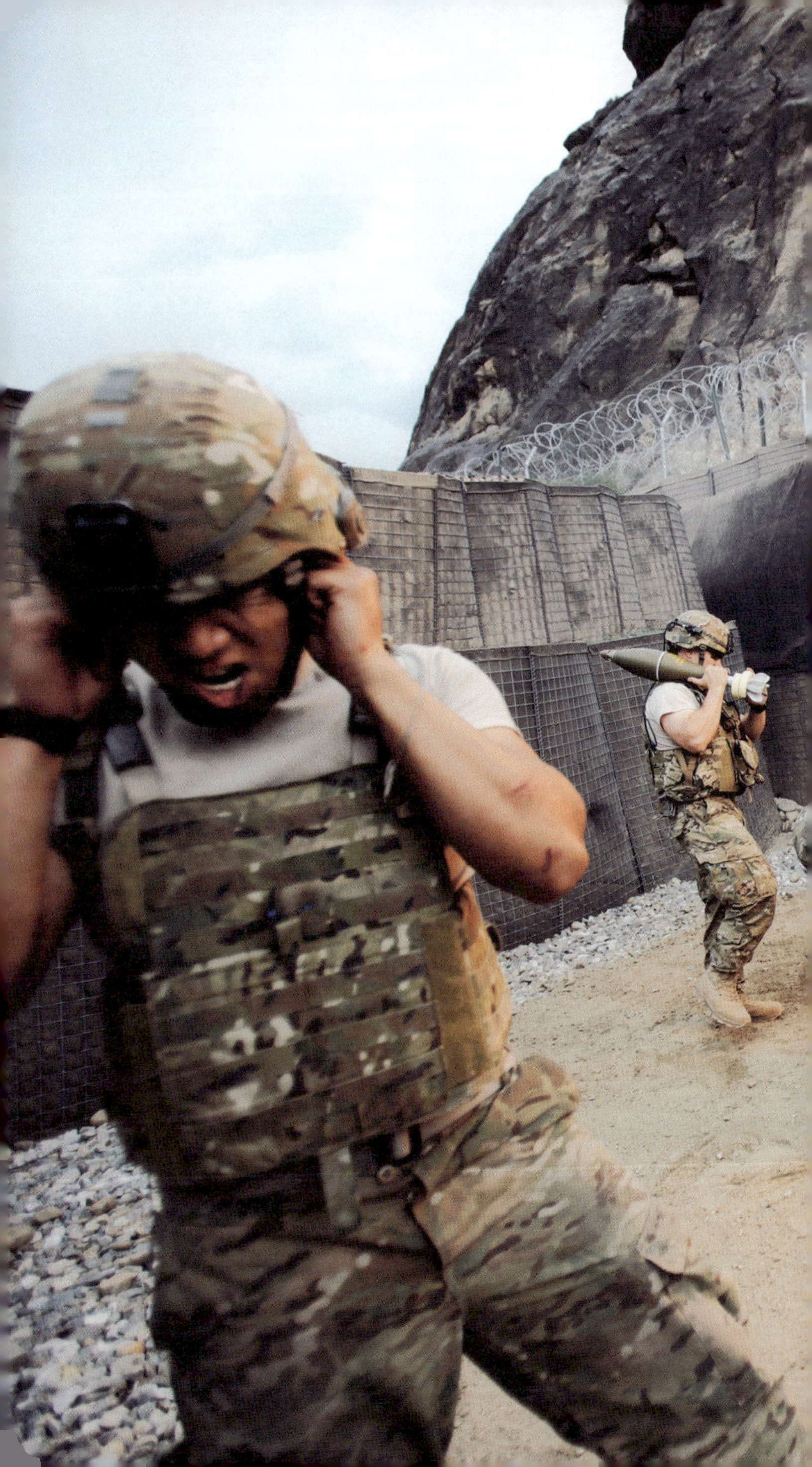

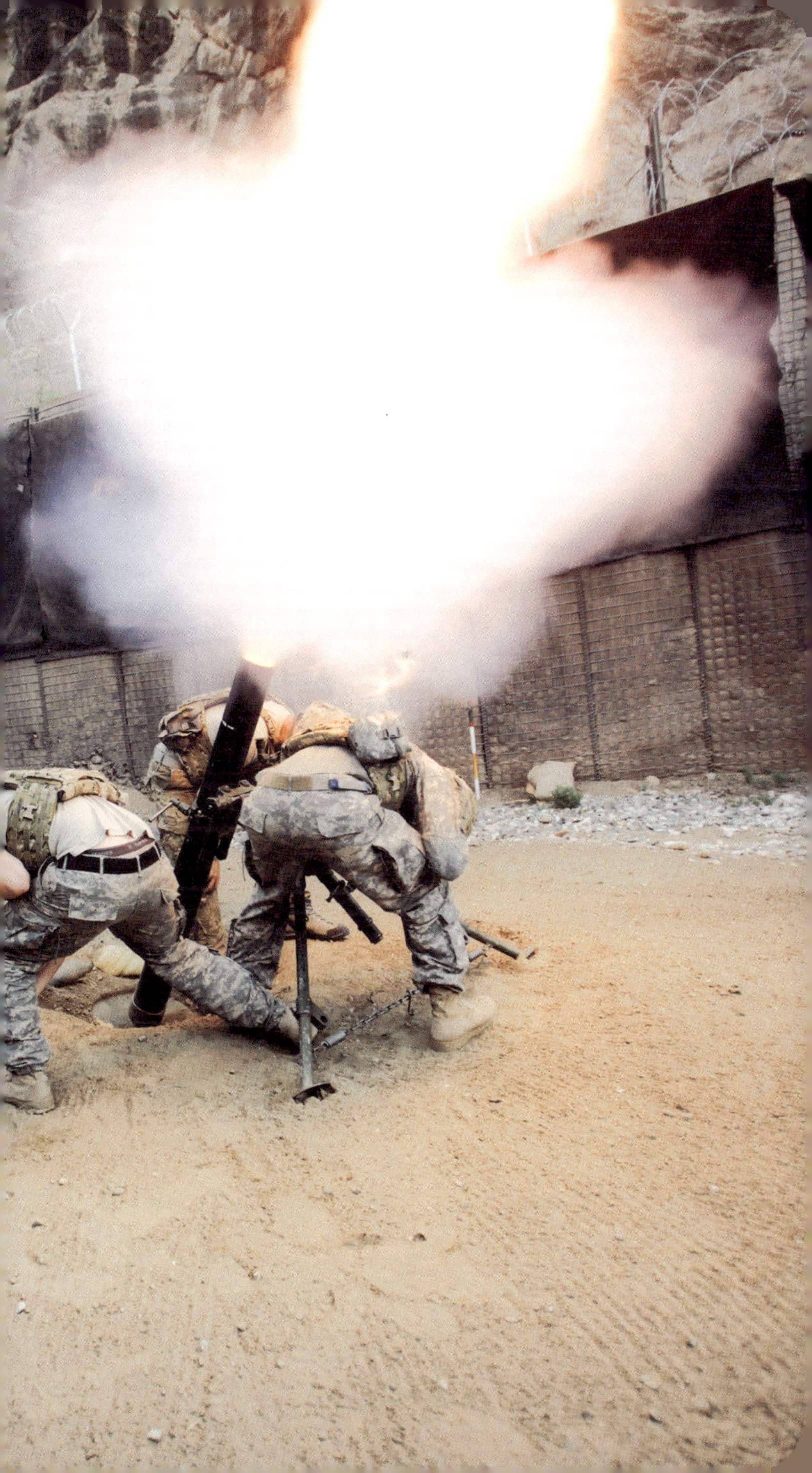

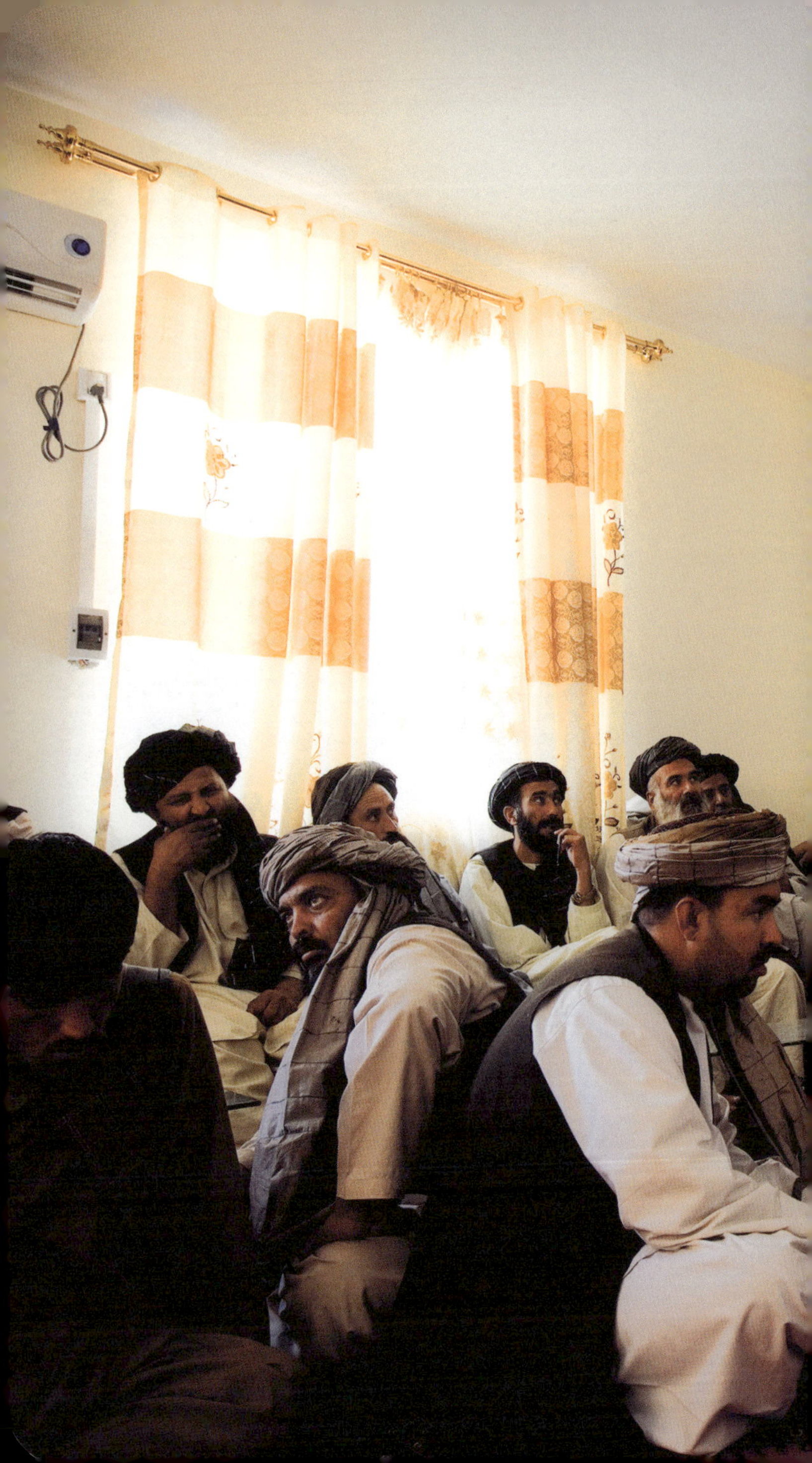

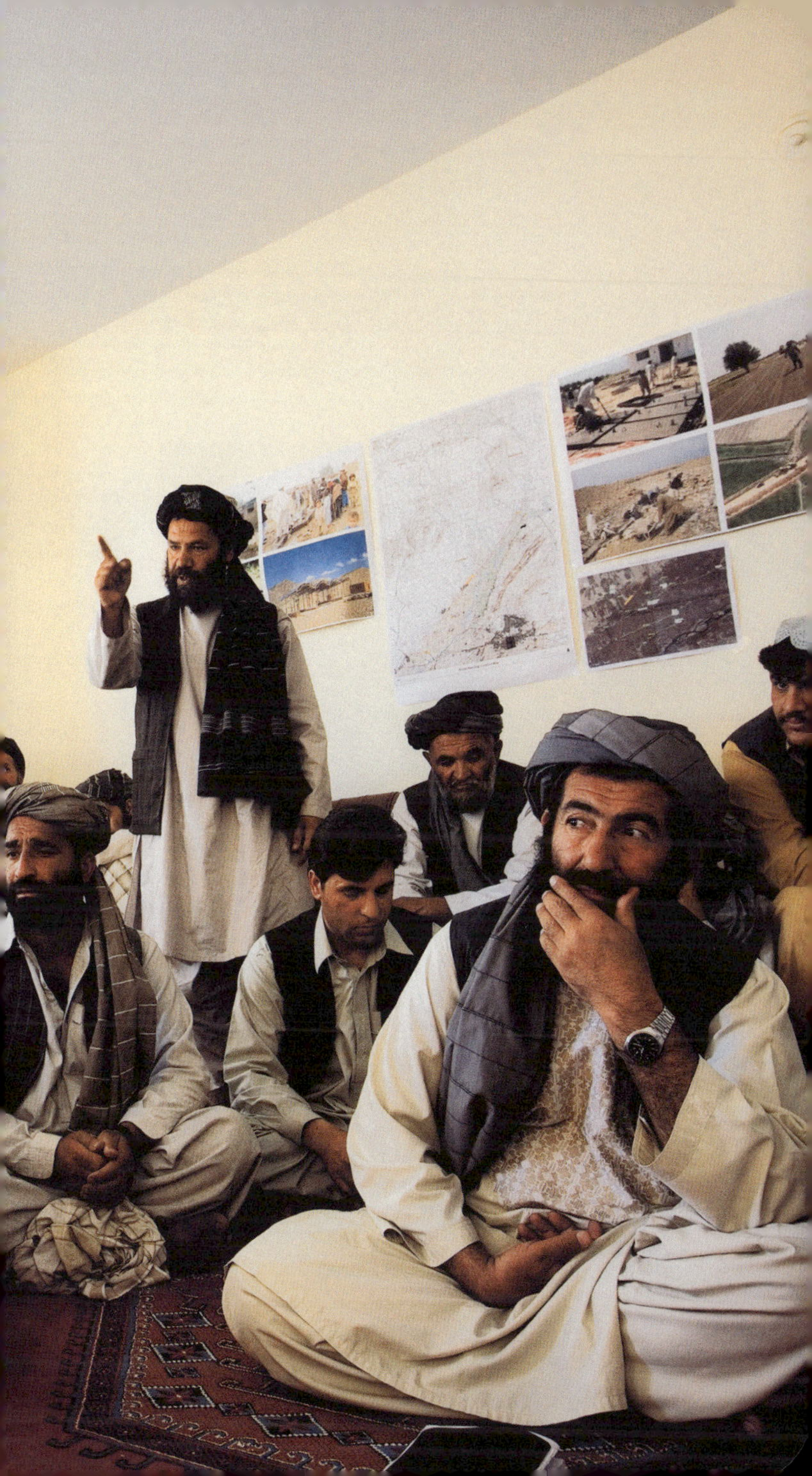

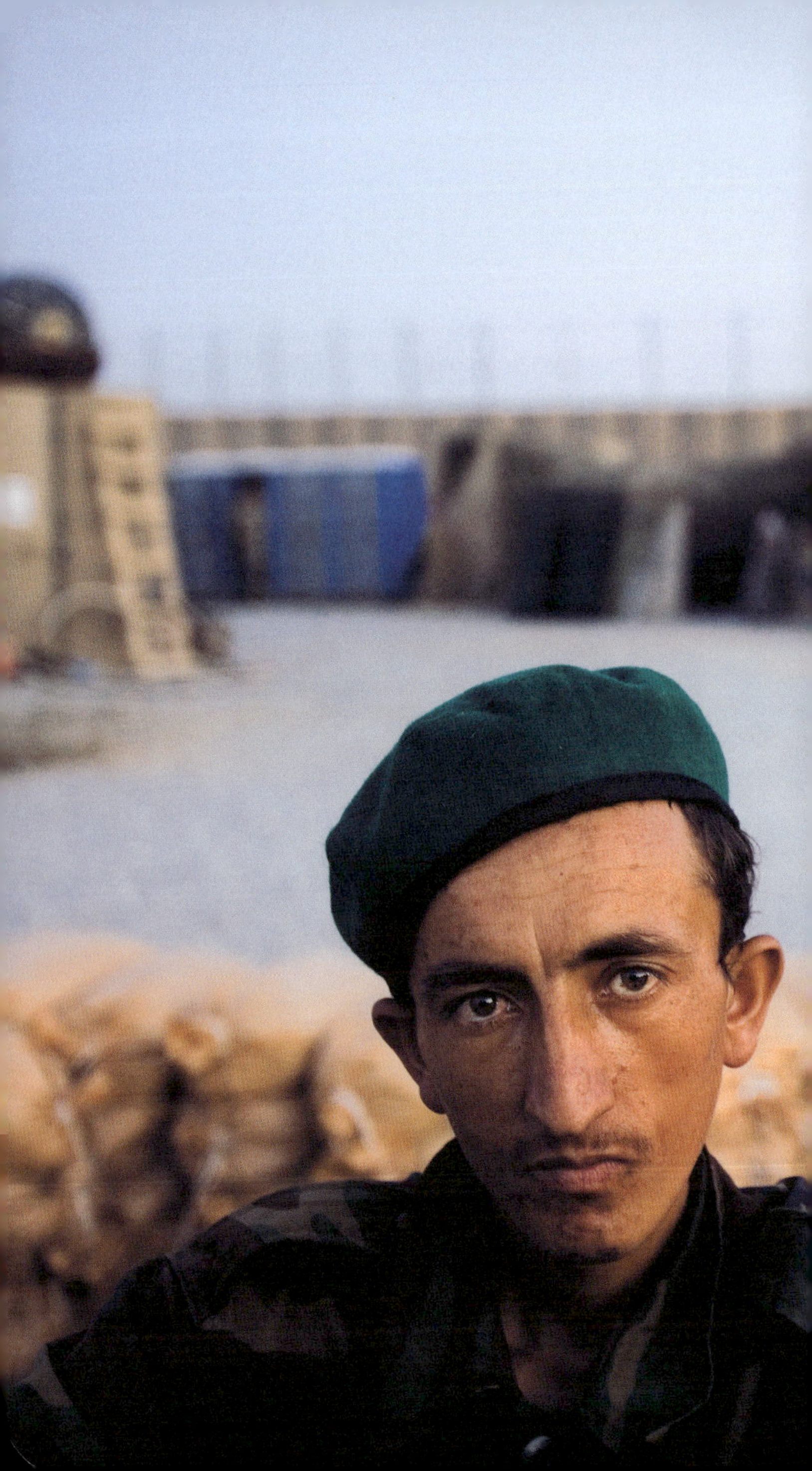

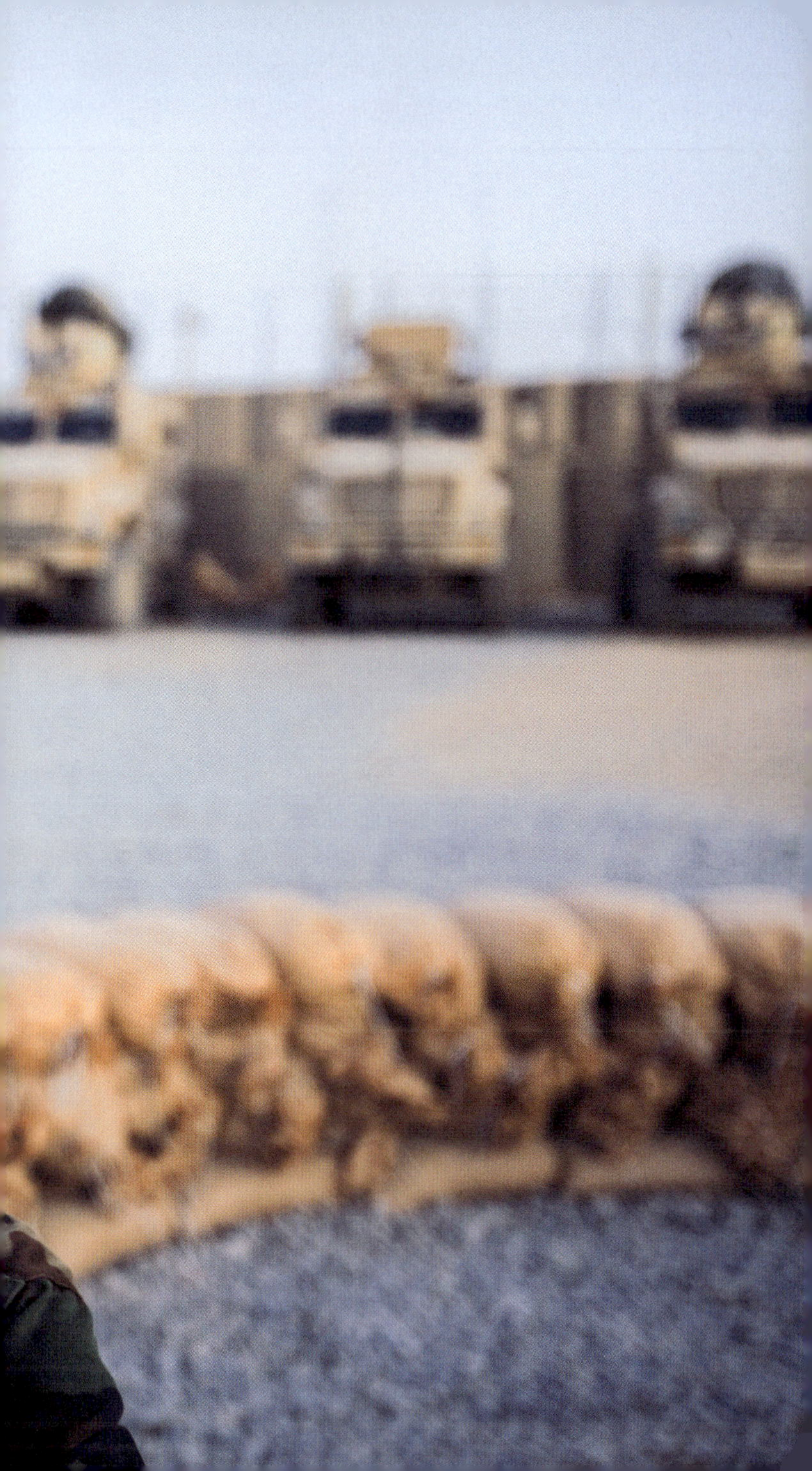

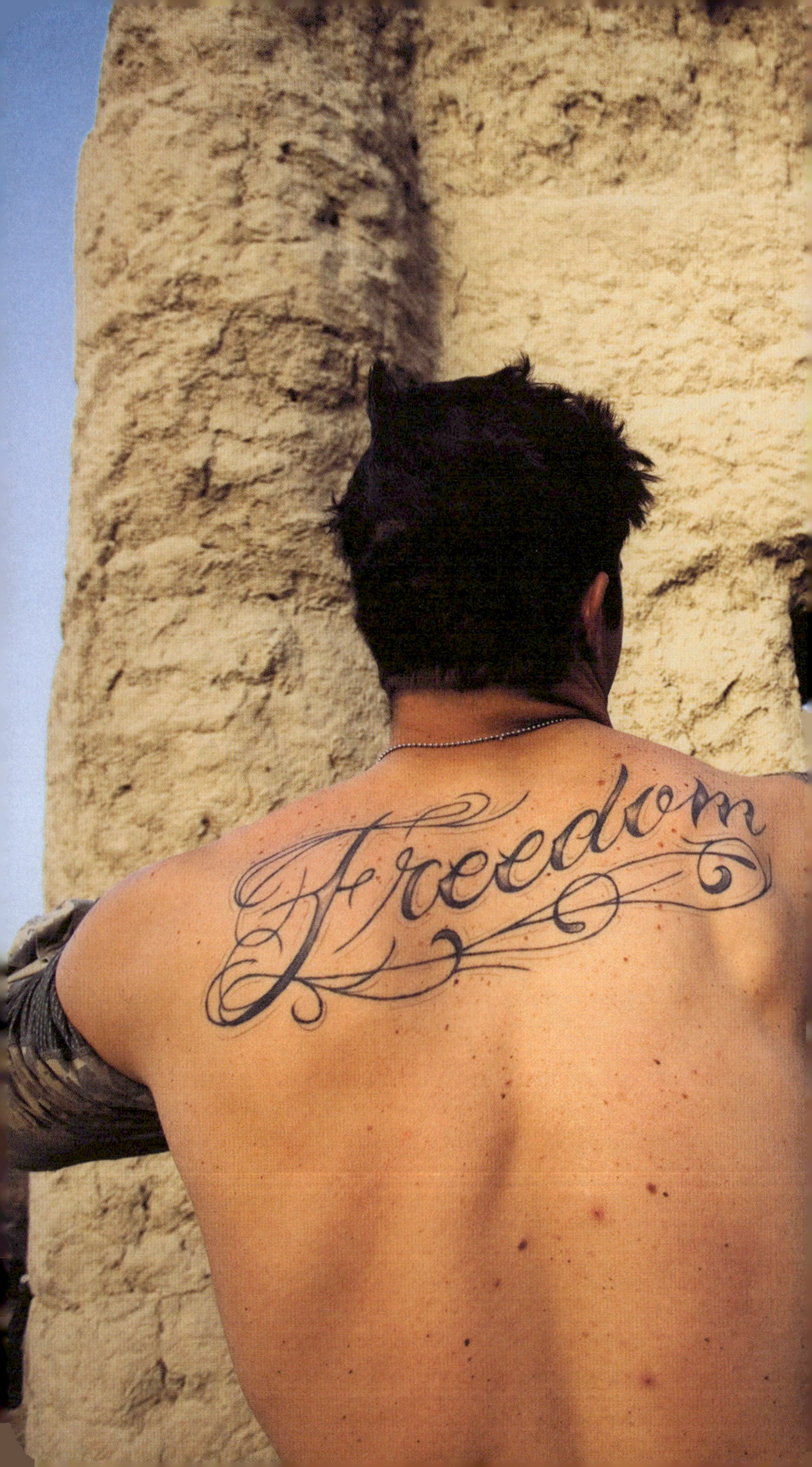
Freedom

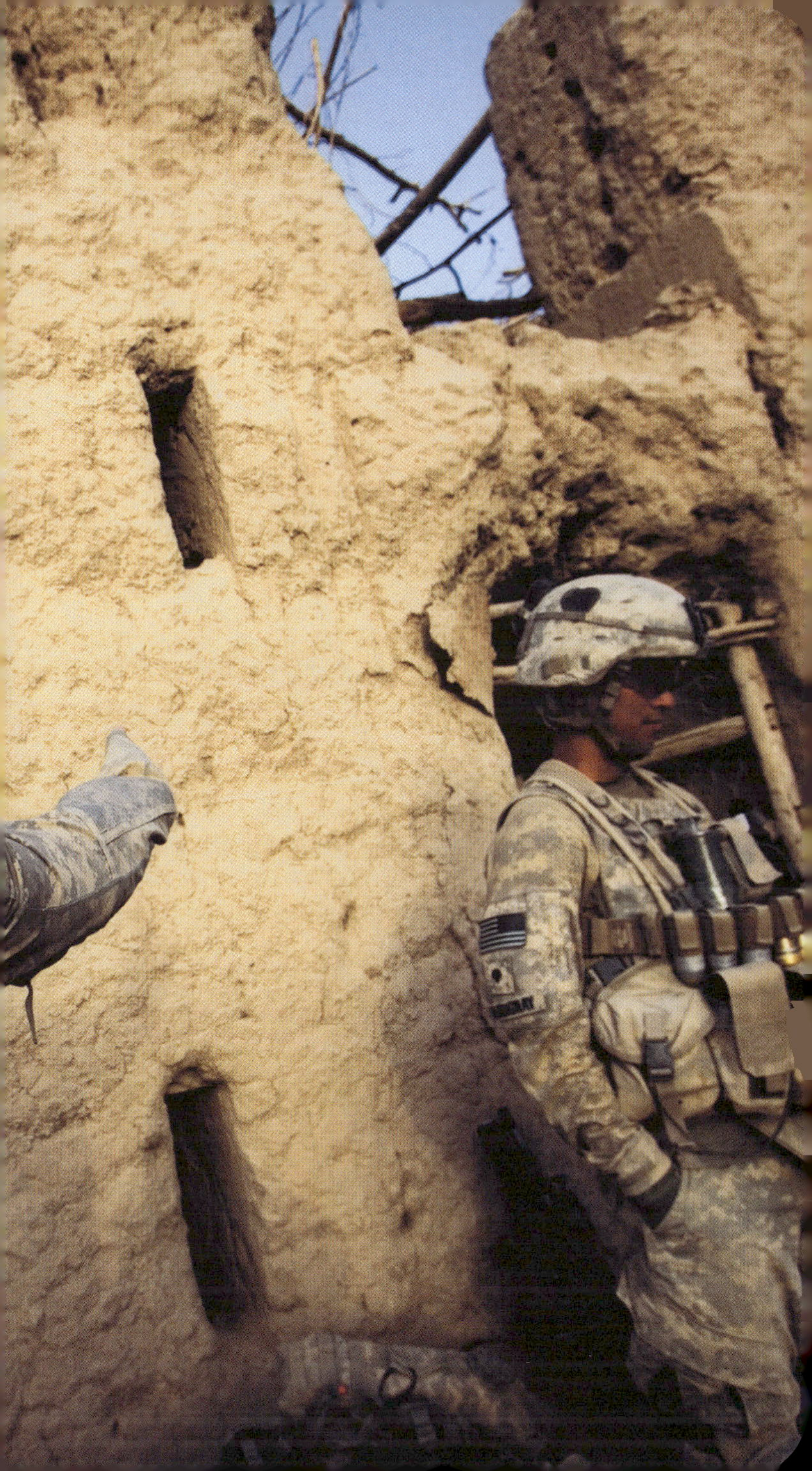

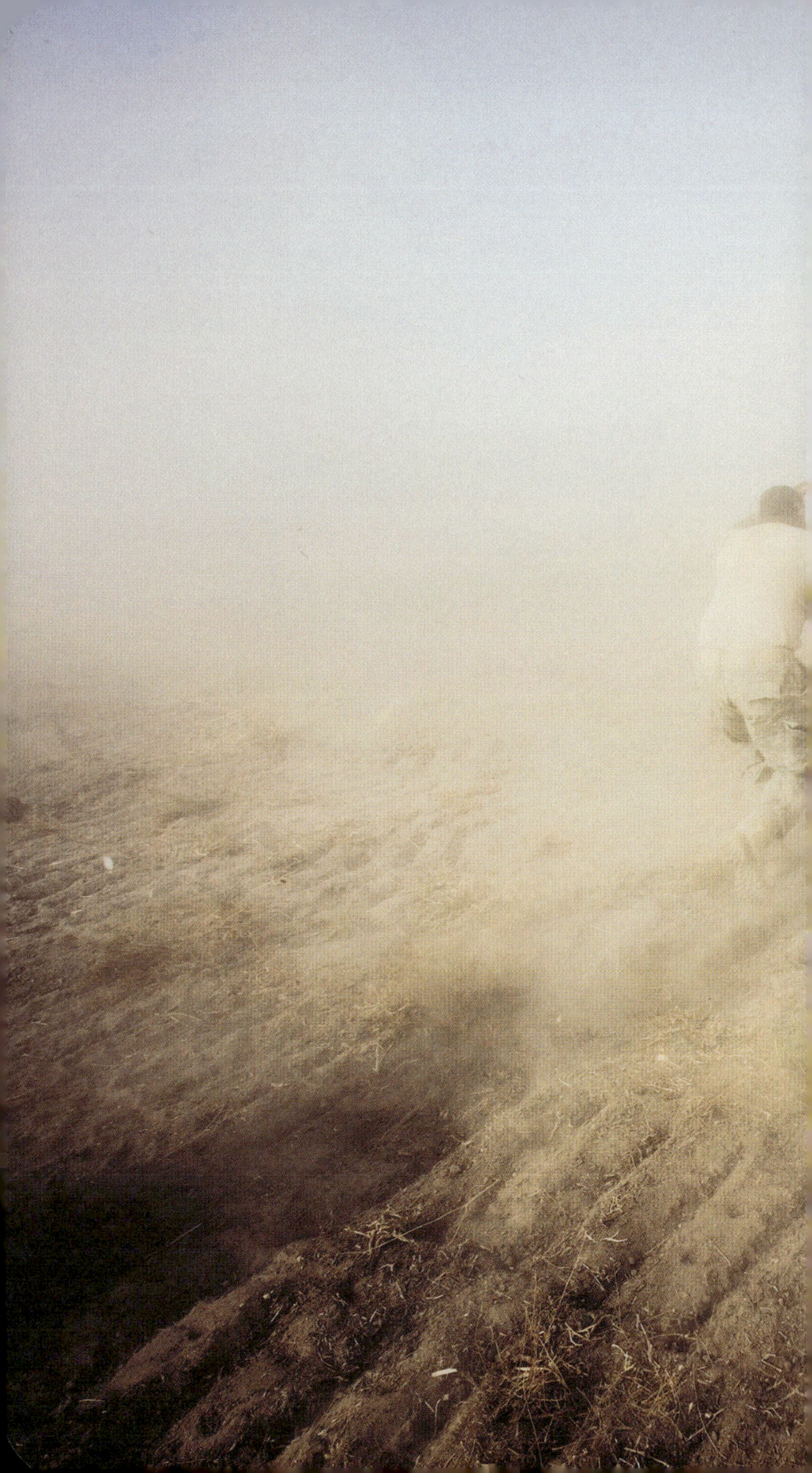

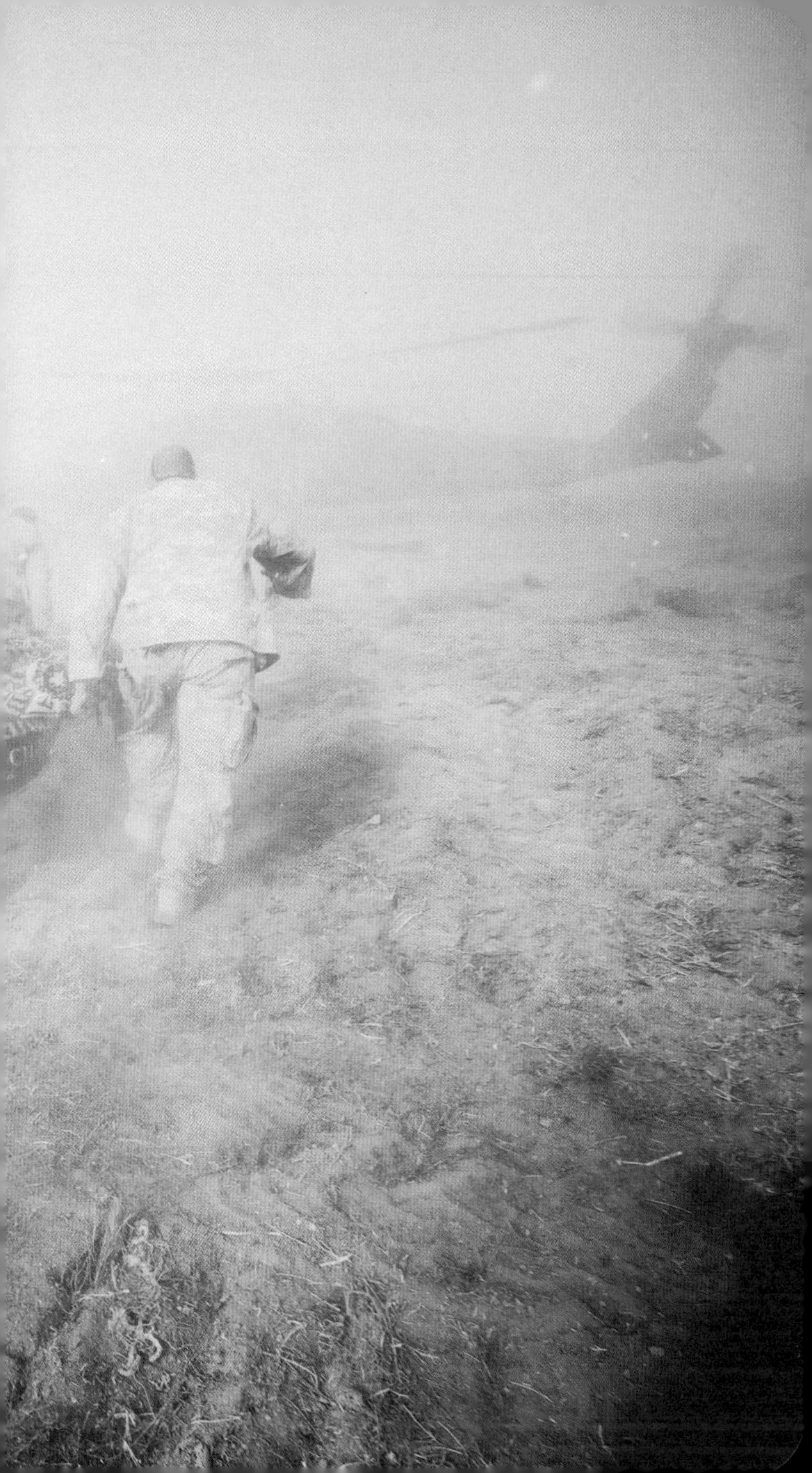

24. Juni 2013, on the plane to Istanbul

Here we go again. I hope this is not going to be one of the many journal-notebooks that are only 1/8 the filled and are today decorating my book shelf. This is another attempt of keeping a real journal on my travels. And this journal will be different, because for the first time it's a visual journal. I brought my brand new Fuji instax mini camera, and I'm intending to use it...

I'm on my way to Afghanistan. I can't believe I'm going back there.

'll be working
for these people →
again for six weeks.
believe I'm now
e longest-serving
Iraq/Afghanistan -NYT-
otation photographer.
verybody else stopped
overing wars, like
ike Kamber, ~~Jeff~~ Ben
owy, Scott Nelson or
no longer working
r the paper like
Jehad Nga, Eros Hoagland,
x Becherer. Others got
jured like Joao or
uit photography, like
Johan. Anyway –

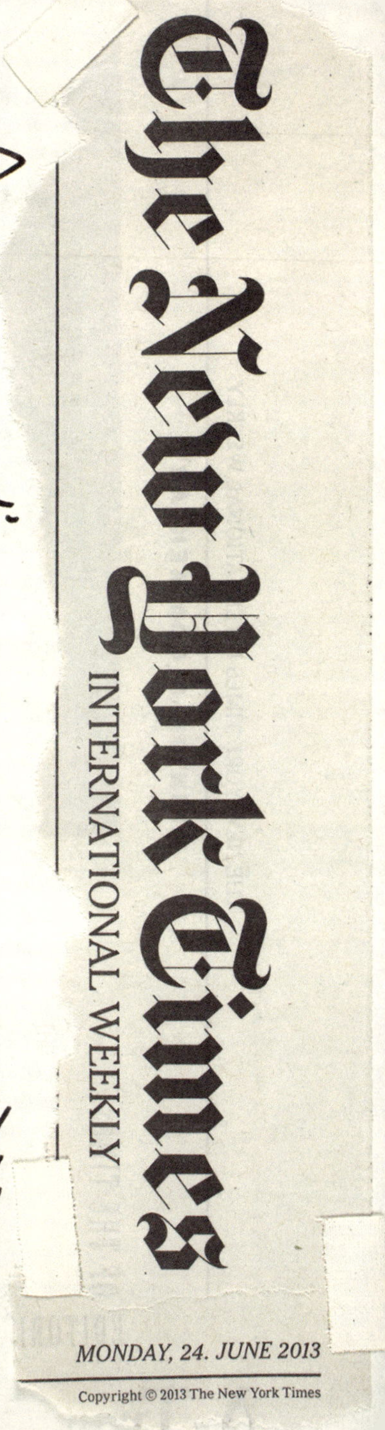
The New York Times
INTERNATIONAL WEEKLY
MONDAY, 24. JUNE 2013

It makes me feel kind of old. And slightly ~~a~~ suspicious. Why am I the last one standing? Is it because I am the only one who is diplomatic enough to deal with all the NYT-madness for so long? Or is it plain stupidity? I guess my long breaks in 2007/2008 in Africa and again in 2012 ~~—~~ contributed to me being able to still do this work. And when all is said and done it's a good thing, I guess. The New York Times is my Life Magazine.

I should use it. And produce!

The last few days were busy. They are always busy. The days before my departure.

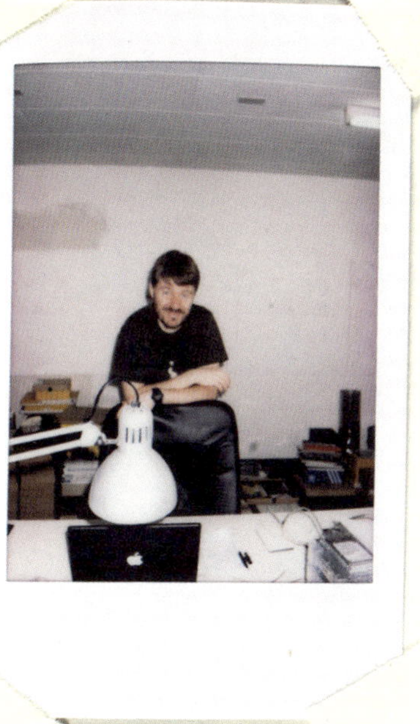

This is me in our office. I love that place. I'm very grateful to have found a true working space, where I can edit, write, think, plan and envision (dream).

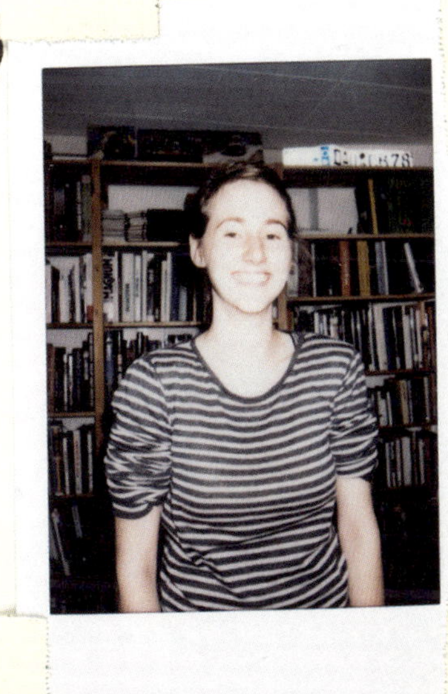

This is Lena. ⟶ She has been working with [illegible] and me for the last three months or so. I asked her to archive and re-pack a large part of my analog archive. Lena put thousands of slides and negatives into sleeves and filed them into archival folders. A gigantic task, but now it's a huge relief to have everything properly stored.

This is a copy of my Afghan visa:

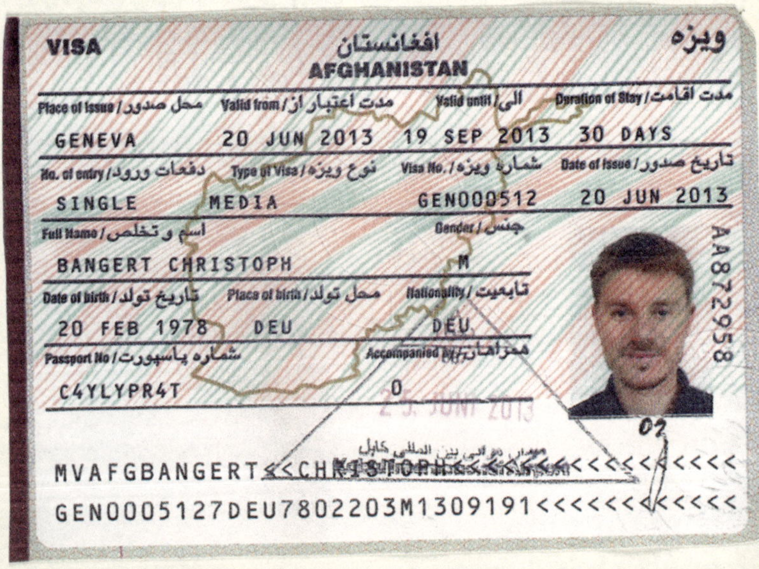
VISA افغانستان ویزه
AFGHANISTAN

Place of issue / محل صدور	Valid from / مدت اعتبار از	Valid until / الی	Duration of Stay / مدت اقامت
GENEVA	20 JUN 2013	19 SEP 2013	30 DAYS

No. of entry / دفعات ورود	Type of Visa / نوع ویزه	Visa No. / شماره ویزه	Date of issue / تاریخ صدور
SINGLE	MEDIA	GEN000512	20 JUN 2013

Full Name / اسم و تخلص: BANGERT CHRISTOPH
Gender / جنس: M

Date of birth / تاریخ تولد	Place of birth / محل تولد	Nationality / تابعیت
20 FEB 1978	DEU	DEU

Passport No / شماره پاسپورت: C4YLYPR4T
Accompanied by / همراهان: 0

AA8722958

25. JUNI 2013

MVAFGBANGERT<<CHRISTOPH<<<<<<<<<<<<<<<<<<<<
GEN0005127DEU7802203M1309191<<<<<<<<<<<<<<

It was a huge drama to get it this time. It's just a cheap sticker in my passport.

but boy, it took me about 20 phone calls and a last minute drive to Geneva (6 hours!) to get it. Bloody bureaucracy. Bloody self-serving, incompetent, lazy, fat bureaucrats.

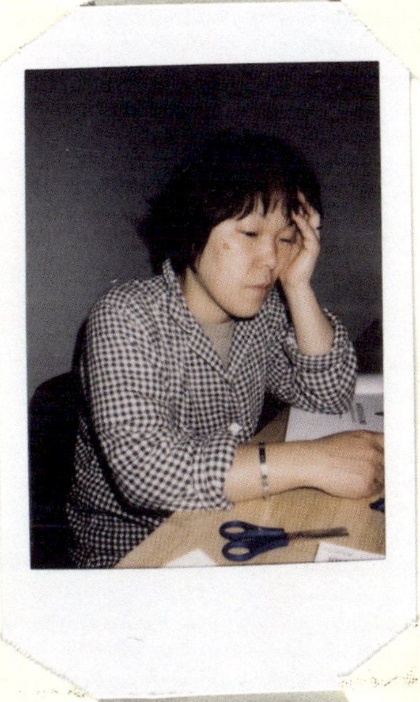

Chiho late at night. Exhausted. She is the hardest working person in the family. She does most of the work with the children. She cleans and washes and cooks. She sleeps very little and works about three days a week in the office, designing websites and doing all this other shit that I through at her. Without her, I would do nothing.

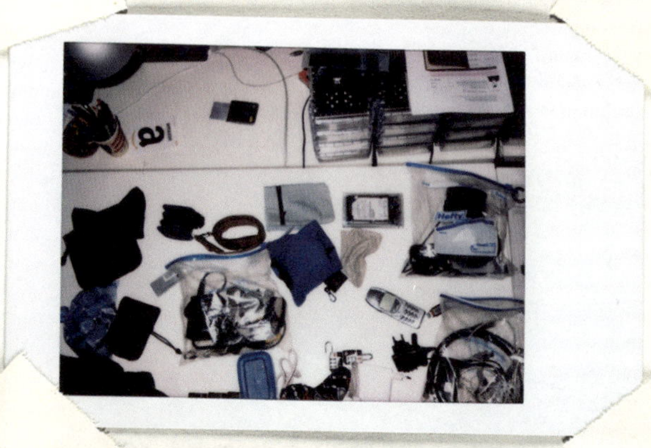

my stuff.

I'm working long hours, typically from 9:30 AM to 10:00 PM. But I like it that way. I love my work.

Money is a problem, but I don't care.

I'm living in one of the most capitalistic and materialistic societies in the world, Switzerland, and I really struggle with that very fact. Not sure if we'll stay forever. I'm still not into money. I'm into work. Photography. I'm planning to write a book about photography.

Today was the day of my departure. Always a tough day. A day filled with great doubts. Guilt. Fear. As soon as you're on the way everything's good. But the last day is hell.

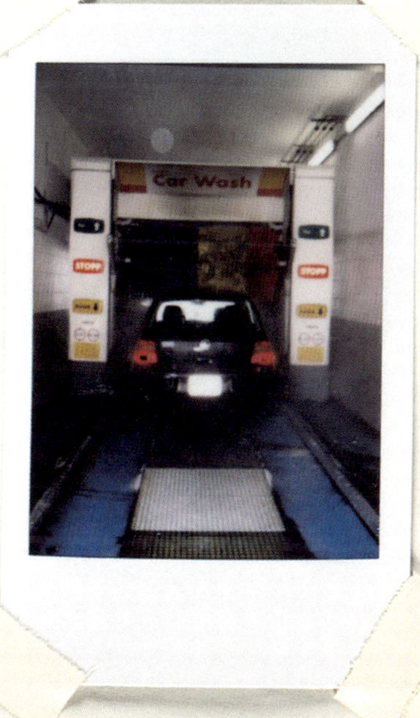

I went to wash my car before I left. I'm doing this for my father. It makes him happy if I wash my car.

Chiho was
with me and
she was holding
the antenna of
the car.

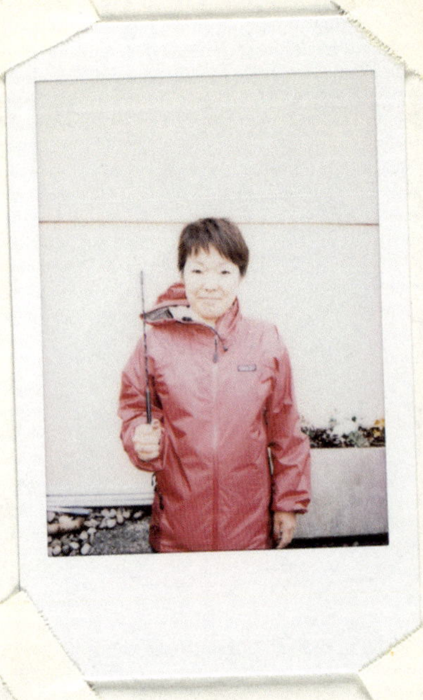

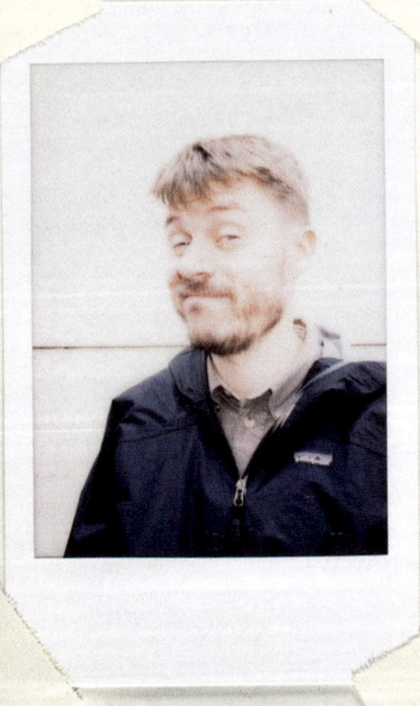

She was also
taking a picture
of me. I guess
that is what I
look like these
days....

I said goodbye to Lilli...

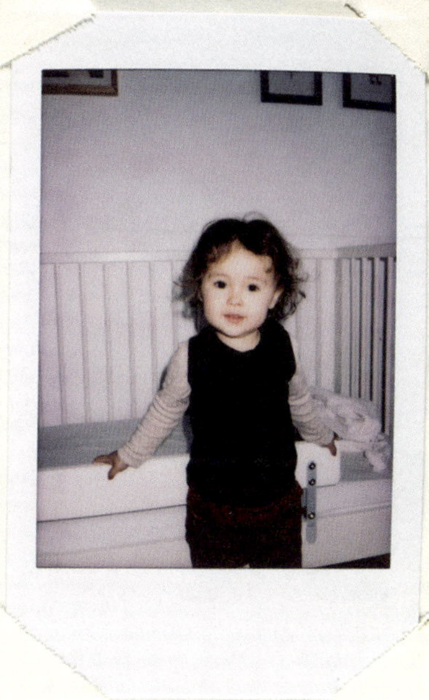

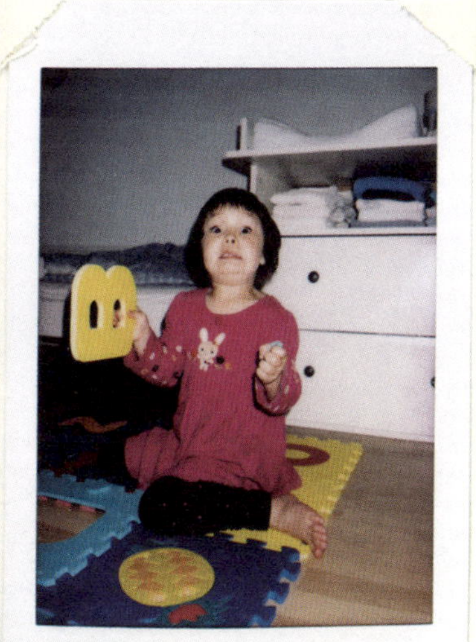

...and to Anna, who is doing her "scary face" for the camera.

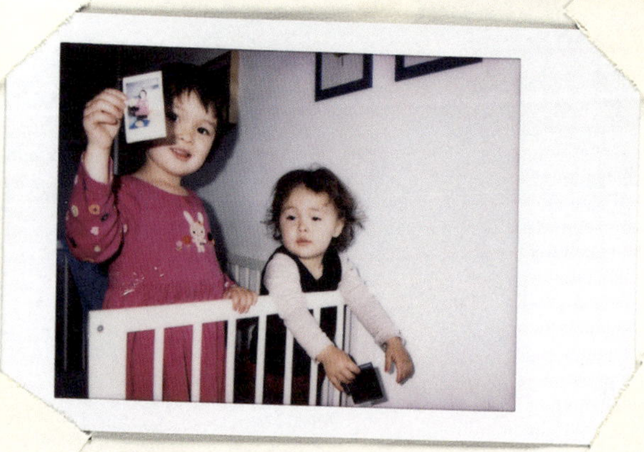

I love these two children.
They make me laugh every day. I miss them already, although it's just been a few hours since I took this picture.

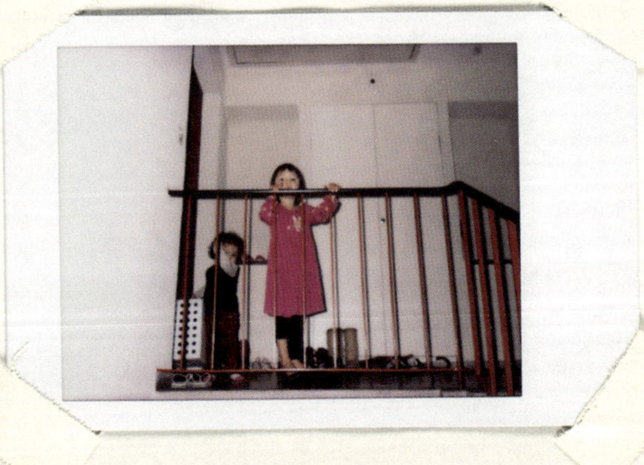

I wave goodbye.

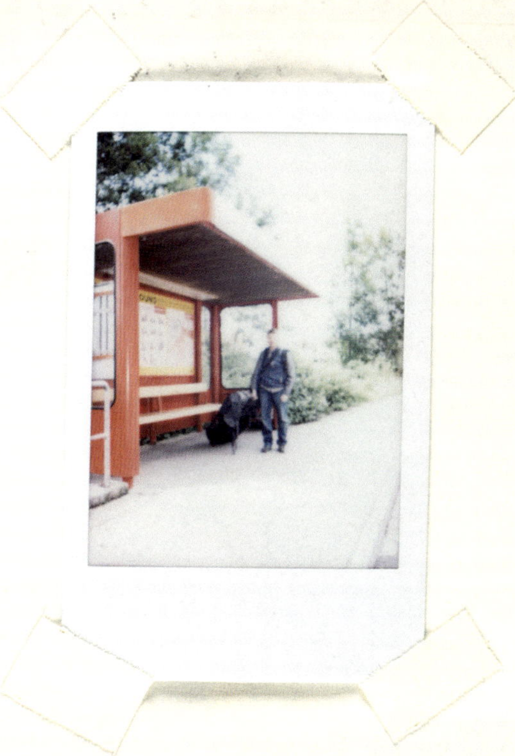

And I'm gone.

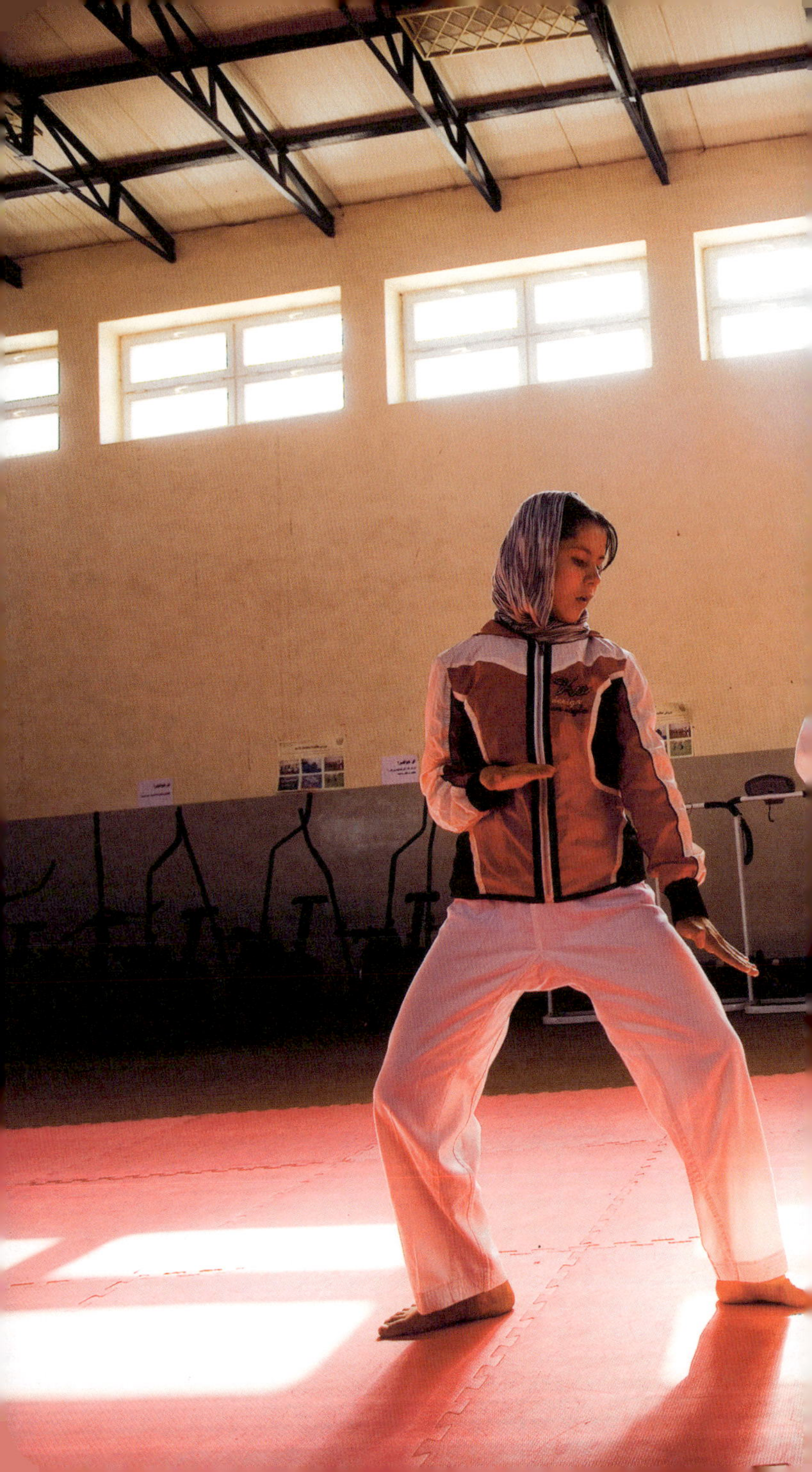

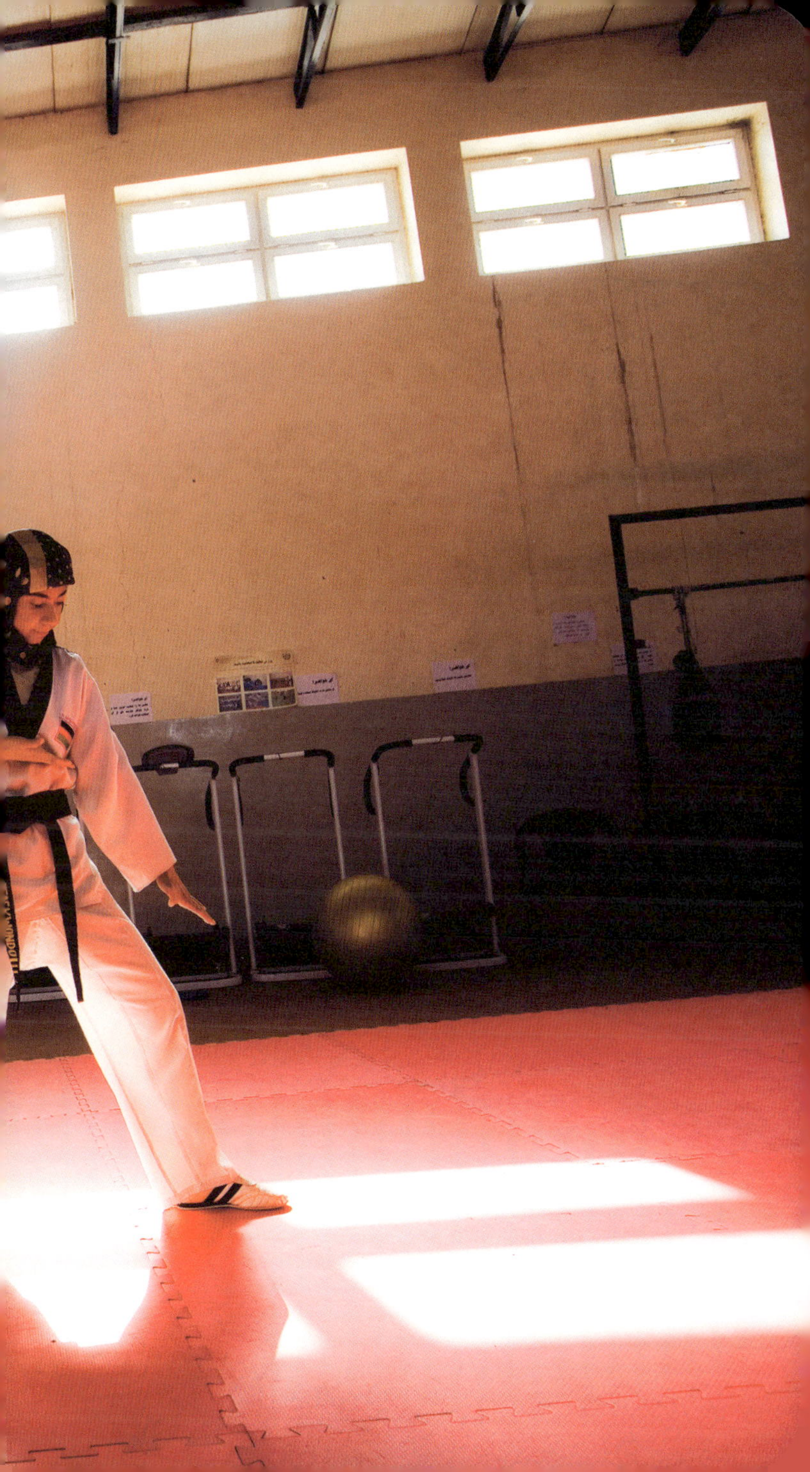

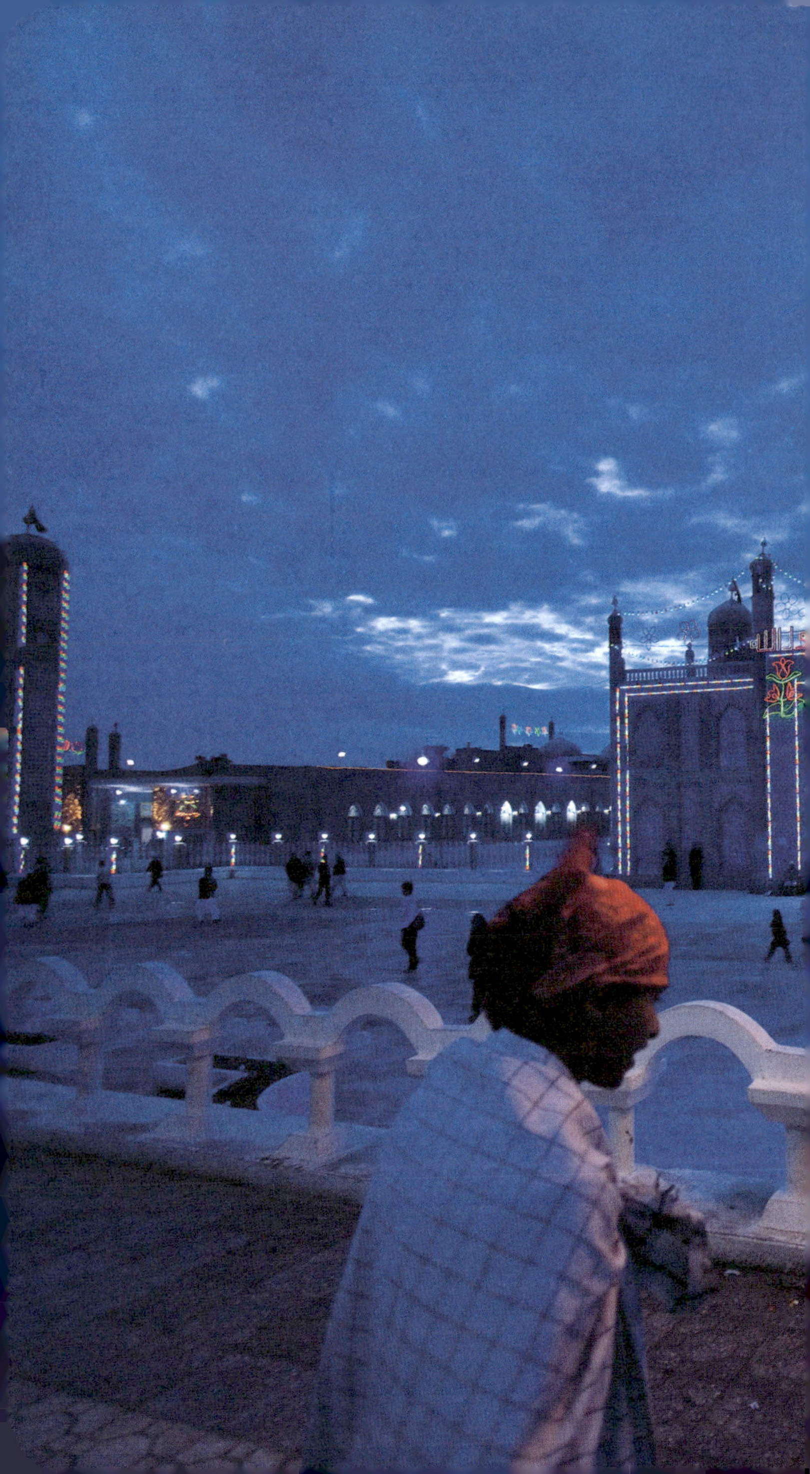

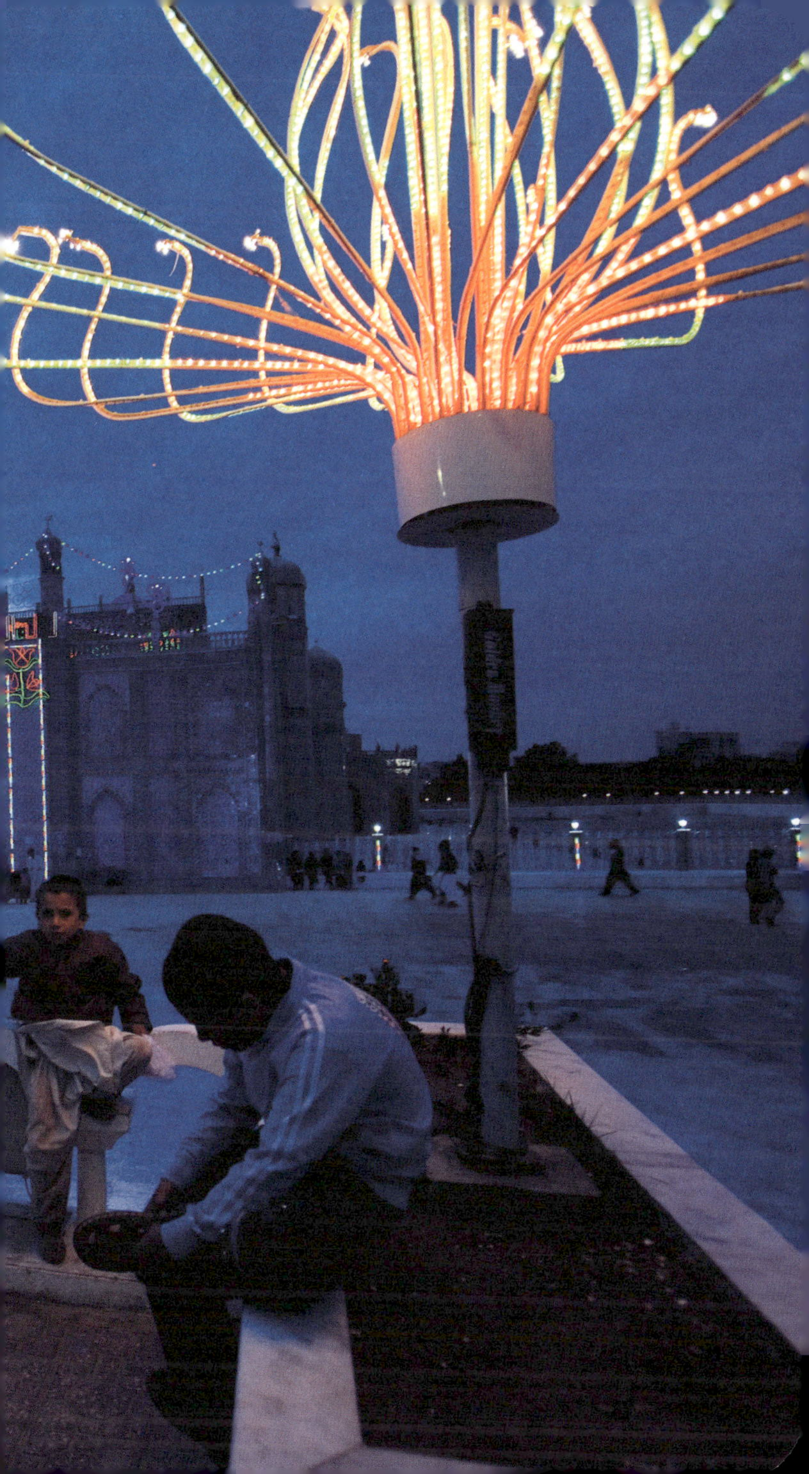

I take bus 811 to Uster Station. Train S5 to Zürich Station. Train S16 to Zürich Airport. Flight TK 1910 to Istanbul. Flight TK0706 to Kabul.

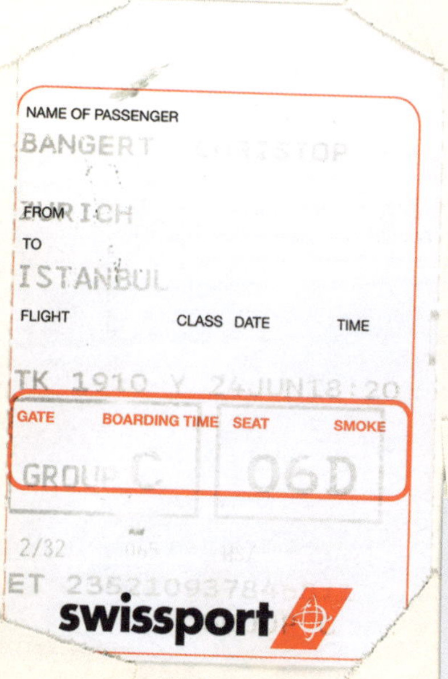
NAME OF PASSENGER
BANGERT CHRISTOP
FROM
ZURICH
TO
ISTANBUL

FLIGHT	CLASS	DATE	TIME
TK 1910	Y	24JUN	18:20

GATE	BOARDING TIME	SEAT	SMOKE
	GROUP C	06D	

2/32
ET 2352109378
swissport

I eat chicken and rice.

I leave the salad.

Airplanes. The ultimate
time machines.

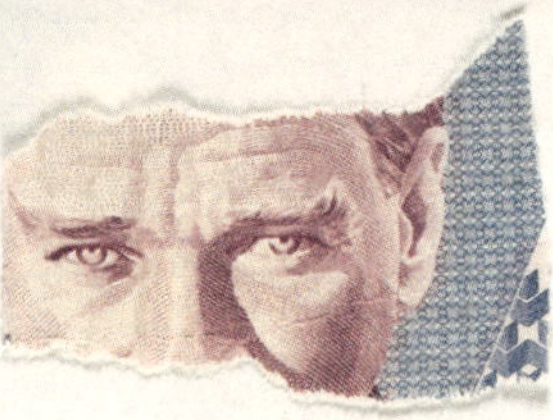

... and Atatürk smiles ...

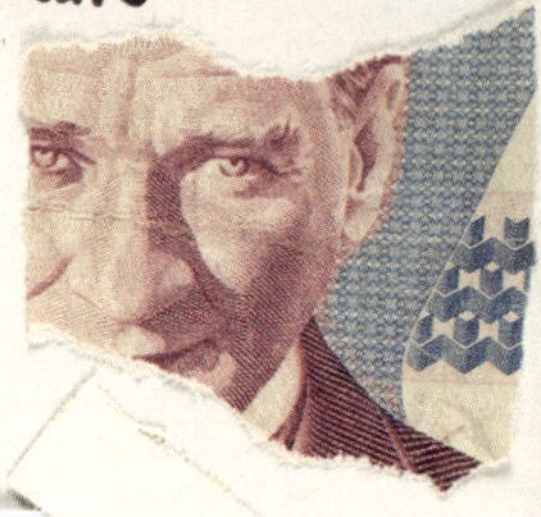

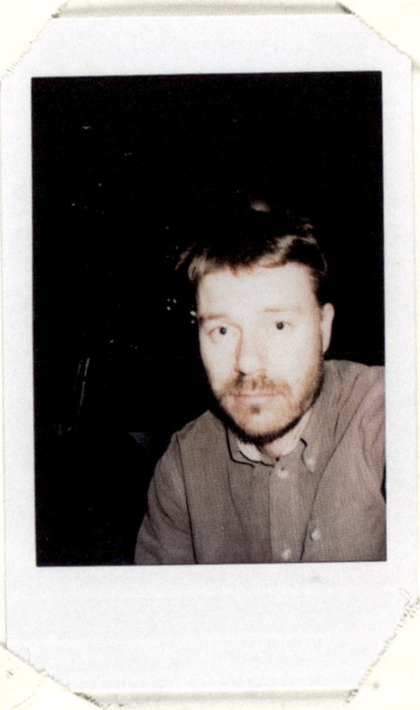

... and watches me ...

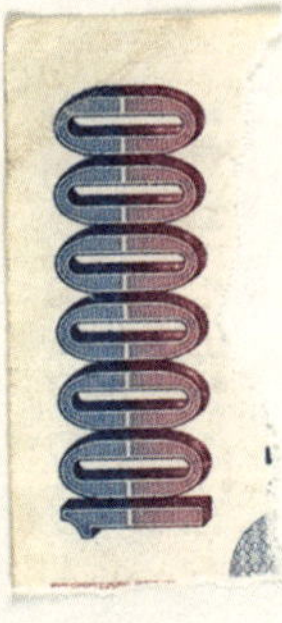

This is me at about 2:30 AM after spending four rather miserable hours "sleeping" on an impressively uncomfortable seat at Istanbul International Airport.

During my stop-over I try to get rid of some old turkish bank notes that I found in a shoe box at home. The clerk at the exchange counter looked at me. Looked at the money. Looked at me. And started laughing. I guess the bills are worthless by now...

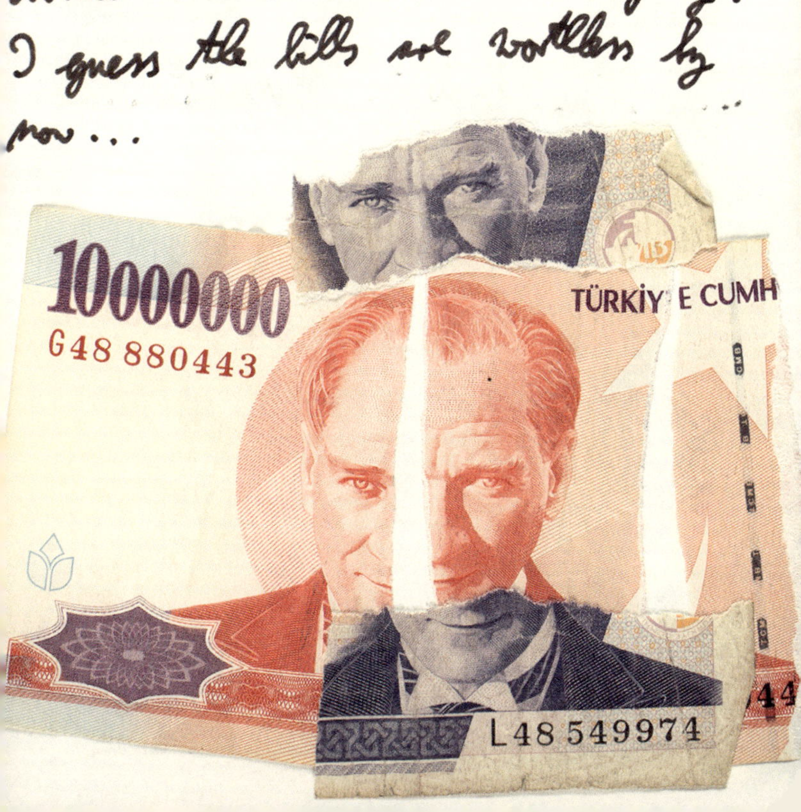

And suddenly ...

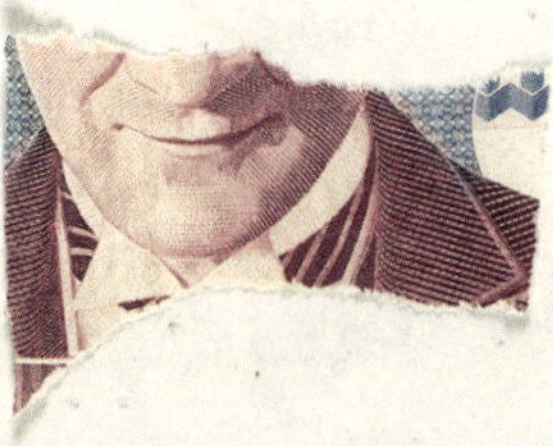

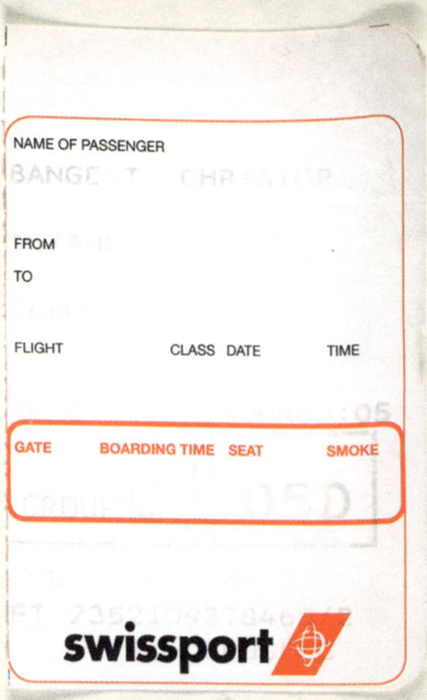

... I'm back in Afghanistan.

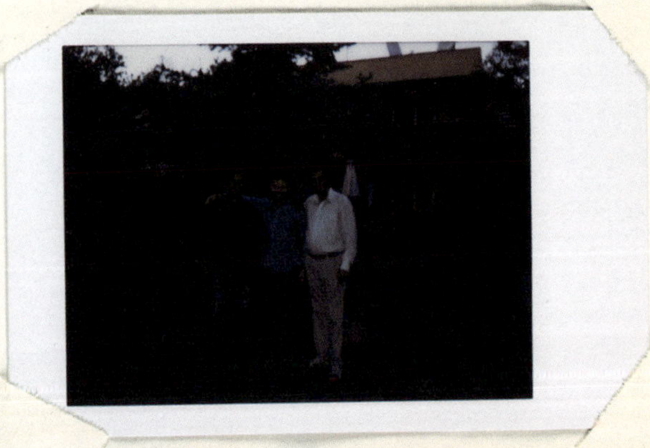

Reunited with some old friends.
Dr. Sangar and Saifullah and I in

the New York Times' house's garden. The gardener passed away. He was very old. His son has taken over his job. I wonder for how many generations the family has tended that ~~garden~~ beautiful garden. A romantic idea.

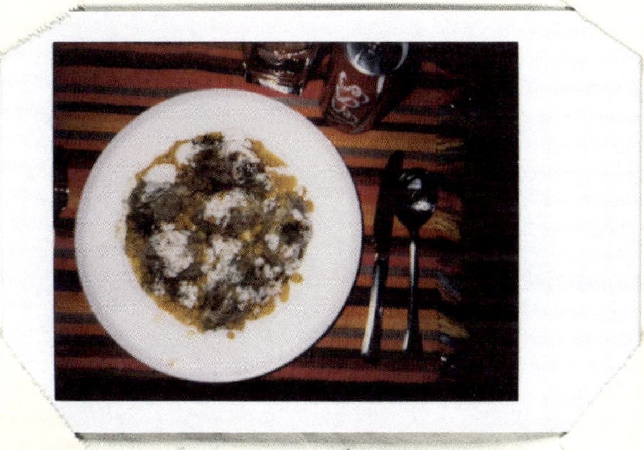

I eat my first Afghan meal in a long time. Dumplings filled with beef. Delicious! Sardar's cooking has improved much since my last visit. His father Haji retired.

I get an Afghan phone number and businesscards:

Christoph Bangert
Photographer

The New York Times

Kabul Bureau:
Afghanistan
Office Phone: 020 210 10 88
Mobile: +93(0)793-41-44-45
Email address: me@christophbangert.com

27.6.2013

I'm in the kitchen talking with Sadar, the cook. I like Sadar, he's a smart man. We talk about the Dhal he made and I ask him if he knows ful, the lentil mush eaten in the Middle East and North-Africa. And he goes: „Every thing has a fool."

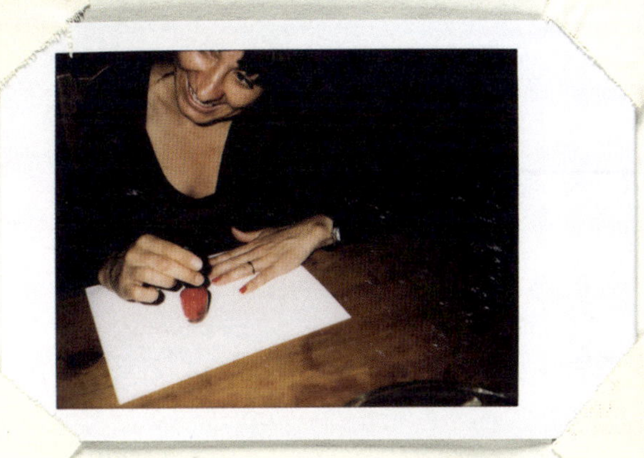

I'm photographing Lynsey Addario doing her nails. We overlapped for one day.
I enjoyed her company.

I'm actually happy to be back in Kabul.

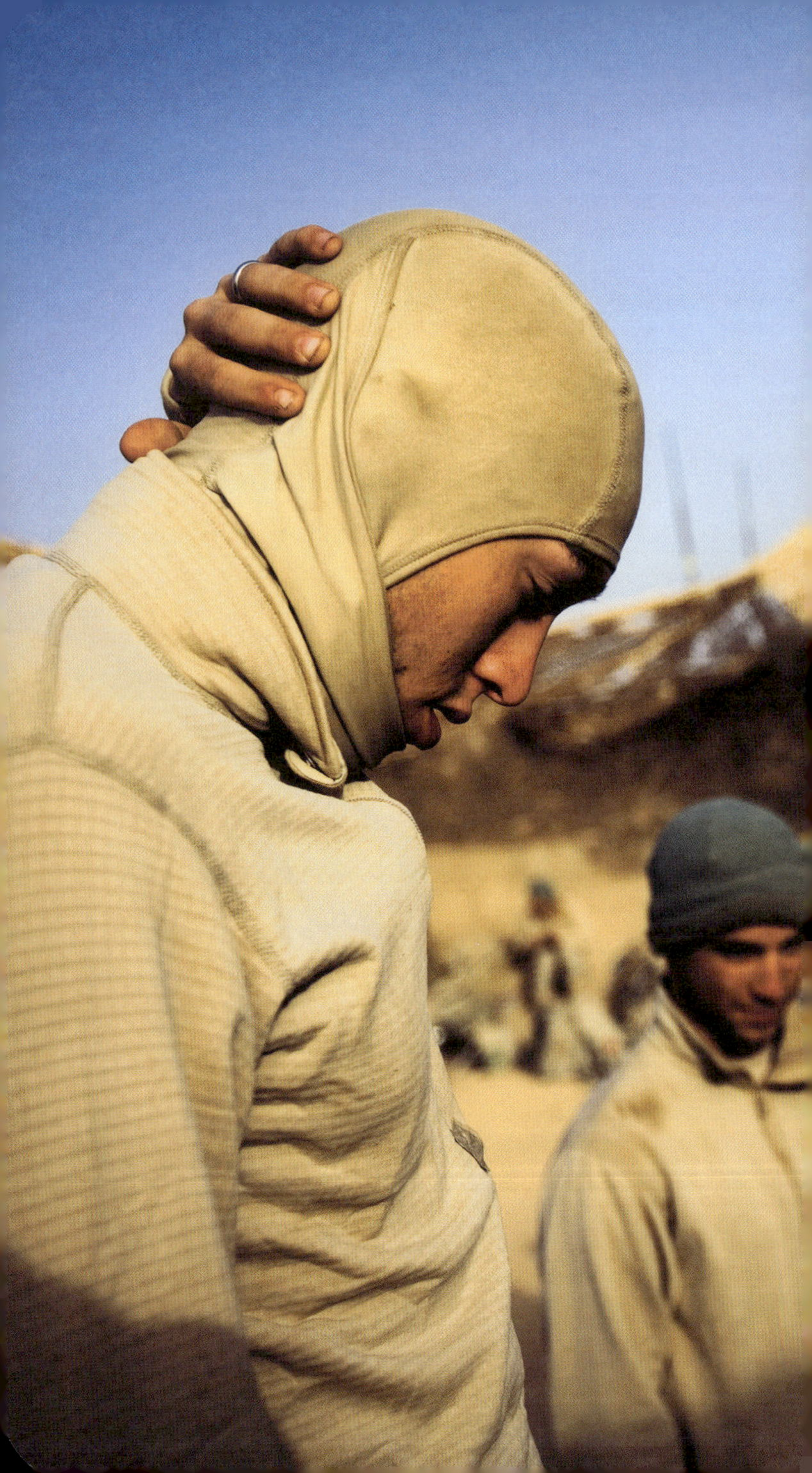

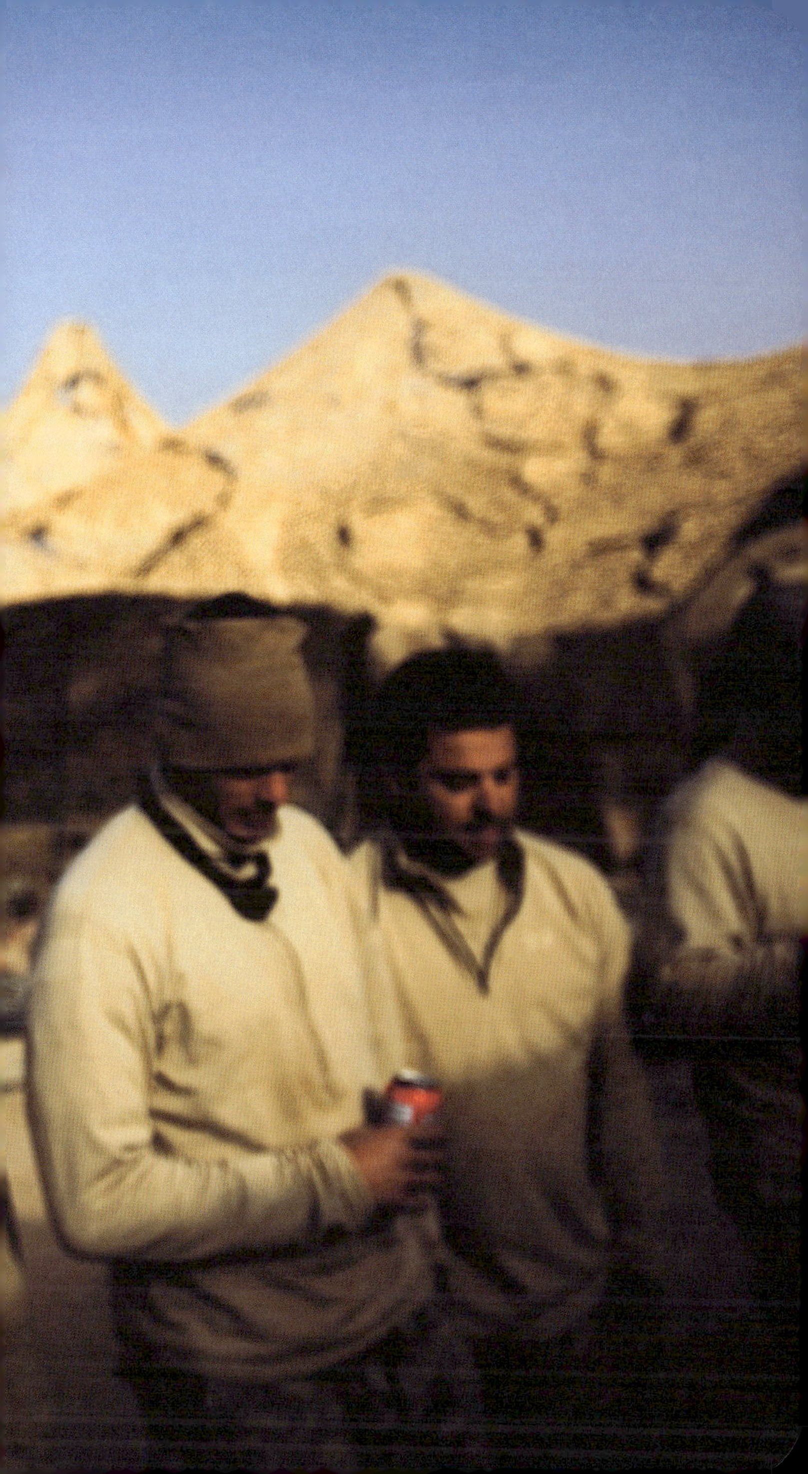

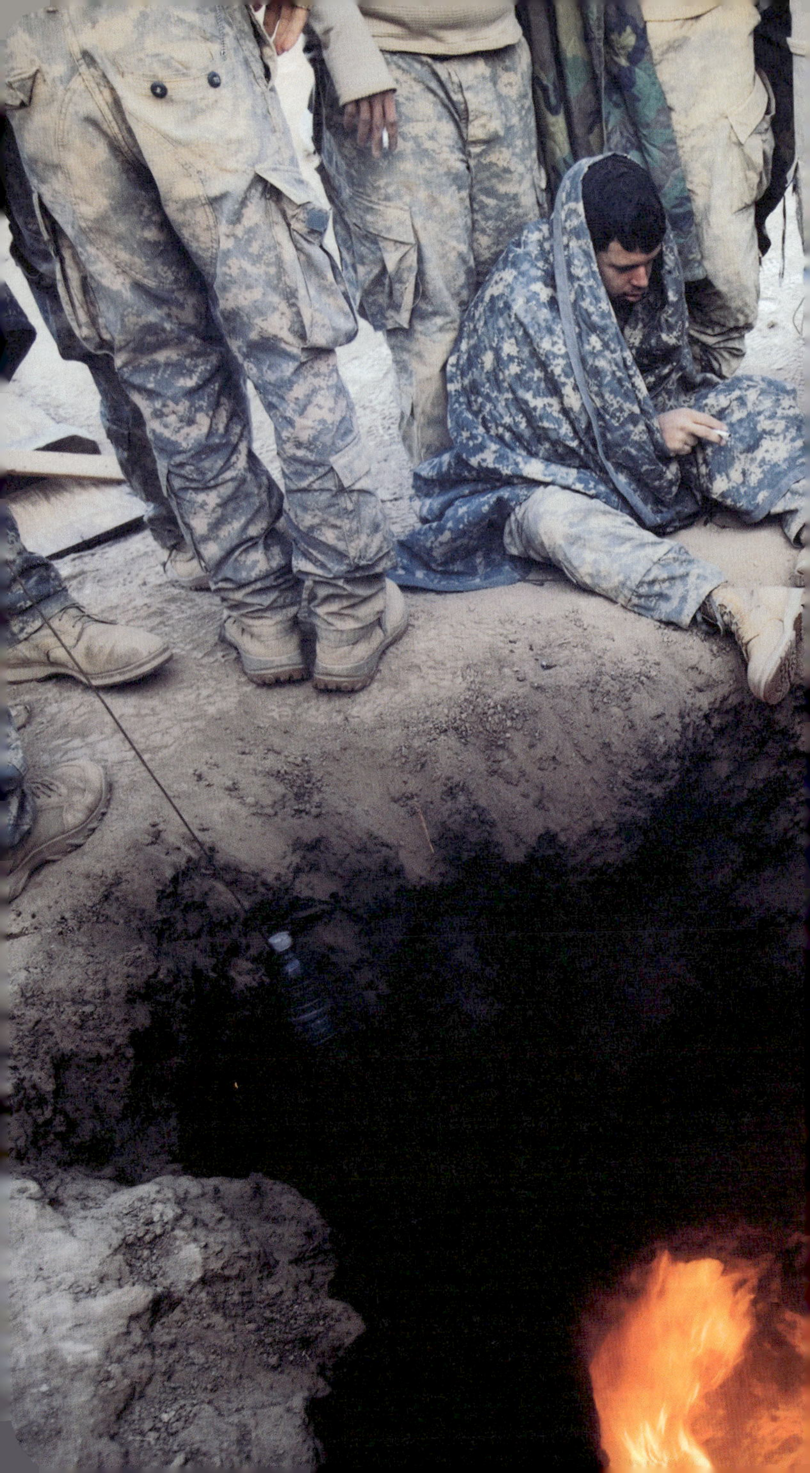

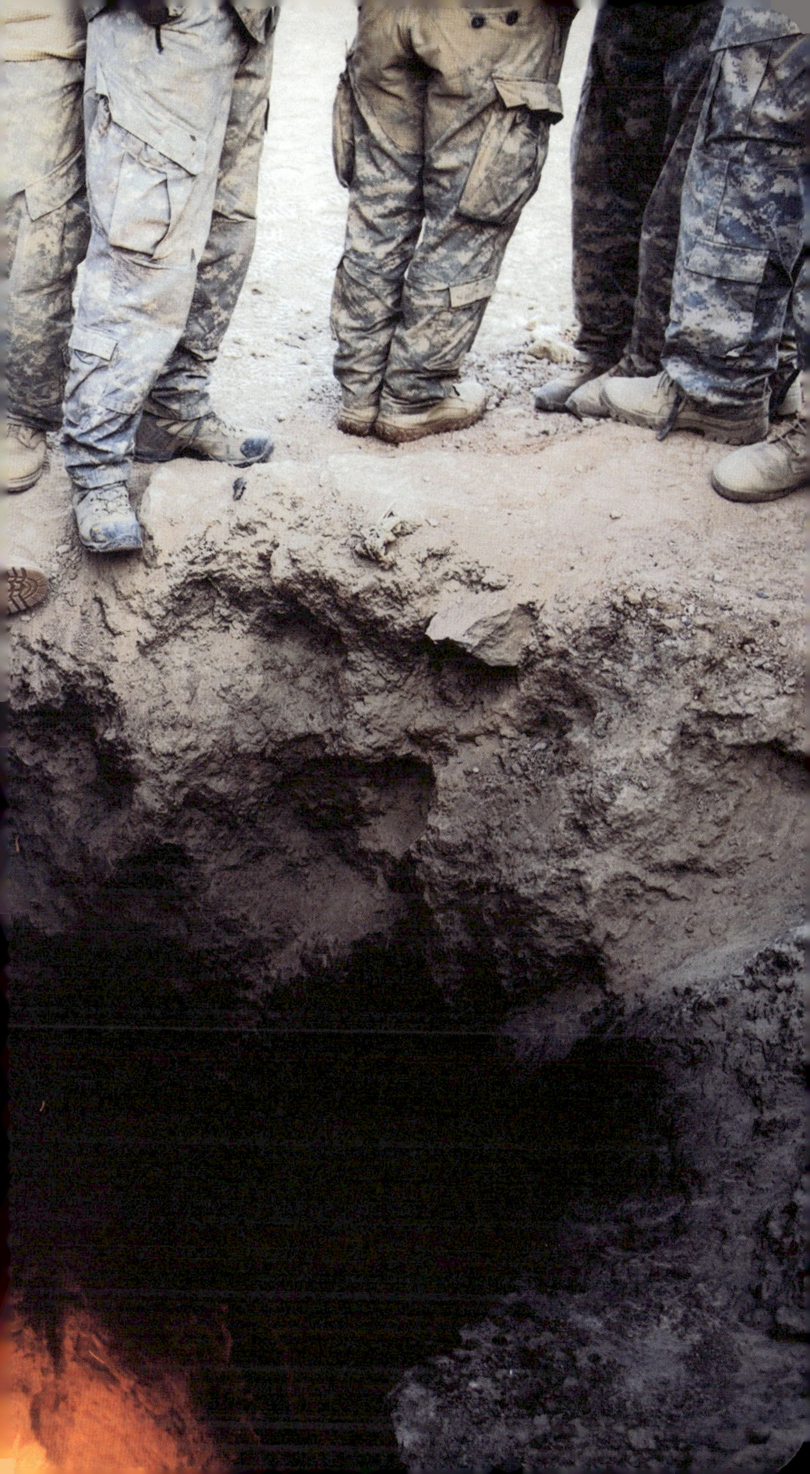

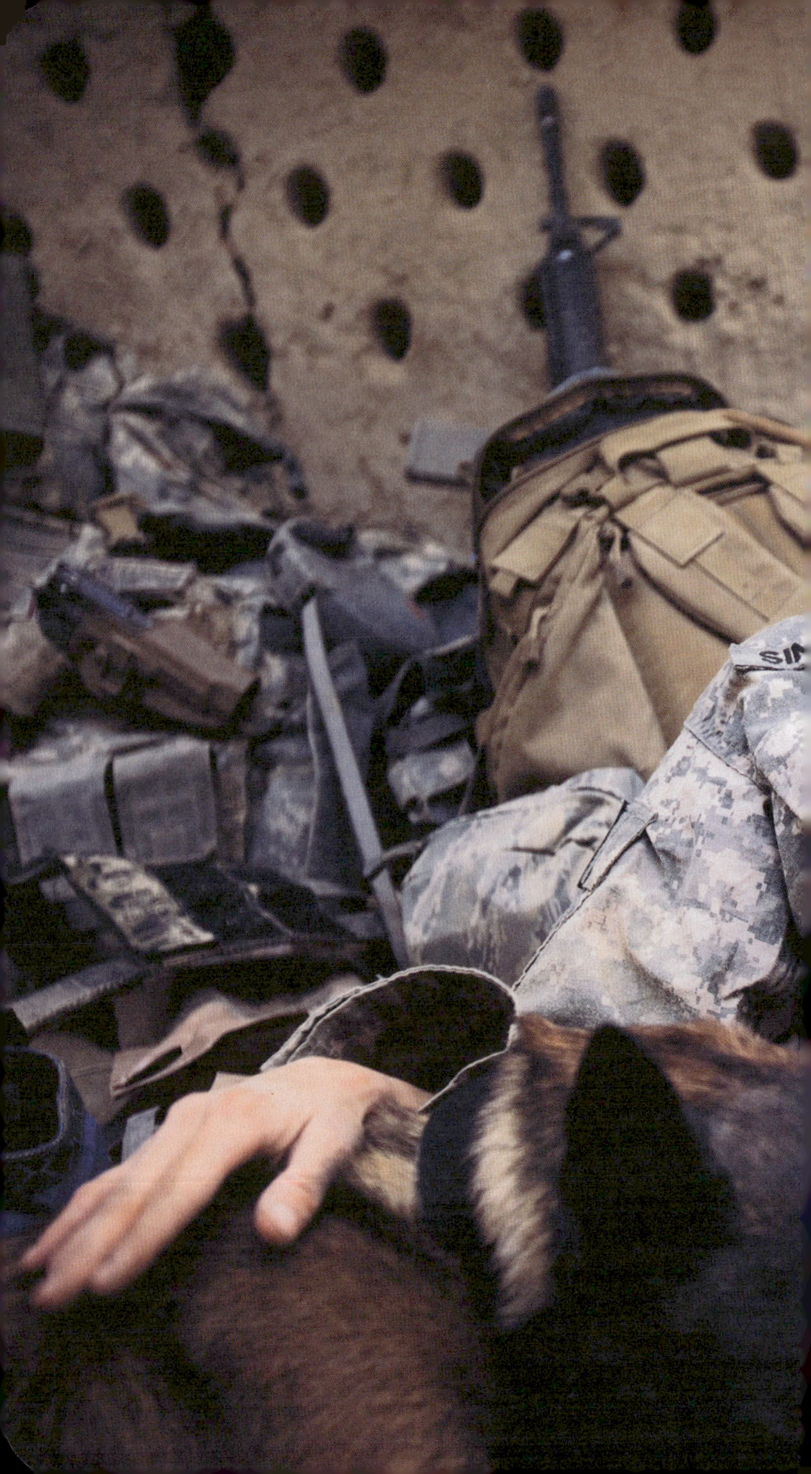

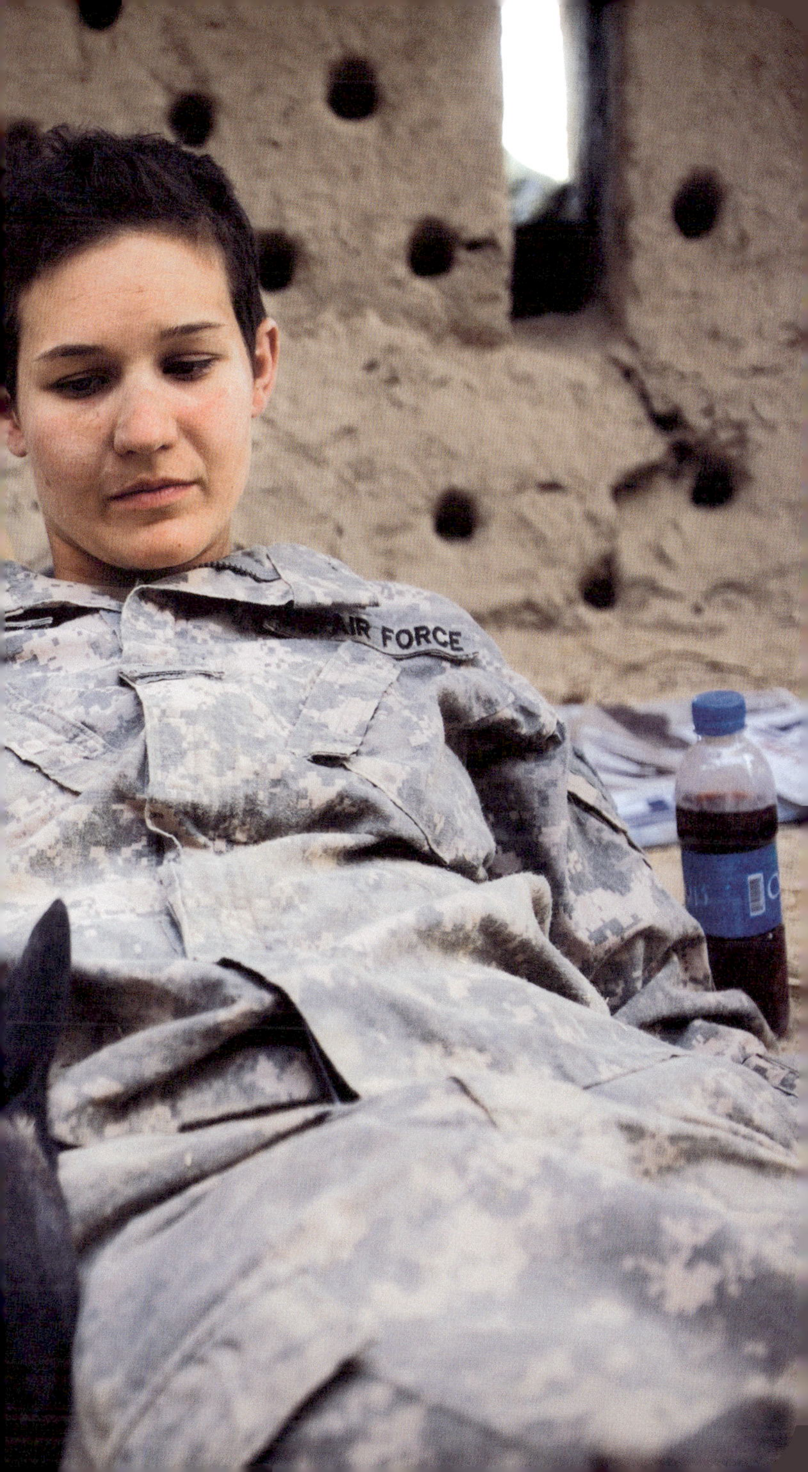
AIR FORCE

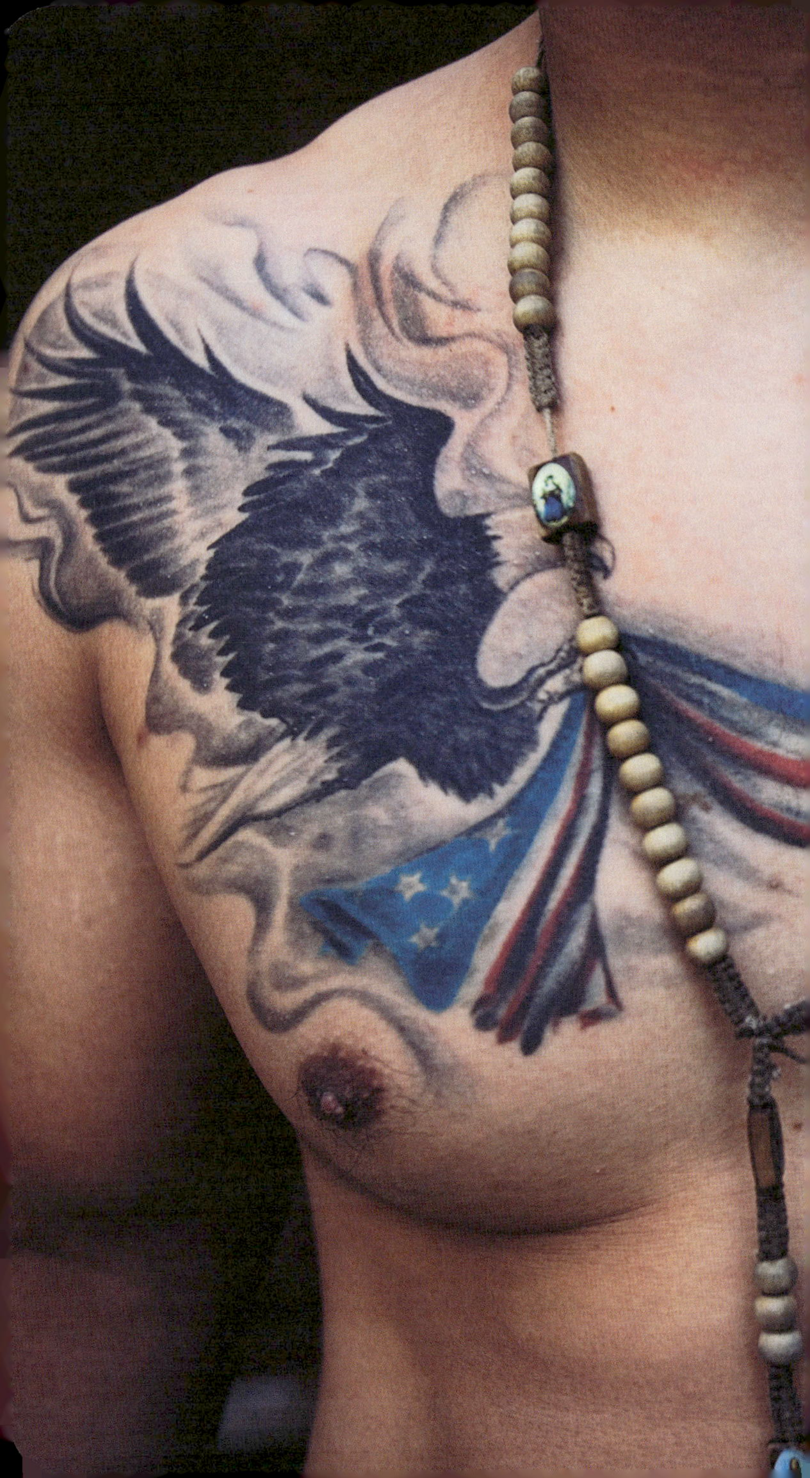

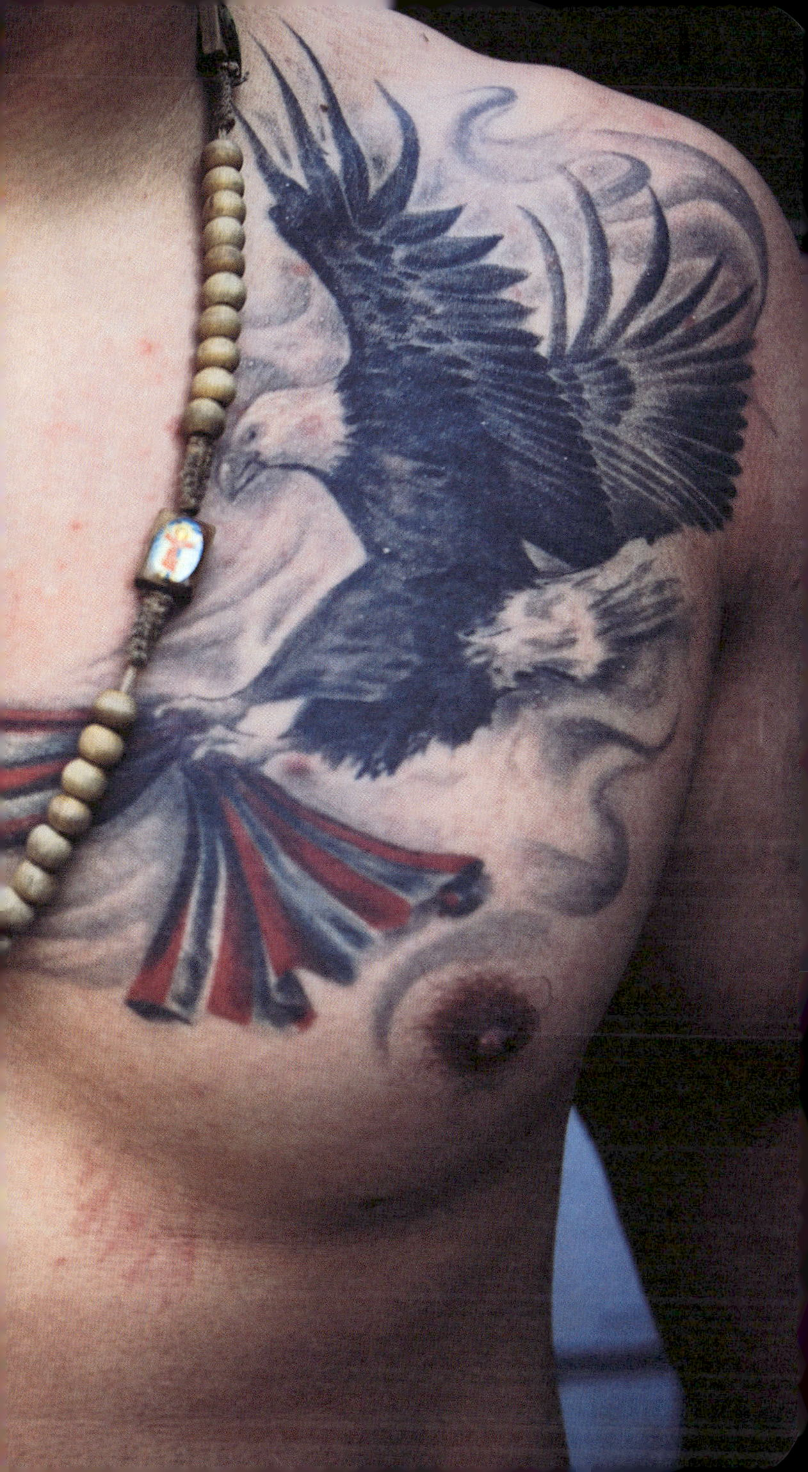

Flashback:

I'm lying on my belly on the floor of the bedroom. It's that little space between the side of the bed and the wall where you can't be seen if you're entering the room. I'm playing hide and seek with Lilli and Anna. The problem is that Lilli, Anna and me are all hiding in the apartment while Shikaranka, ~~Anna's imaginary friend~~, is searching for us. Shikaranka is Anna's imaginary friend, so this can take a while. I'm lying on my belly

and I'm watching the dust flakes, toys and lost socks that have been accumulating under the bed.
Anna is almost four. Lilli almost two. Tomorrow I'm leaving for six weeks to Afghanistan.
Why am I doing this? Fool!
I'd better come home with some good pictures.

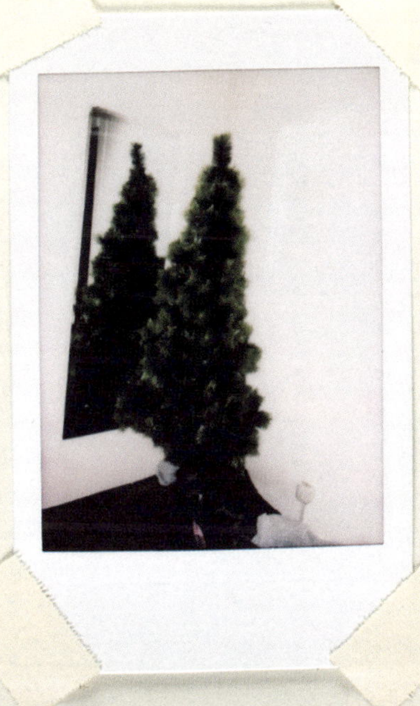

found plastic Christmas tree in the NYT house. It must be the only one in Afghanistan. Christmas is not that huge around here. It's illegal to be christian…

What the hell am I doing

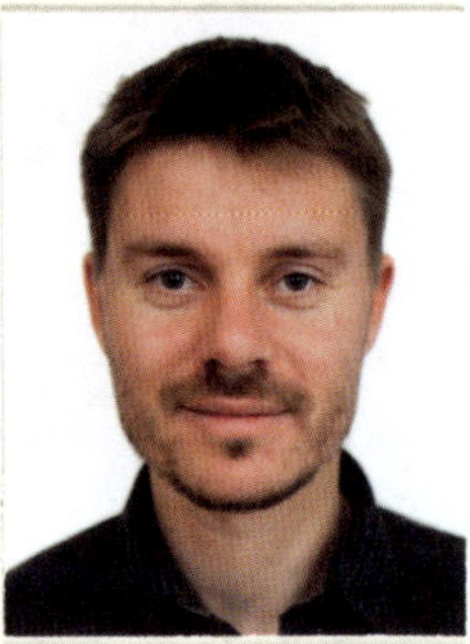

here.

Books. Books. Books.
I have to publish books. And I should get out of Switzerland. Soon.

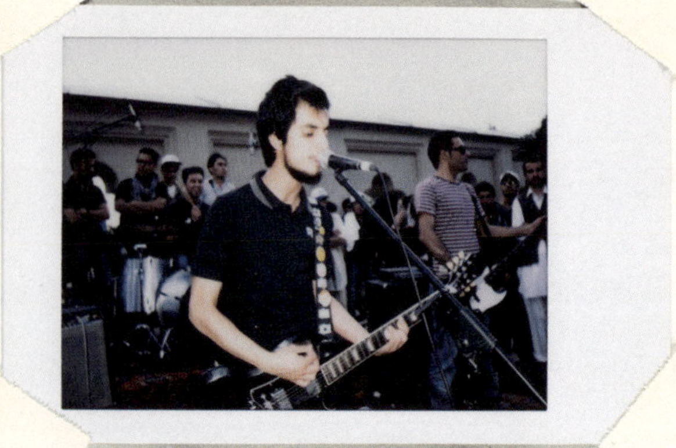

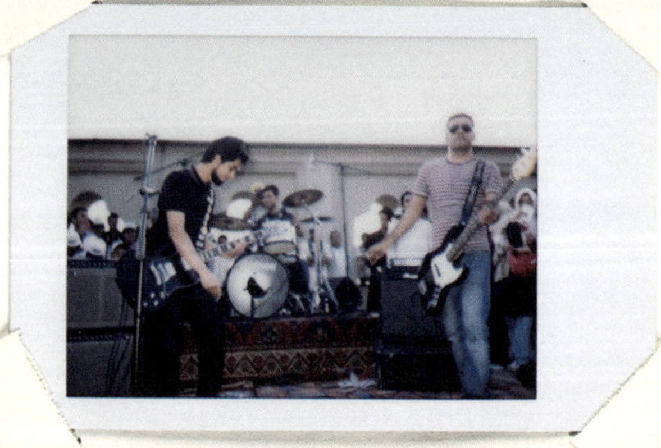

ROCK AND ROLL!

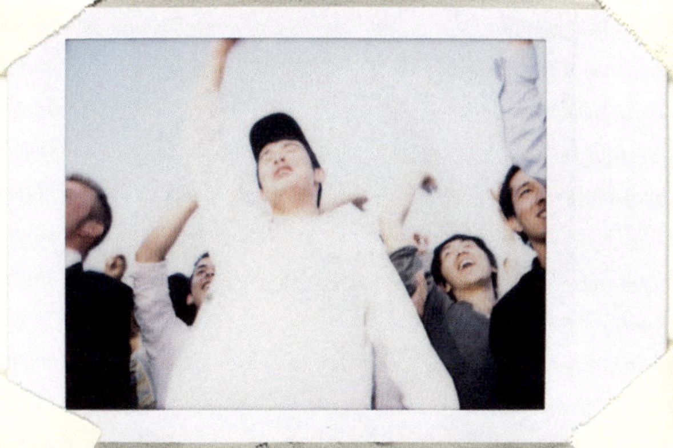

27. 6. 2013

I photograph at a rock concert
at Babur Gardens in Kabul.
The band Kabul Dreams is playing,
Afghanistan's most famous, and maybe
only proper rock band.
I liked it a lot.

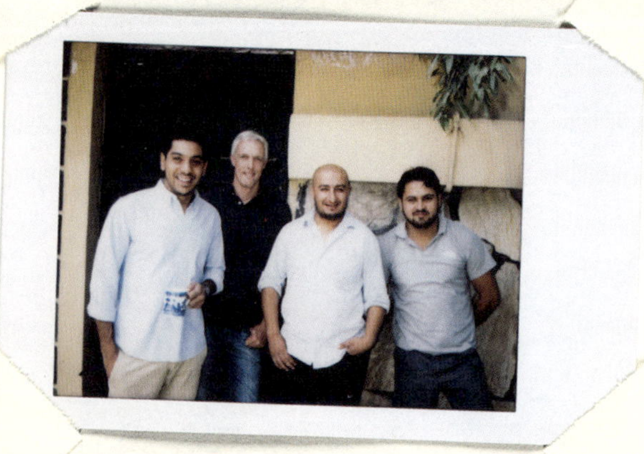

I meet Azam, Charlie, Habib and Satar. I like them instantly. I'm so glad to have these guys here.

I'm busy immediately, which I'm very grateful for. There is nothing worse than sitting around the NYT office in Kabul with nothing to do.

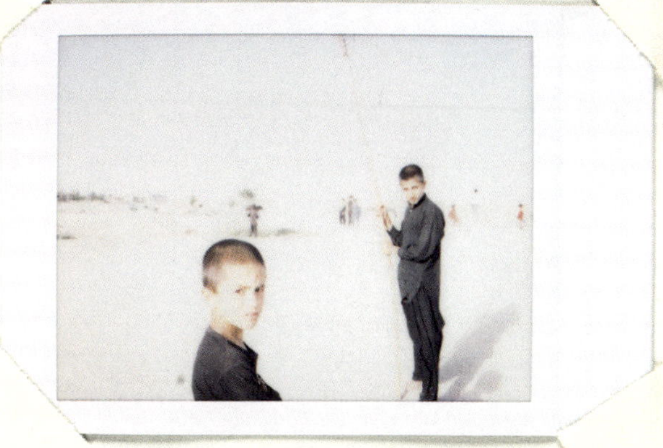

I'm really happy with this image. A different version of it appeared in "pictures of the day" on the Times blog. Nice surprise. Even the printed paper picked it without a story. :)

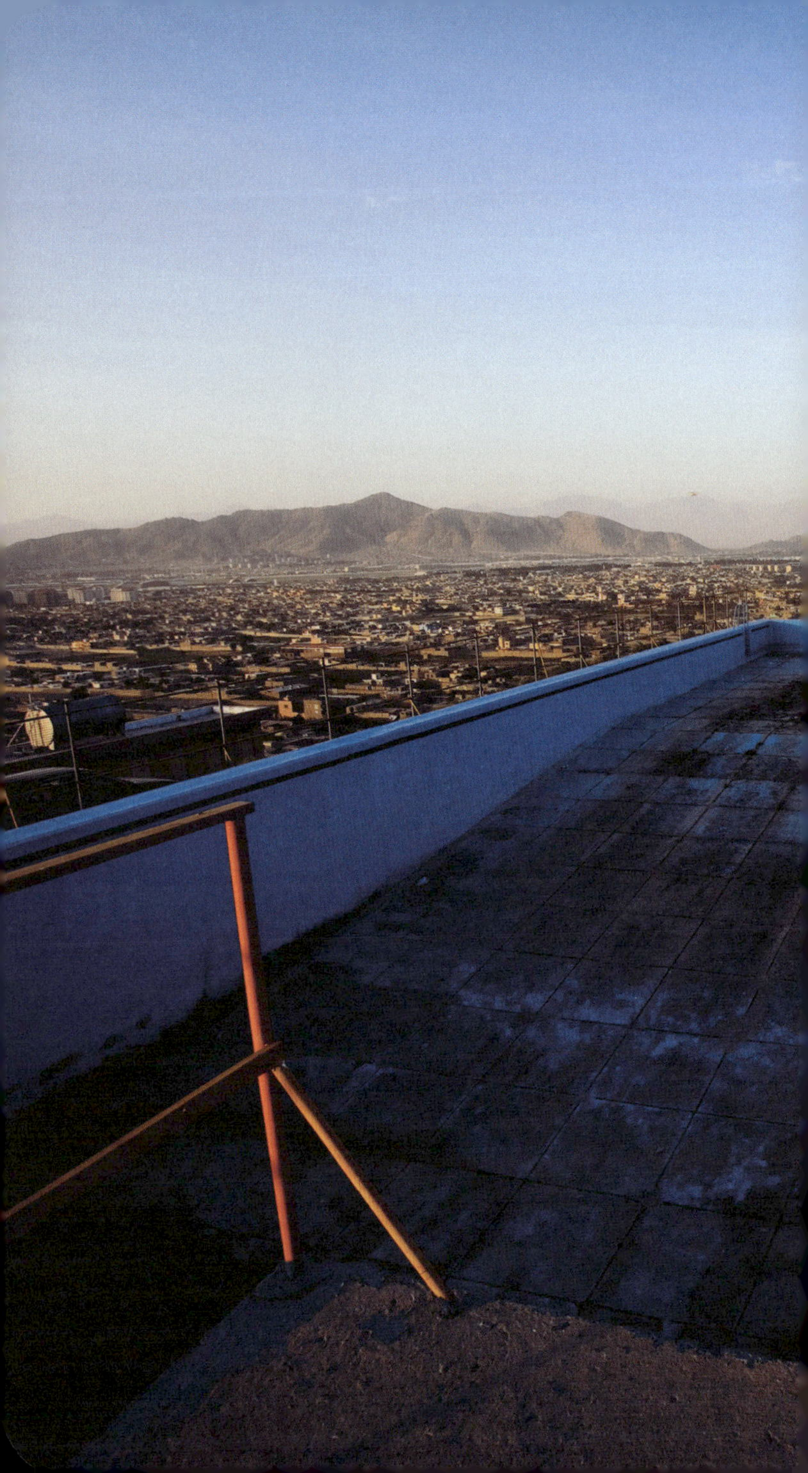

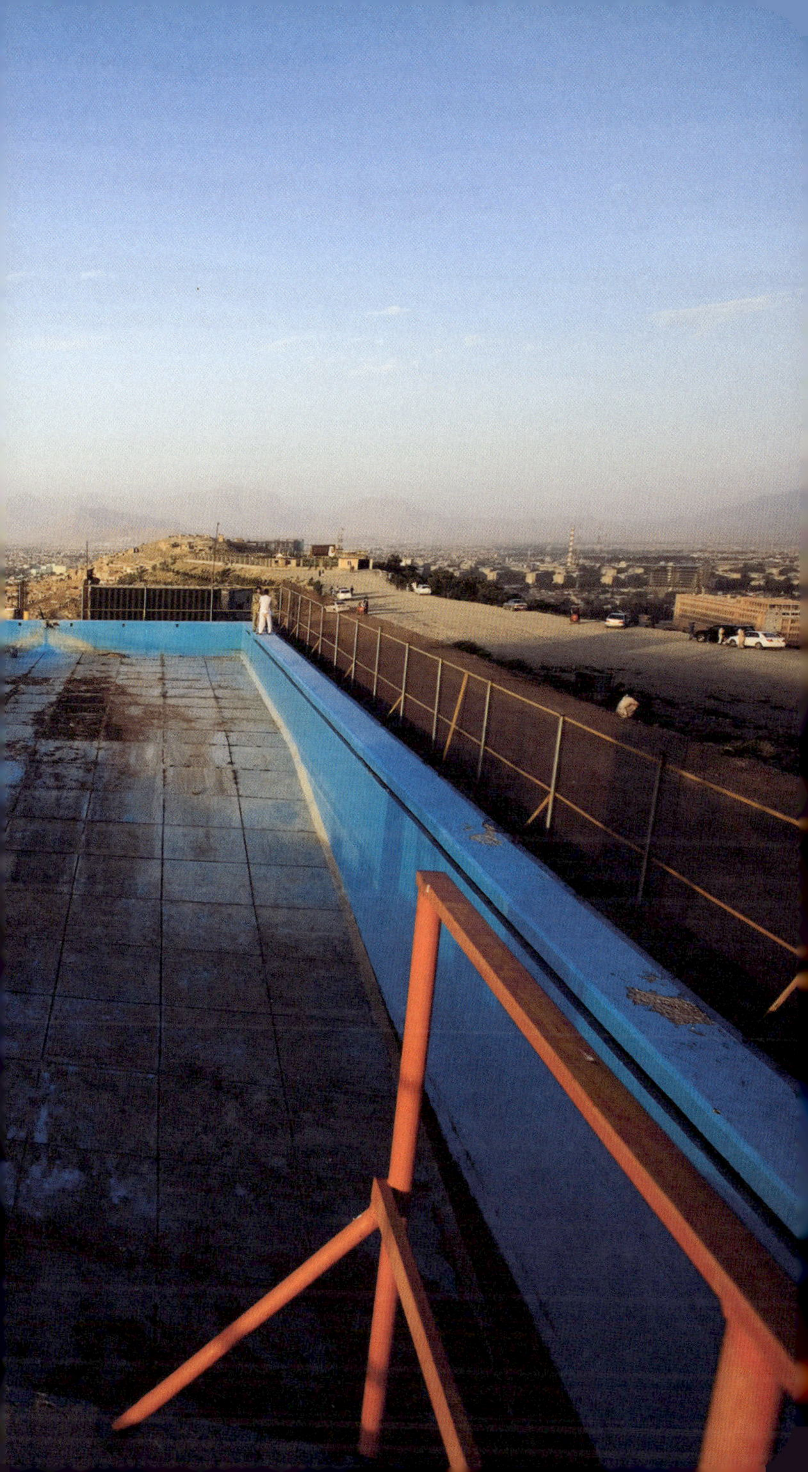

I go to take pictures on "swimming pool" hill. I think I'm the only foreign photographer

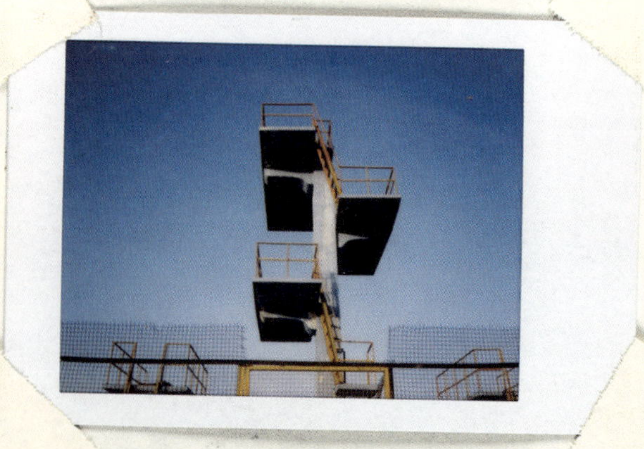

who visited Kabul and never took

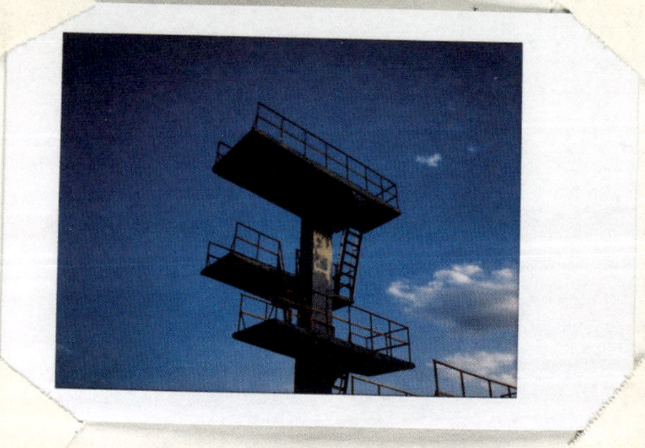

a picture of the old Russian swimming pool.

Another riddle solved. Another myth demystified.

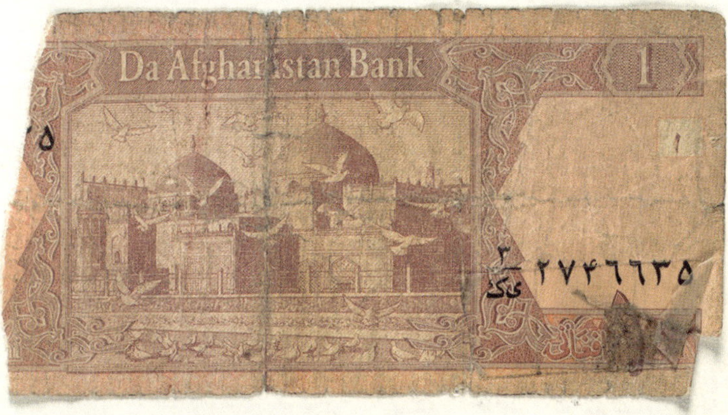

"Da Afganistan Bank"

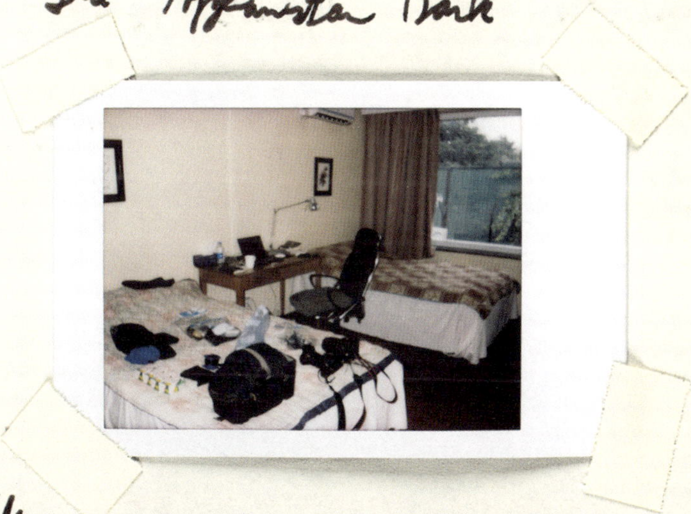

My room.
It's the smallest one in the house,
but I like it.
I spent a LOT of time here

in the last years. Like months. I gave birth to a kidney stone here. And this is where my medical emergency – nightmare started two years ago. I sleep here (on the bed next to the window) and work here as well. There's a Gauguin hanging on the wall.

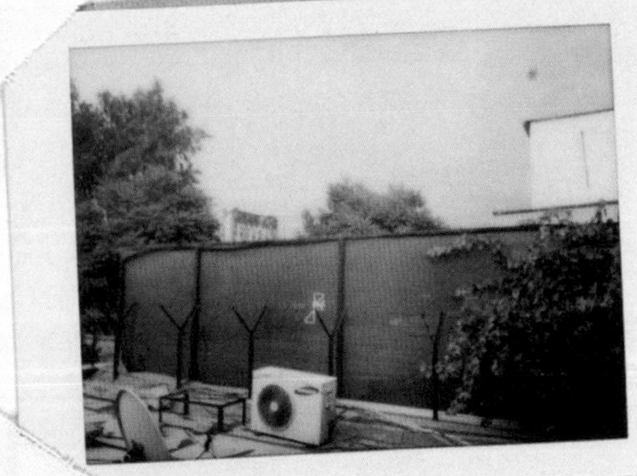

The view from my window.

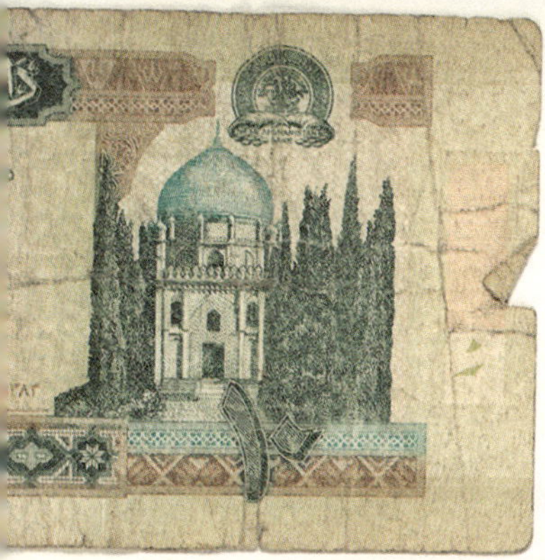

Charlie gave us
a first aid class
today. When he
took out the needle
my imagination took
ver. I almost fainted. All the blood in my
ody went to my legs. I had to go
to my room and lay down with
my legs up. This "war photographer" can't
see blood. It's even worse. Whenever
I hear a story involving blood, needles,
surgery, etc. I faint. But when I photograph
m always fine.
king pictures of
guy who had his
gs blown off?
problem. But if
have no camera,
m in big trouble. I collapse.

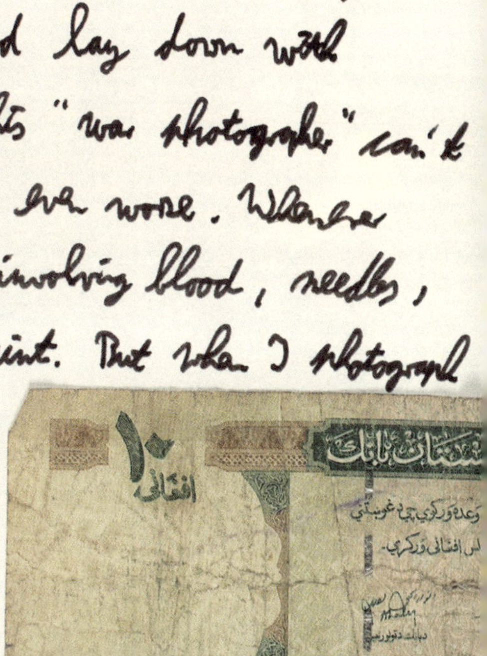

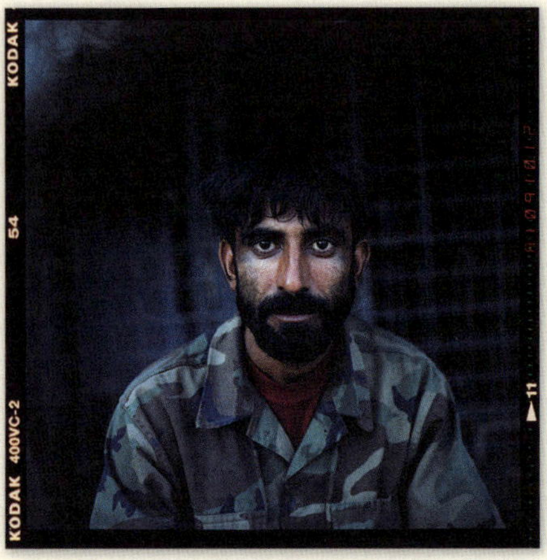
KODAK 400VC-2
54
KODAK
11

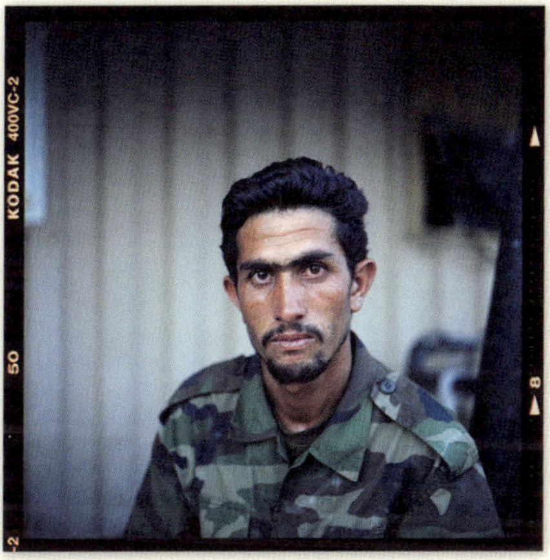
KODAK 400VC-2
50
8

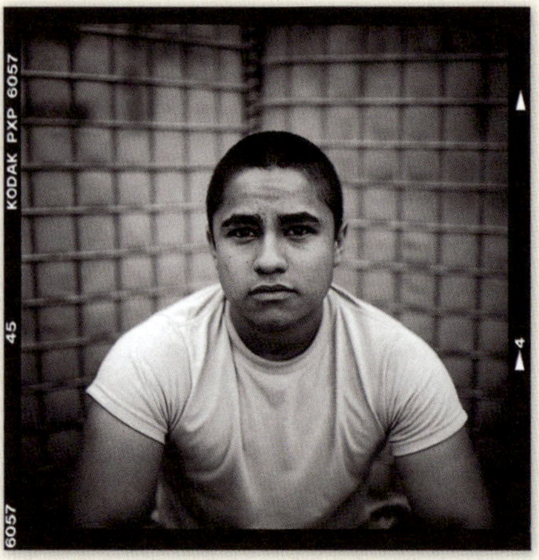
KODAK PXP 6057
45
4
6057

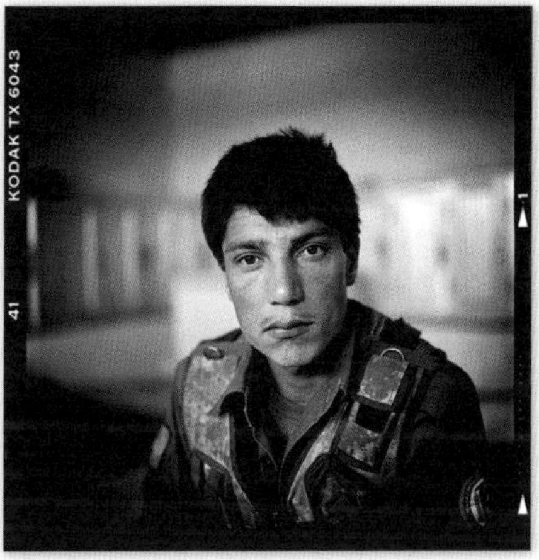
KODAK TX 6043
41

I found this stamp in a copy of John Berger's "About Looking". → 'No longer property of the Queens library'

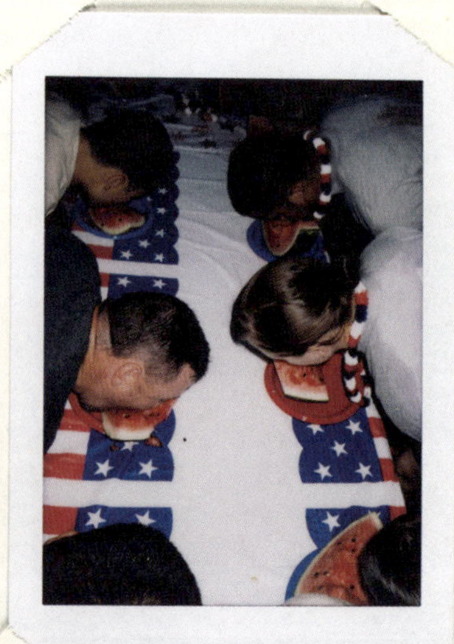

4th of July 2013,
FOB Fenty, Jalalabad Afghanistan.
The water melon eating contest.
We are all so dignified.

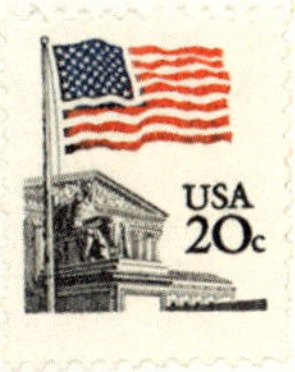
USA
20c

TAKE THE PLEDGE.
BE THE FORCE.

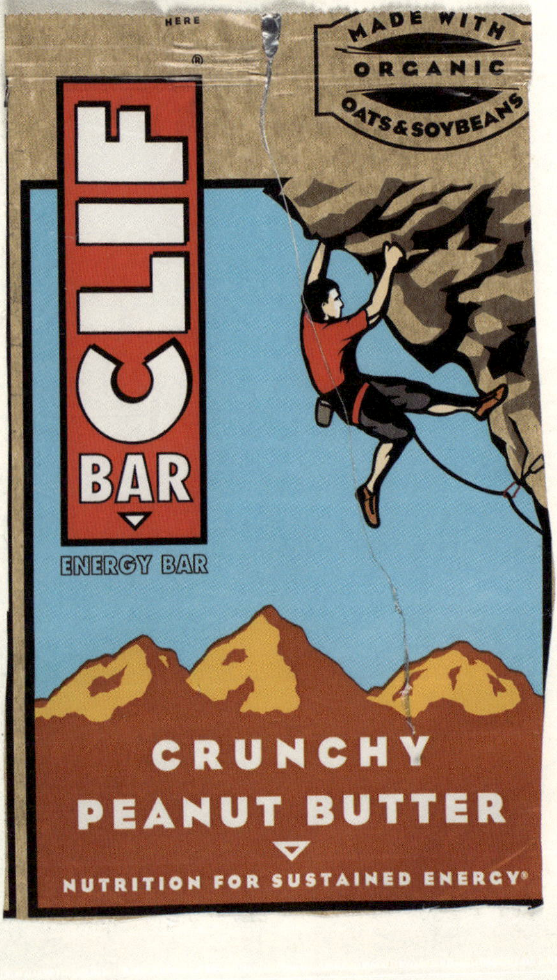

THE FORCE

Loyalty Duty Respect Selfless Service Honor

Sexual Harassment and Sexual Assault

THE FIGHT.

This

FORCE

is fighting on

PURE SUGAR
DIXIE CRYSTALS
SINCE 1917

PURE SUGAR

.

U.S.ARMY

I. A.M.
STRONG
INTERVENE • ACT • MOTIVATE

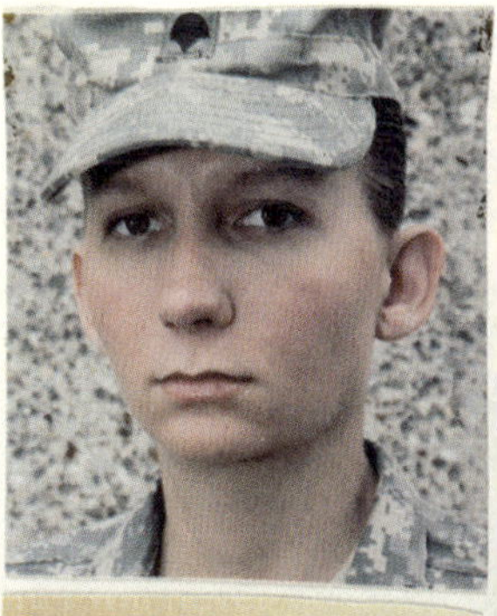

I am committed to preventing all forms of Sexual Harassment and Sexual Assault.

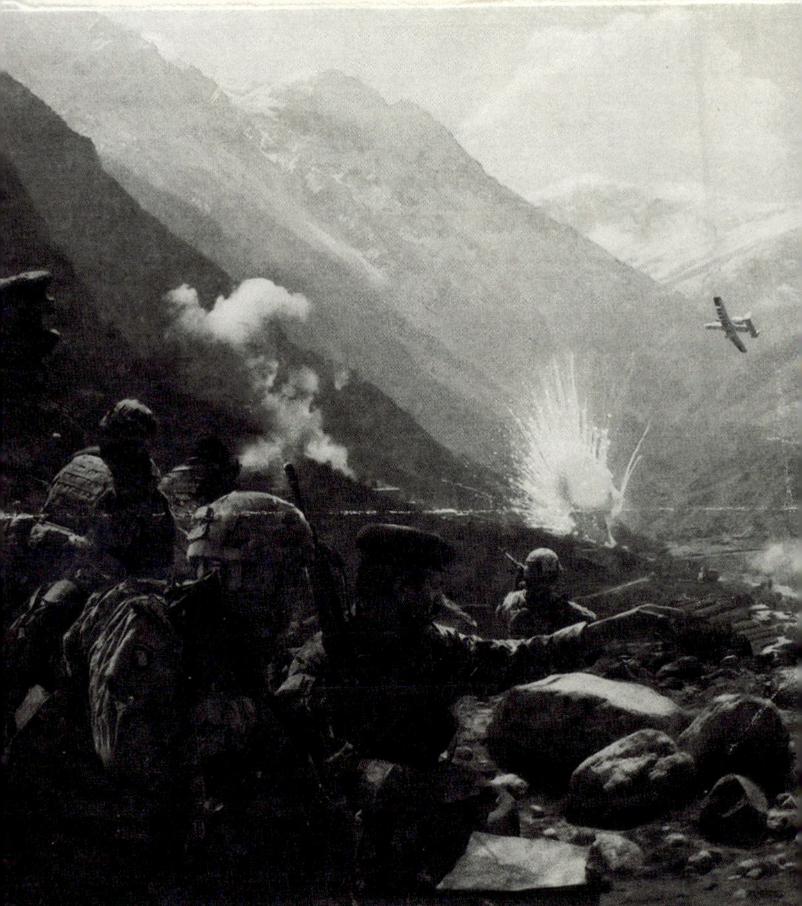

This is what we *think* the war is like.

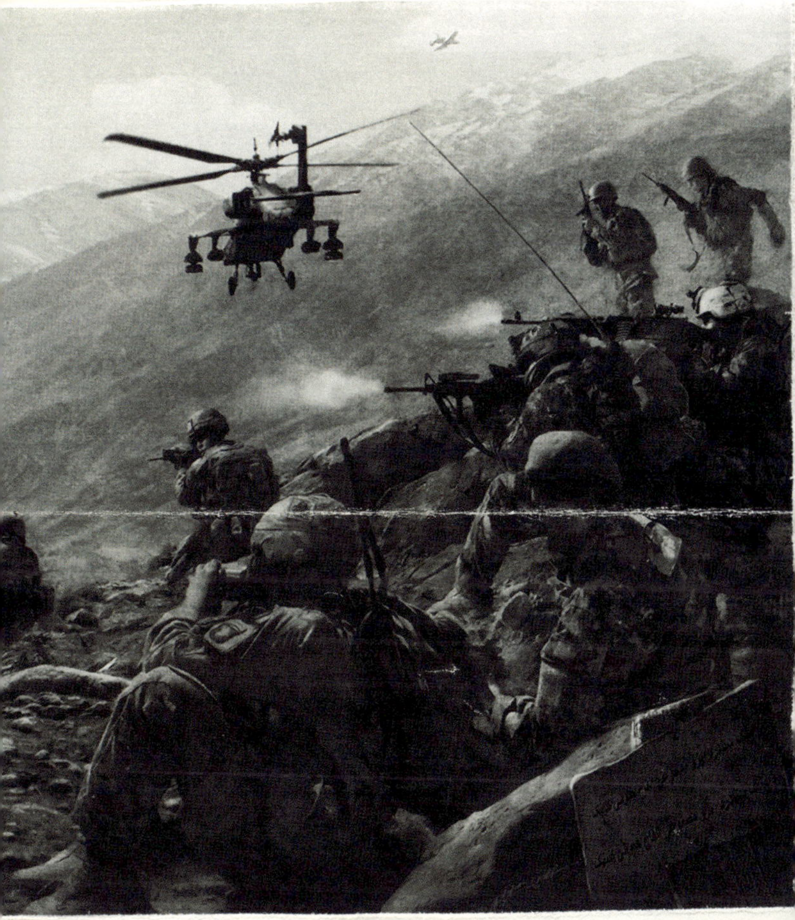

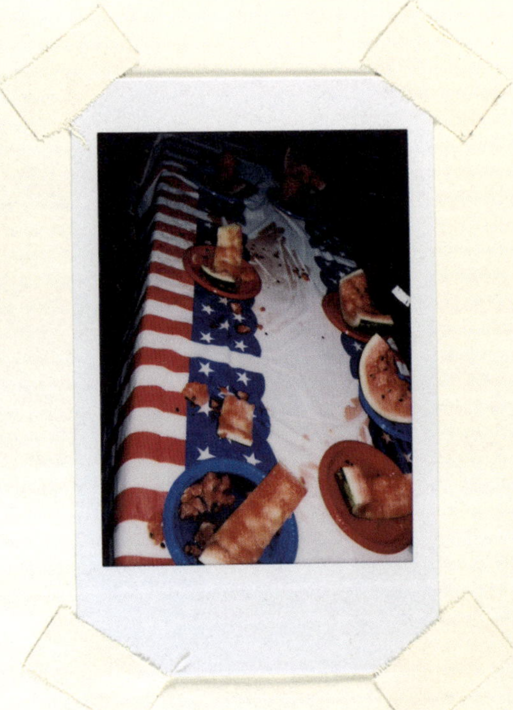

This is what the war is really like.

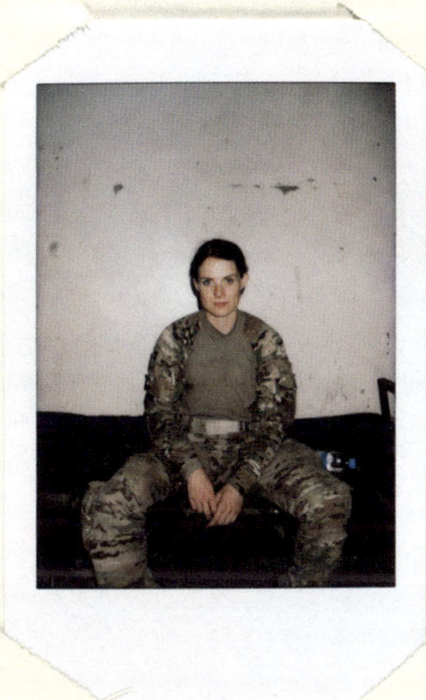

Sgt. Brittney Armstrong.

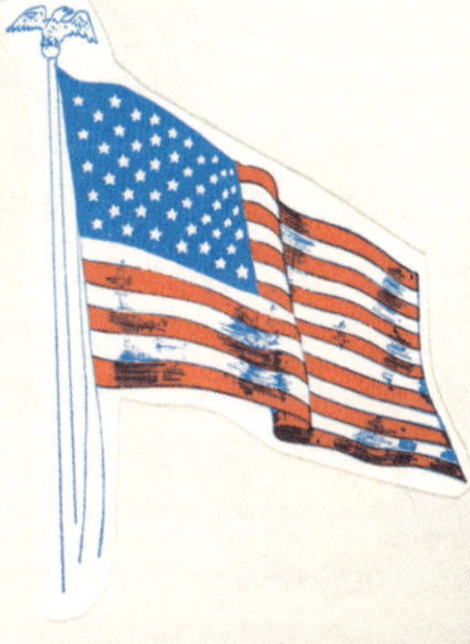

Righteousness exalteth a nation:
but sin is a reproach to any people.
—*Proverbs 14:34*

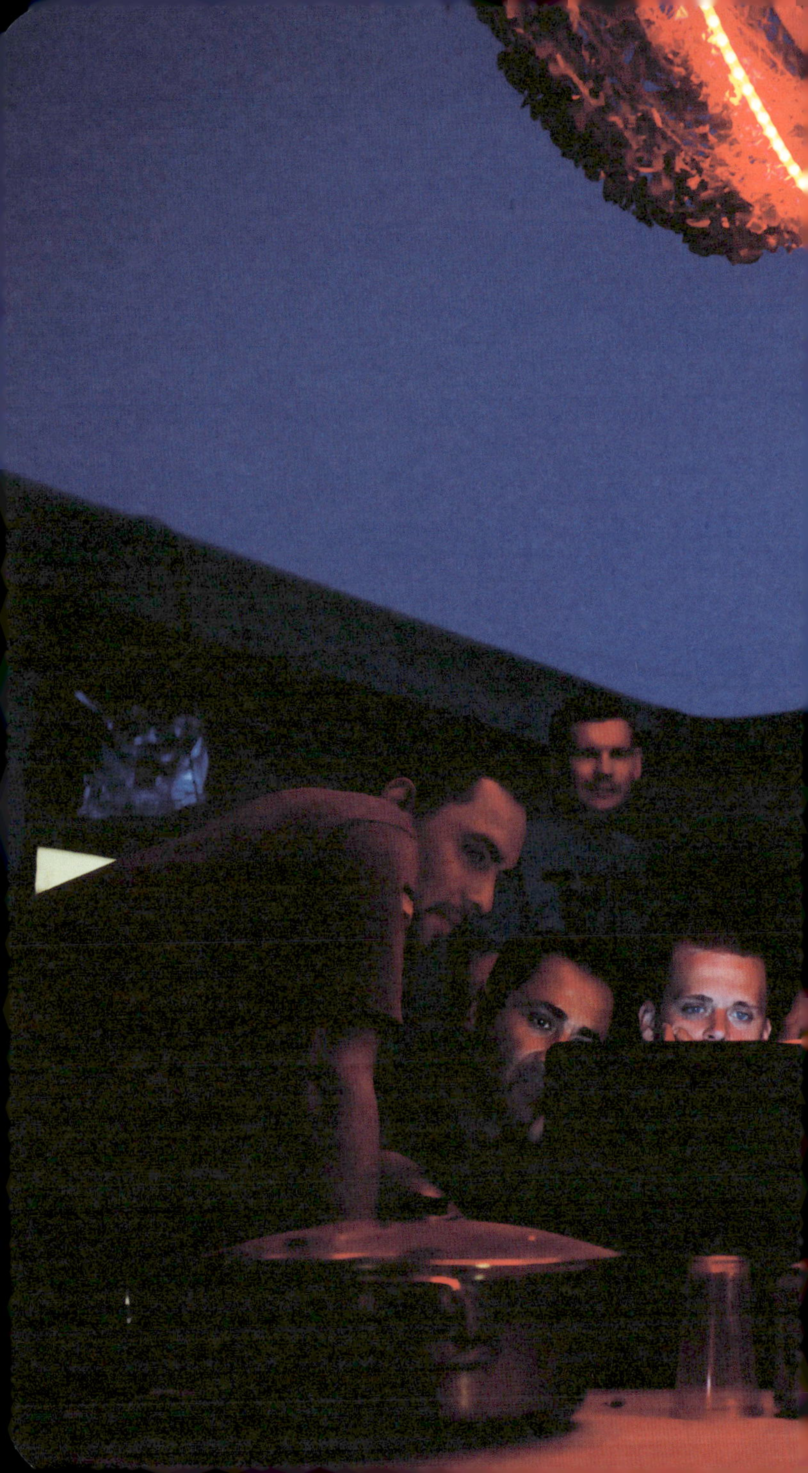

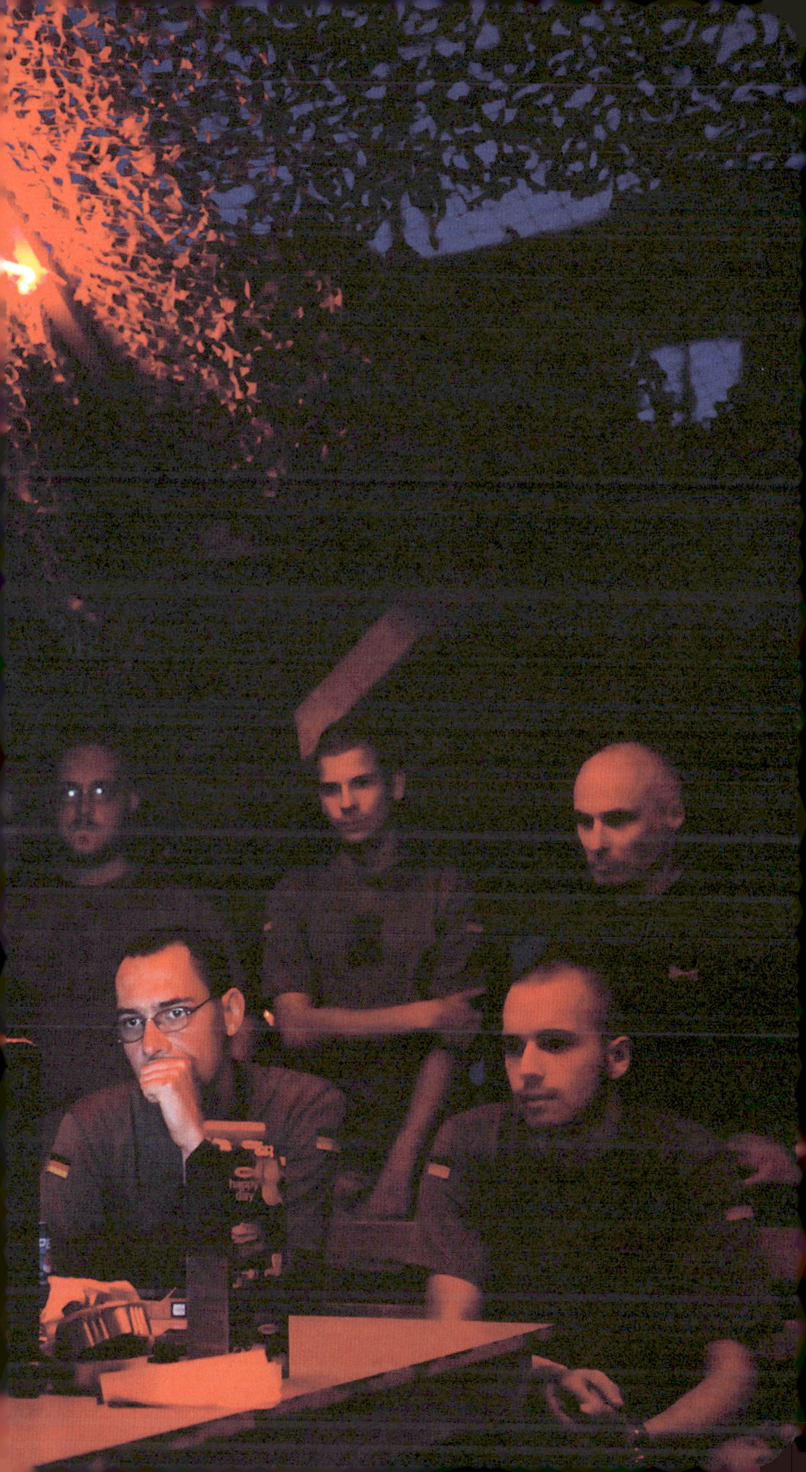

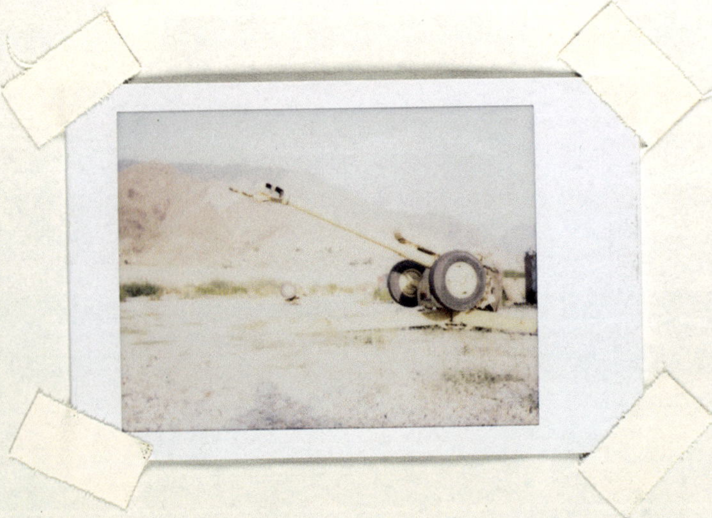

God Loves You

For God so loved the world, that He gave His only begotten Son, that whoever believes in Him should not perish but have everlasting life.

—John 3:16 (page 171)

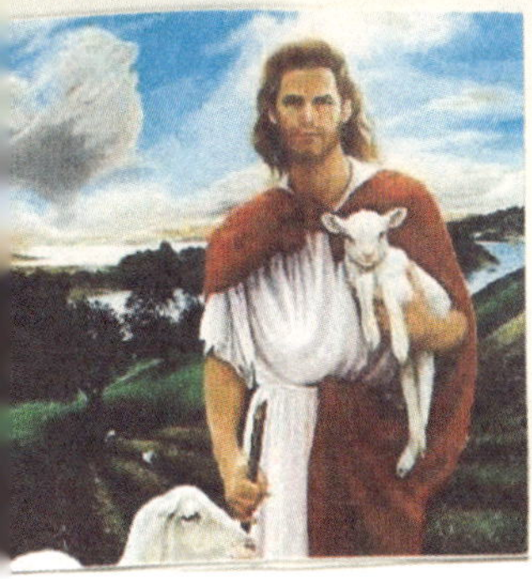

Peace and Protection

4 Yea, though I walk through the valley of the shadow of death, I will
fear no evil: for Thou art with me; Thy rod and Thy staff they comfort me.

FAKE

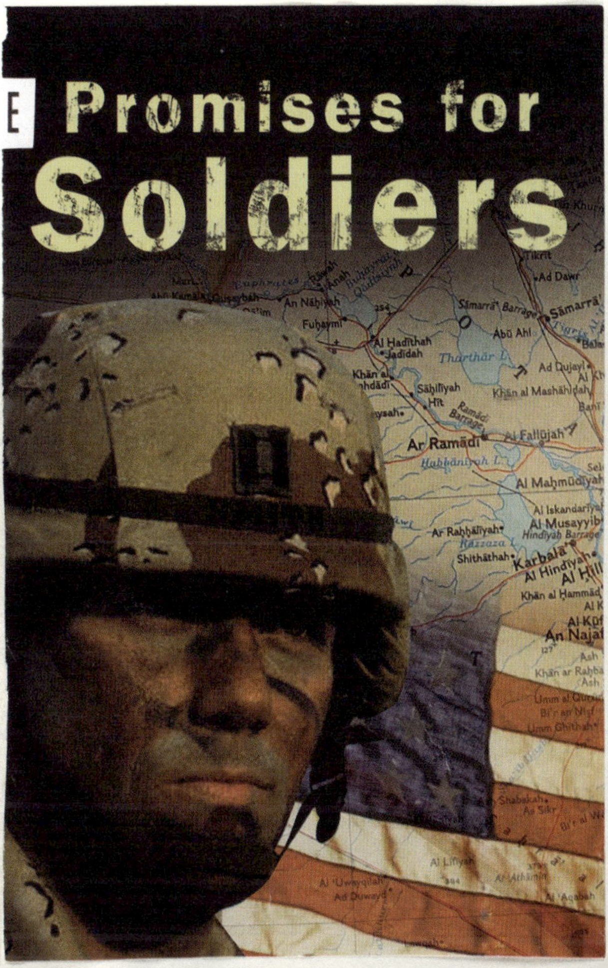

U.S. property

All Are Sinners

For all have sinned and fall short of the glory of God. —*Romans 3:23 (page 282)*

As it is written: *There is none righteous, no, not one.* —*Romans 3:10 (page 282)*

THE NEW YORK TIMES

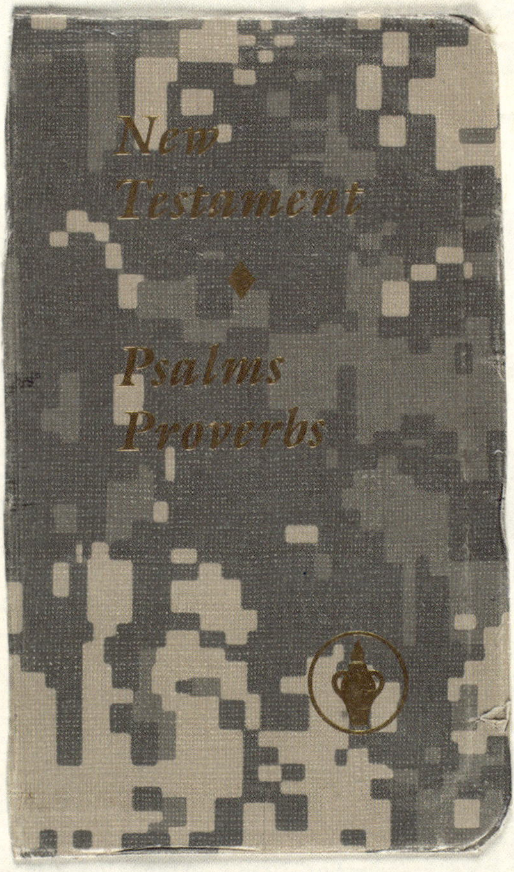

The combat bible :

Famous in The World

Follow Me

Obama

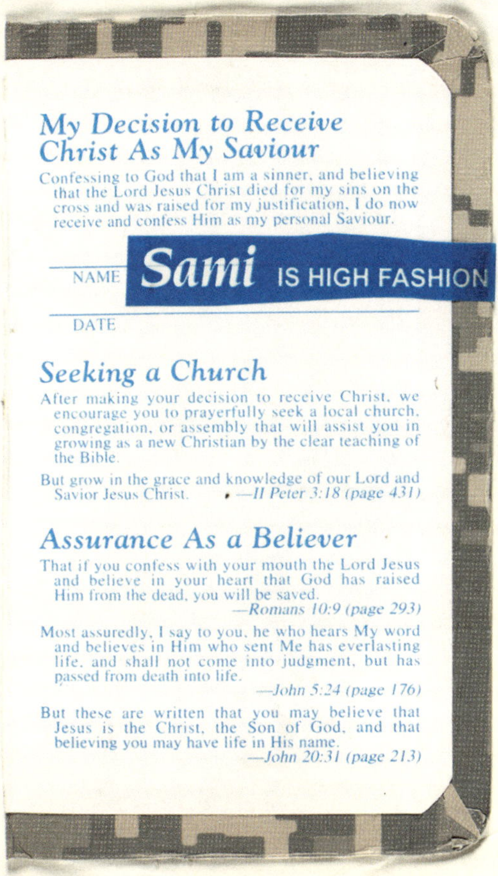

My Decision to Receive Christ As My Saviour

Confessing to God that I am a sinner, and believing that the Lord Jesus Christ died for my sins on the cross and was raised for my justification, I do now receive and confess Him as my personal Saviour.

NAME **Sami** IS HIGH FASHION

DATE

Seeking a Church

After making your decision to receive Christ, we encourage you to prayerfully seek a local church, congregation, or assembly that will assist you in growing as a new Christian by the clear teaching of the Bible.

But grow in the grace and knowledge of our Lord and Savior Jesus Christ. *—II Peter 3:18 (page 431)*

Assurance As a Believer

That if you confess with your mouth the Lord Jesus and believe in your heart that God has raised Him from the dead, you will be saved.
—Romans 10:9 (page 293)

Most assuredly, I say to you, he who hears My word and believes in Him who sent Me has everlasting life, and shall not come into judgment, but has passed from death into life.
—John 5:24 (page 176)

But these are written that you may believe that Jesus is the Christ, the Son of God, and that believing you may have life in His name.
—John 20:31 (page 213)

SPECIALLY MADE FOR EVERY ONE

YOU ARE ASSURED OF YOUR BEST CHOICE

اخليه على احدث موضة

Colgate®

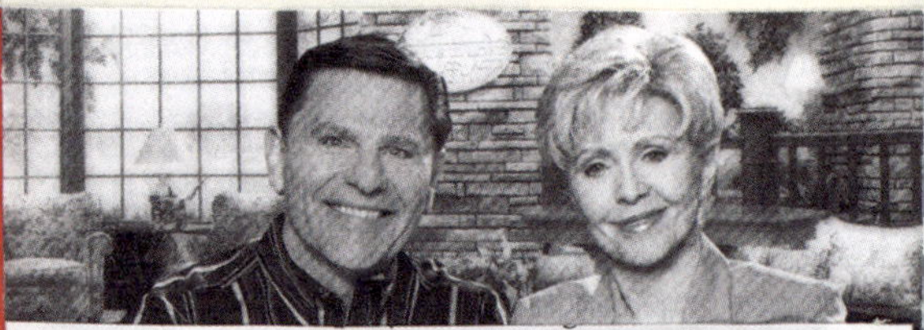

"God, I realize that I have sinned. Thank You for sending Jesus to pay the penalty for my sins so that I would not be separated from You forever. I turn now from my sins and invite You into my life."

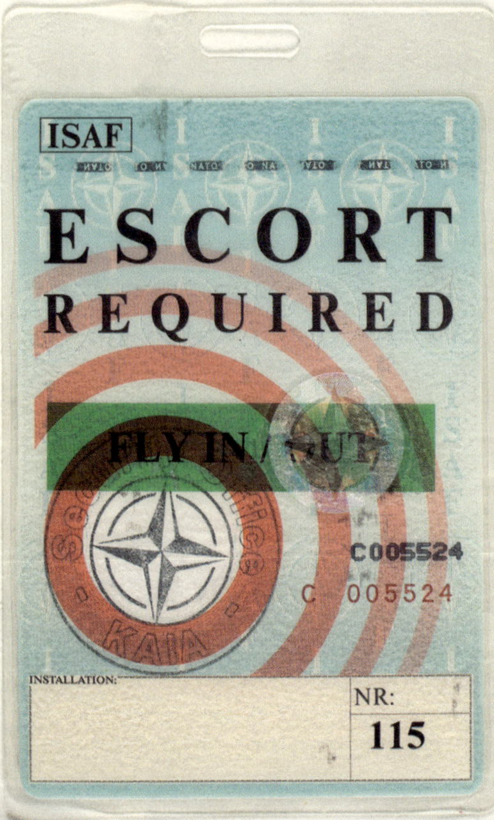

Business

RUMORS OF WAR

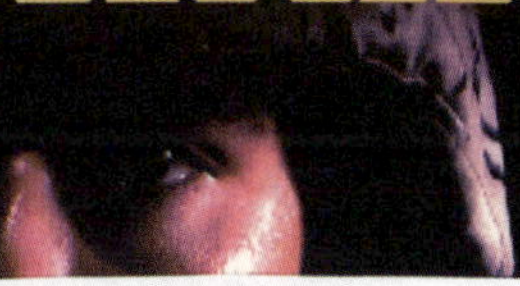

If you'll let him, Satan will use them to fill your mind with worries. He'll use the media to bring to you all the terrors of war. To show you every kind of horrible thing you can think of.

BUSINESS

This war is not about religion.

ONWARD, CHRISTIAN SOLDIERS

1. Onward, Christian soldiers! Marching as to war,
With the cross of Jesus Going on before:
Christ, the royal Master, Leads against the foe;
Forward into battle, See, His banner go!
CHORUS
Onward, Christian soldiers! Marching as to war,
With the cross of Jesus Going on before.

2. Like a mighty army Moves the Church of God:
Brothers, we are treading Where the saints have trod;
We are not divided, All one body we,
One in hope and doctrine, One in charity.

3. Crowns and thrones may perish, Kingdoms rise and wane,
But the Church of Jesus Constant will remain;
Gates of hell can never 'Gainst that Church prevail,
We have Christ's own promise, And that cannot fail.

Onward, then, ye faithful! Join our happy throng,
Blend with ours your voices, In the triumph song;
Glory, praise, and honor Unto Christ the King,
This thro' countless ages Men and angels sing.

Marlboro

right.

THE NEW YORK TIMES

poor, for yours is the king-
dom of God.
21 Blessed *are you* who
hunger now, for you shall
be filled. Blessed *are you*
who weep now, for you
shall laugh.
22 Blessed are you when
men hate you, and when
they exclude you, and re-
vile *you,* and cast out your
name as evil, for the Son
of Man's sake.
23 Rejoice in that day
and leap for joy! For in-
deed your reward *is* great
in heaven, for in like man-
ner their fathers did to the
prophets.
24 "But woe to you who
are rich, for you have re-
ceived your consolation.
25 Woe to you who are
full, for you shall hunger.
Woe to you who laugh
now, for you shall mourn
and weep.
26 Woe to you when all
men speak well of you, for
so did their fathers to the
false prophets.
27 "But I say to you who
hear: love your enemies,
do good to those who hate
you,
28 "Bless those who
curse you, and pray for
those who spitefully use
you.
29 "To him who strikes
you on the *one* cheek, offer
the other also. And from
him who takes away your
cloak, do not withhold
your tunic either.
30 "Give to everyone
who asks of you. And from
him who takes away your
goods do not ask *them*
back.
31 "And just as you want
men to do to you, you also
do to them likewise.
32 "But if you love those
who love you, what credit
is that to you? For even
sinners love those who
love them.
33 "And if you do good
to those who do good to
you, what credit is that to
you? For even sinners do
the same.
34 "And if you lend *to
those* from whom you
hope to receive back, what
credit is that to you? For
even sinners lend to sin-
ners to receive as much
back.
35 "But love your ene-
mies, do good, and lend,
hoping for nothing in re-
turn; and your reward will
be great, and you will be
sons of the Most High. For
He is kind to the unthank-
ful and evil.
36 "Therefore be merci-
ful, just as your Father also
is merciful.
37 "Judge not, and you
shall not be judged. Con-
demn not, and you shall
not be condemned. For-
give, and you will be for-
given.
38 "Give, and it will be
given to you: good mea-
sure, pressed down, shaken
together, and running over
will be put into your bo

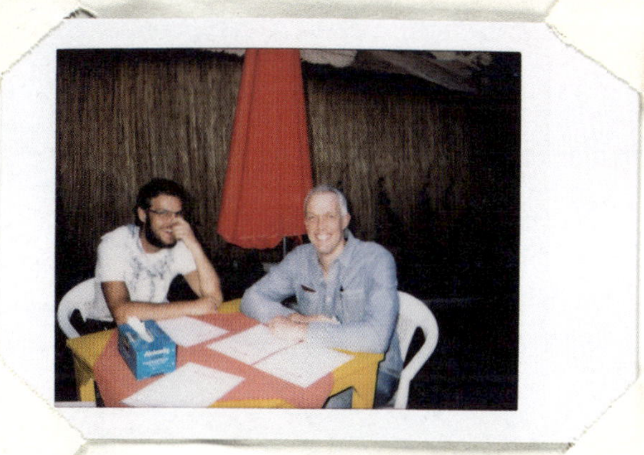

with Thilo and Charlie at 'Le Bistro' in Kabul.

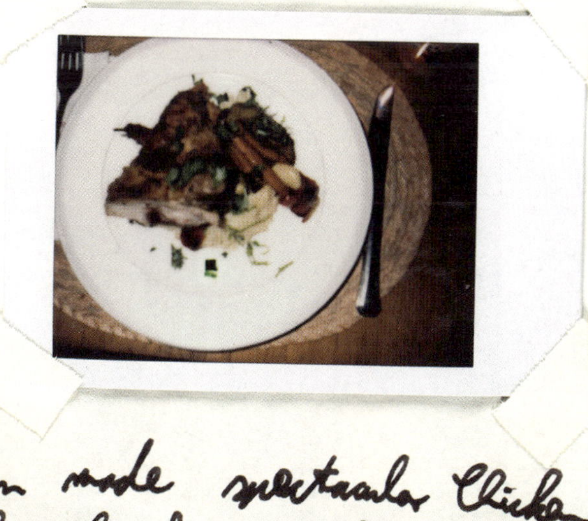

Azam made spectacular Chicken. maybe the best meal in Afghanistan ever.

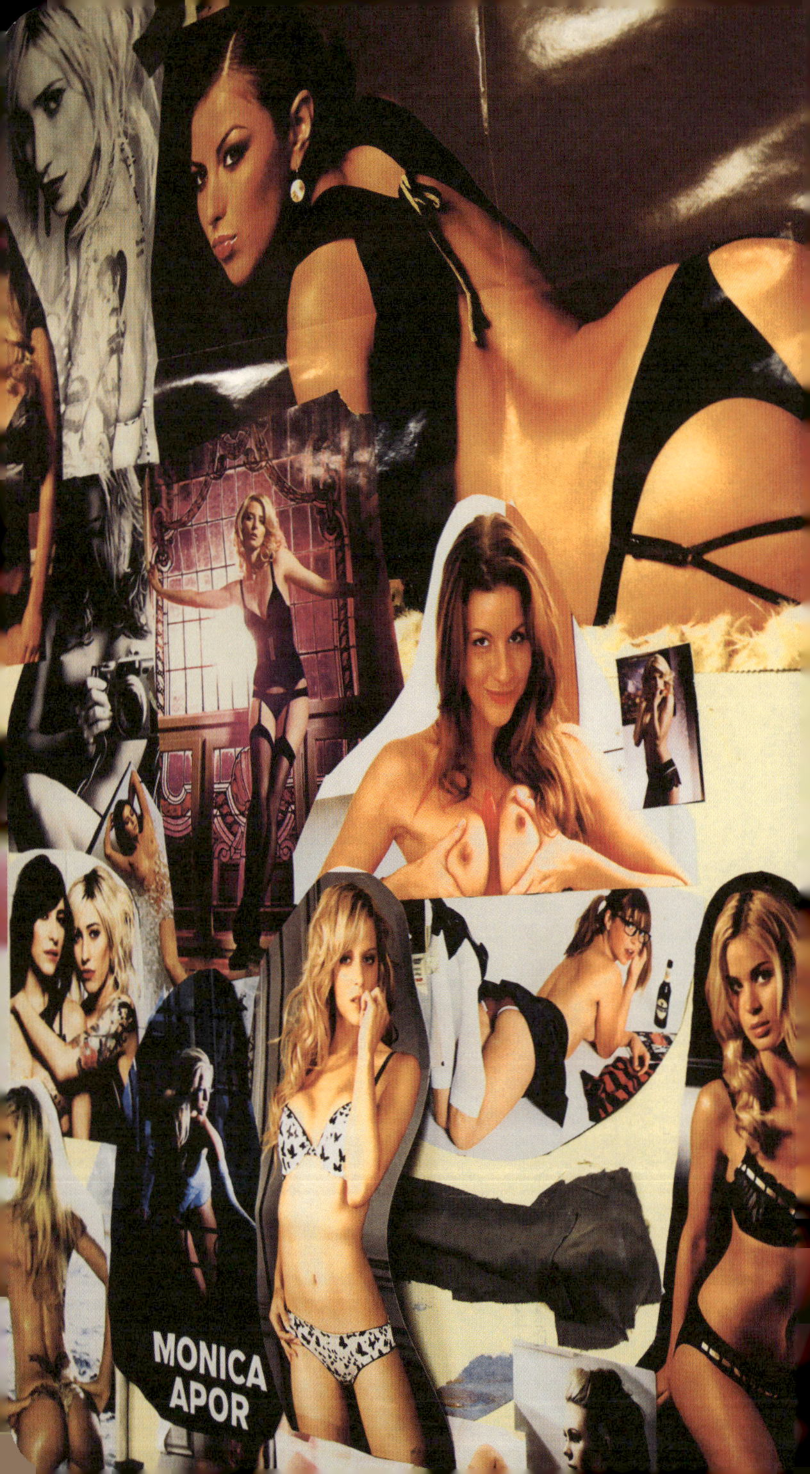
MONICA
APOR

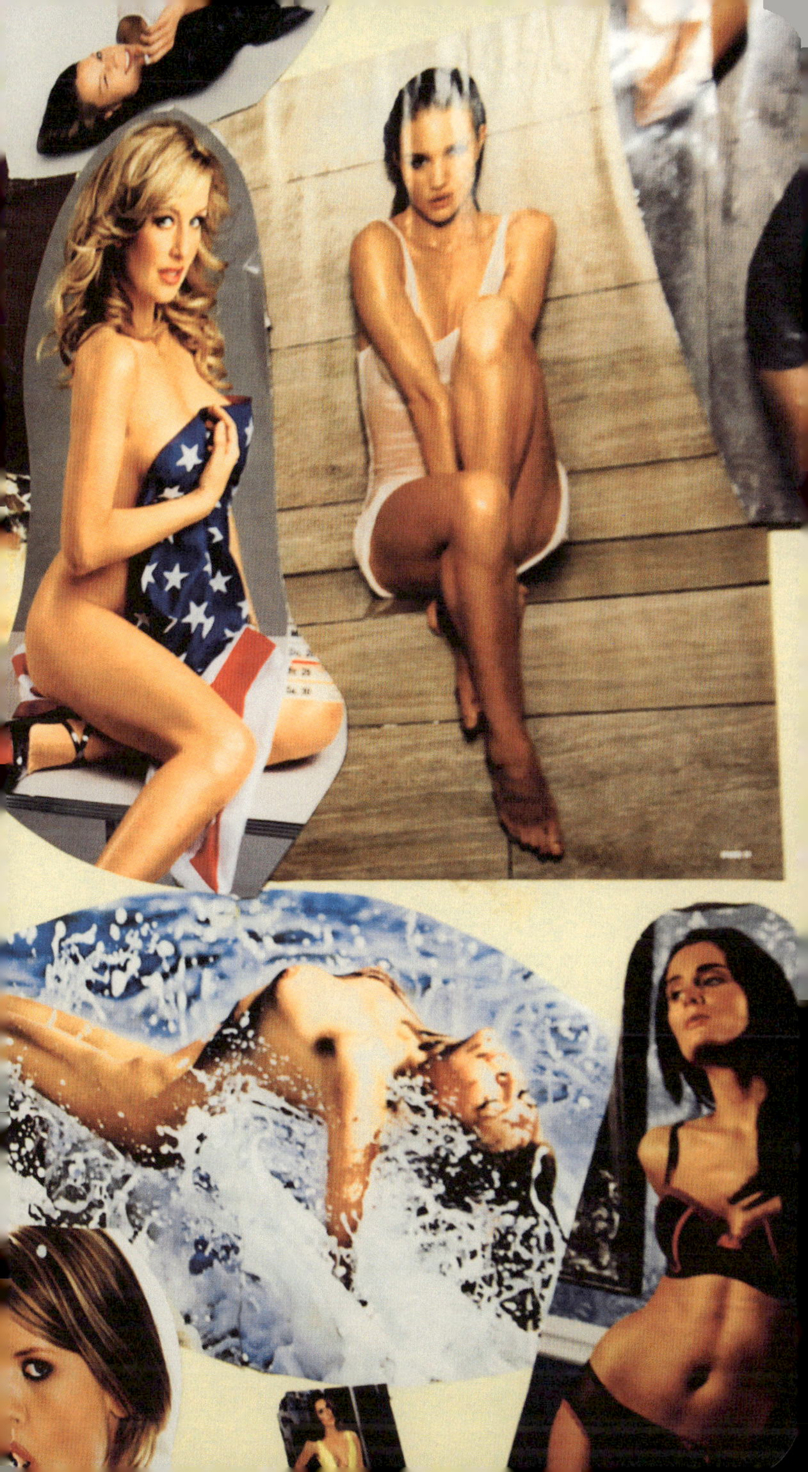

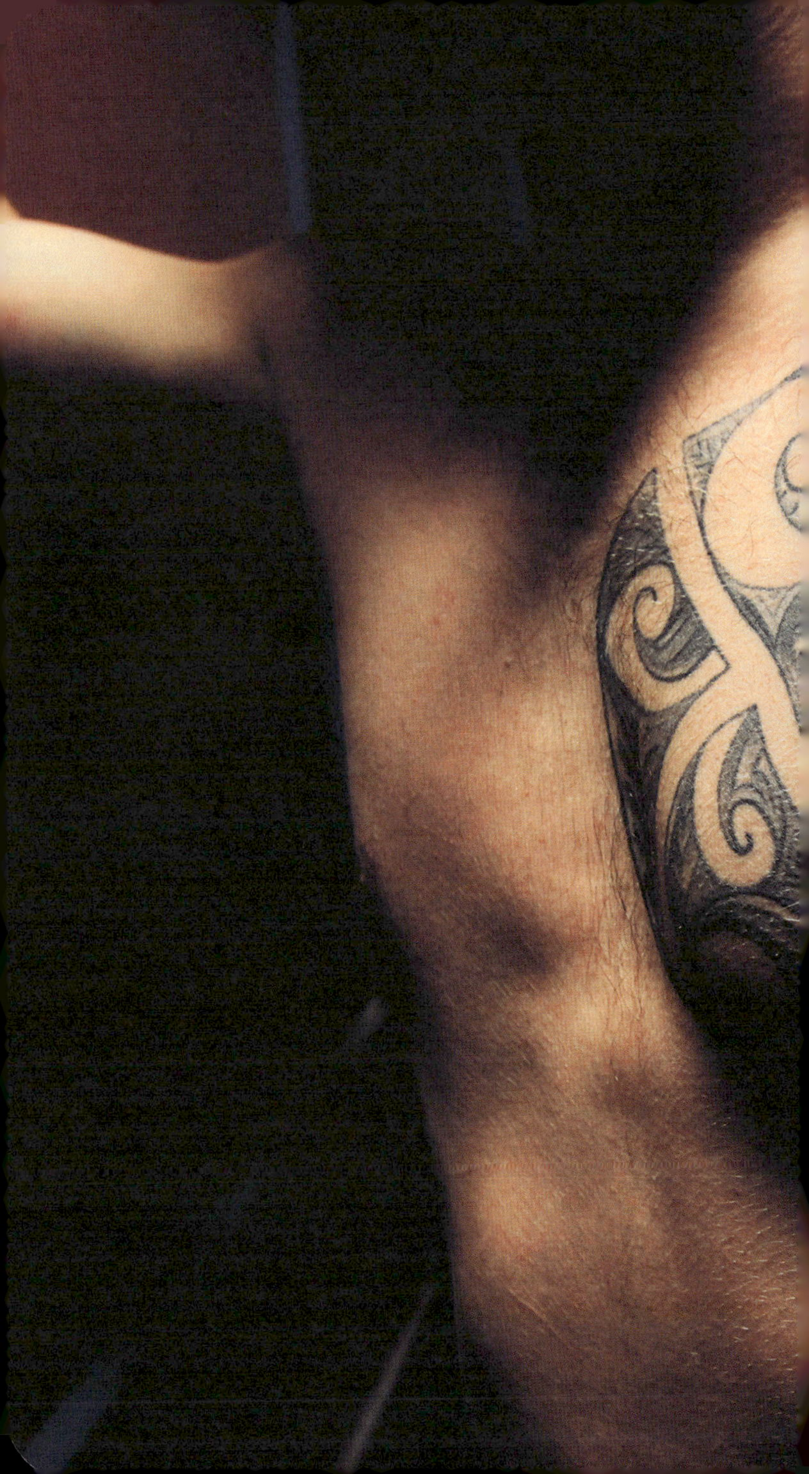

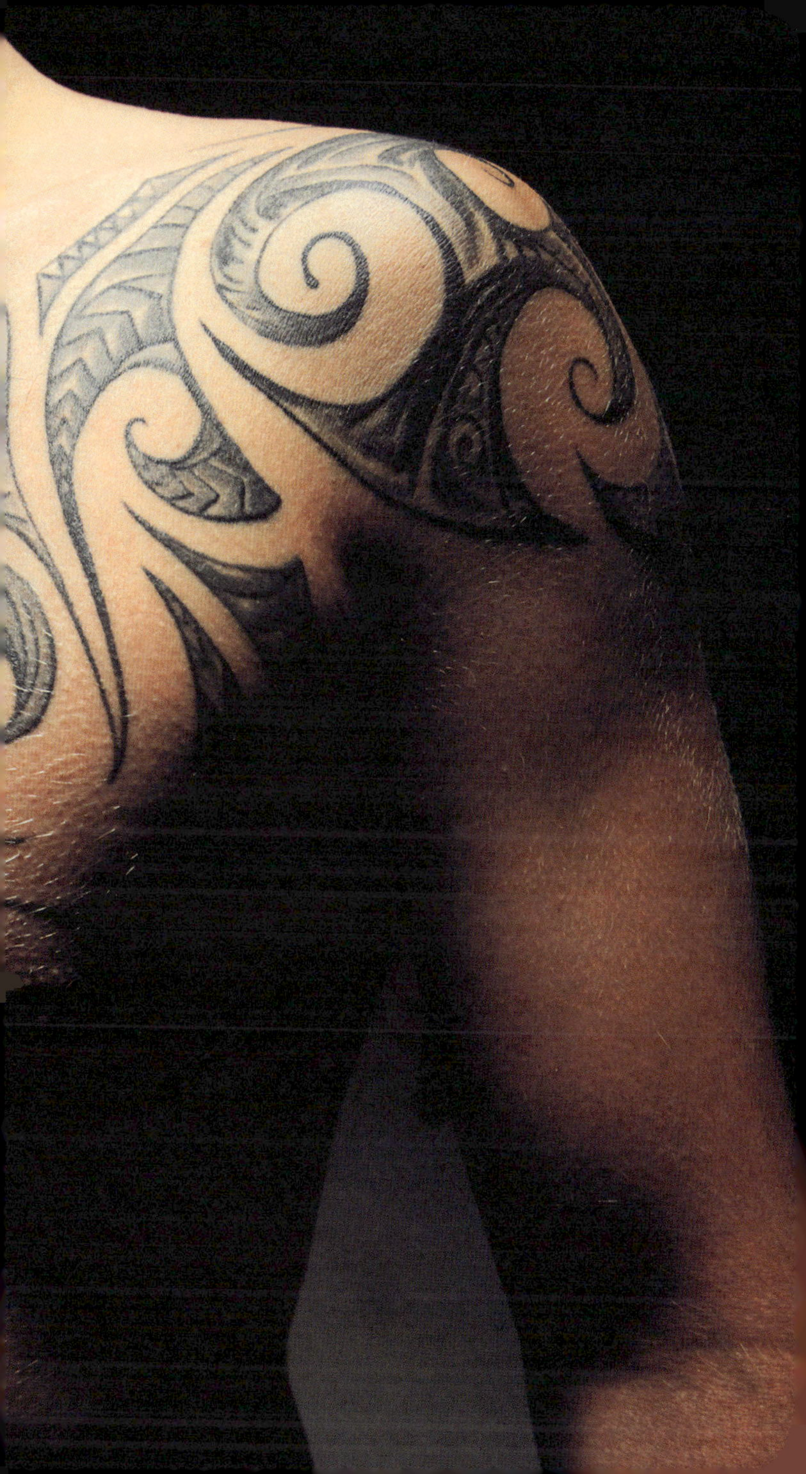

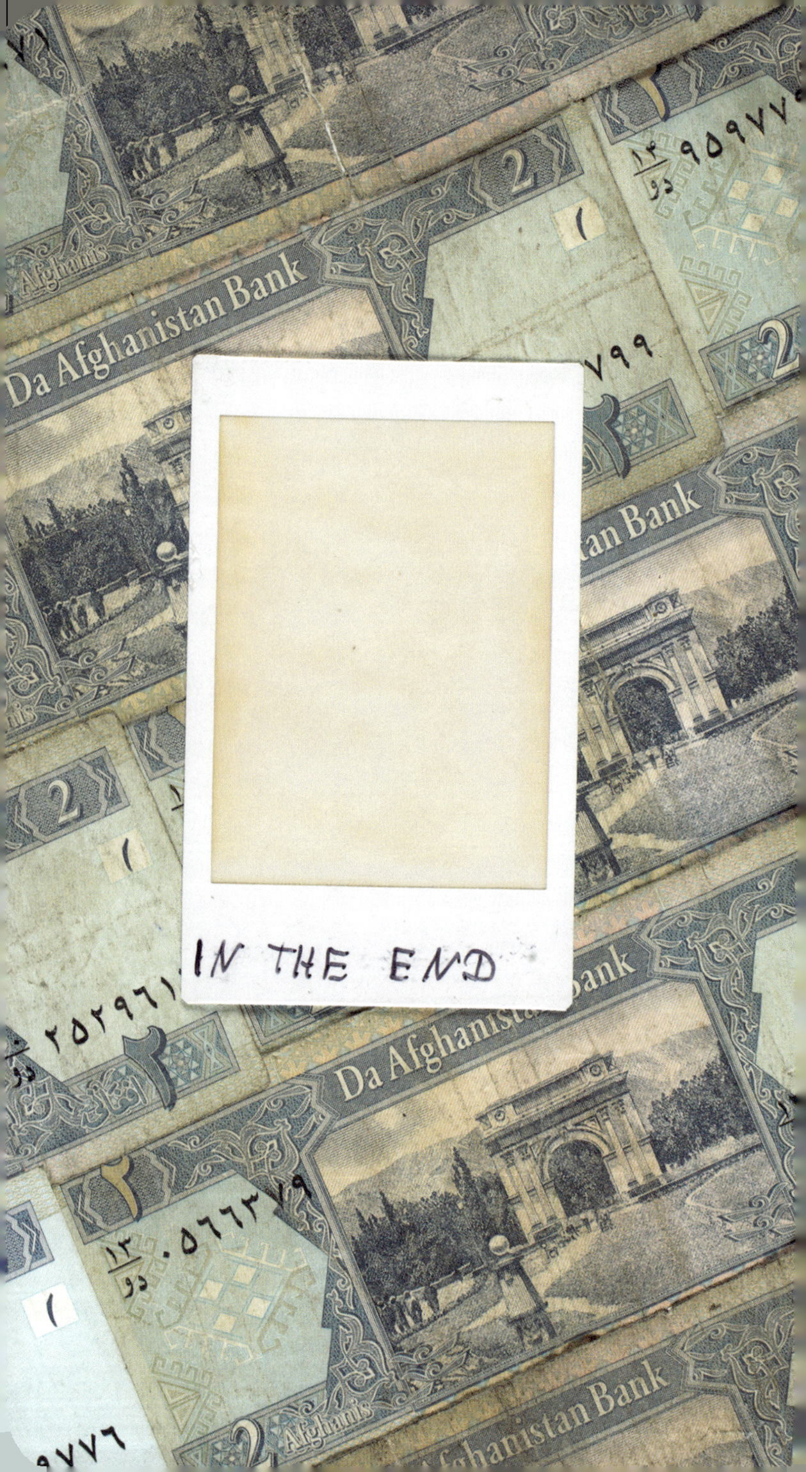
IN THE END
Da Afghanistan Bank
Afghanis

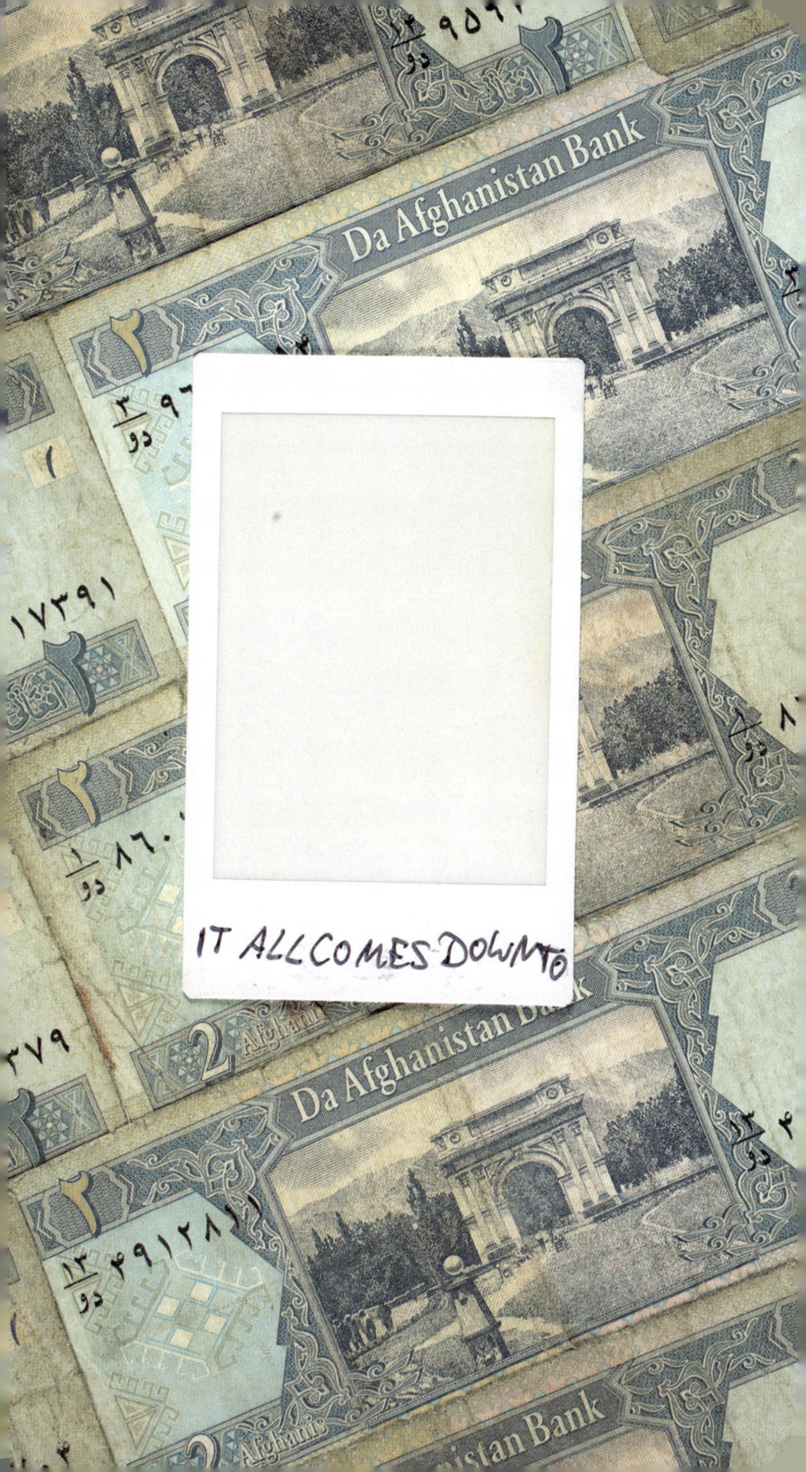
Da Afghanistan Bank
IT ALLCOMES DOWNTO
Da Afghanistan Bank

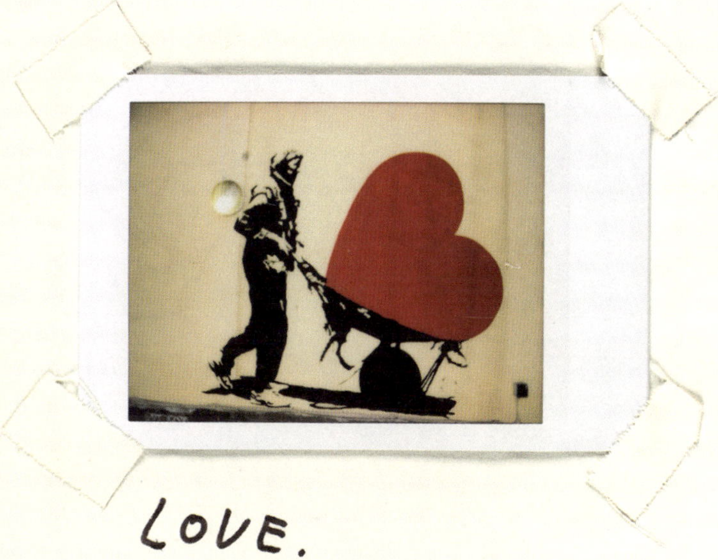

LOVE.

The NYT Magazine gives me the assignment to photograph the president of Afghanistan.
What a drama!
The appointment is at 21:45 at night. It's Ramadan and everybody works at night and sleeps during the day. Even the president.
The magazine asks me to shoot a possible cover. How can I possibly shoot a cover for the NYT Magazine at 10 o'clock at night without lights?
Impossible. I've seen pictures from inside the palace. The lighting is a disaster. Dark.

Dark. Dark.

I'm nervous. Tear myself apart. Walk up and down in my room for a day. Should I try to

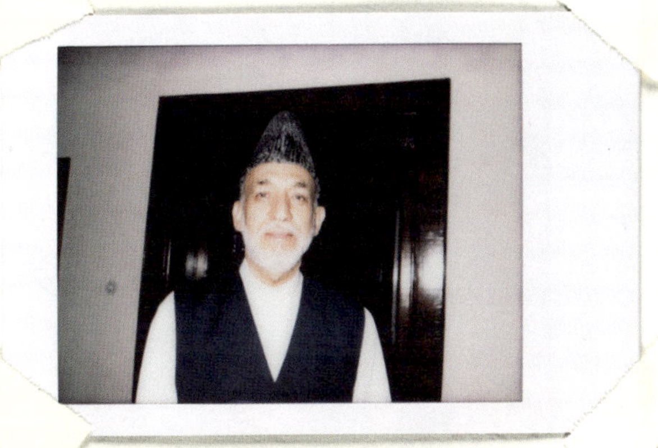

set lights? Would they allow me to ~~sen~~ set them up or even bring them into the palace? Even if I wanted lights, I would not really know how to use them. The last time I used studio lights was when I was photo student more than 10 years ago. I email back and forth with Kathy Ryan. She is very understanding and the plan is that I will try to get as much as possible and then purvey them that I can come back in day light hours.

I meet the writer.

A madman. Historian, Posh Bolt, living in India. Is Public schooler. He makes me even more nervous. He talks relentlessly. About himself.

Then I go to the place. The writer is late. Security check. K-9 dogs. X-Ray machine. Security check.

K 9- dogs. Full body check.
X-Ray machine. No pens allowed.
I have to leave my cell phone and
watch and get a cheaply laminated
card for it.
My escort is called Khwaja. Nice
guy. We wait in a waiting room
with oil paintings of Afghan
landscapes. ~~[illegible]~~ My cameras
are taken away from me. We wait.
Suddenly the door flies open,
and the president of Afghanistan,
Hamid Karzai, storms in. Every
photographer's worst nightmare: The
country's president enters the room
and I have to cameras!!
He warmly greets me and shakes

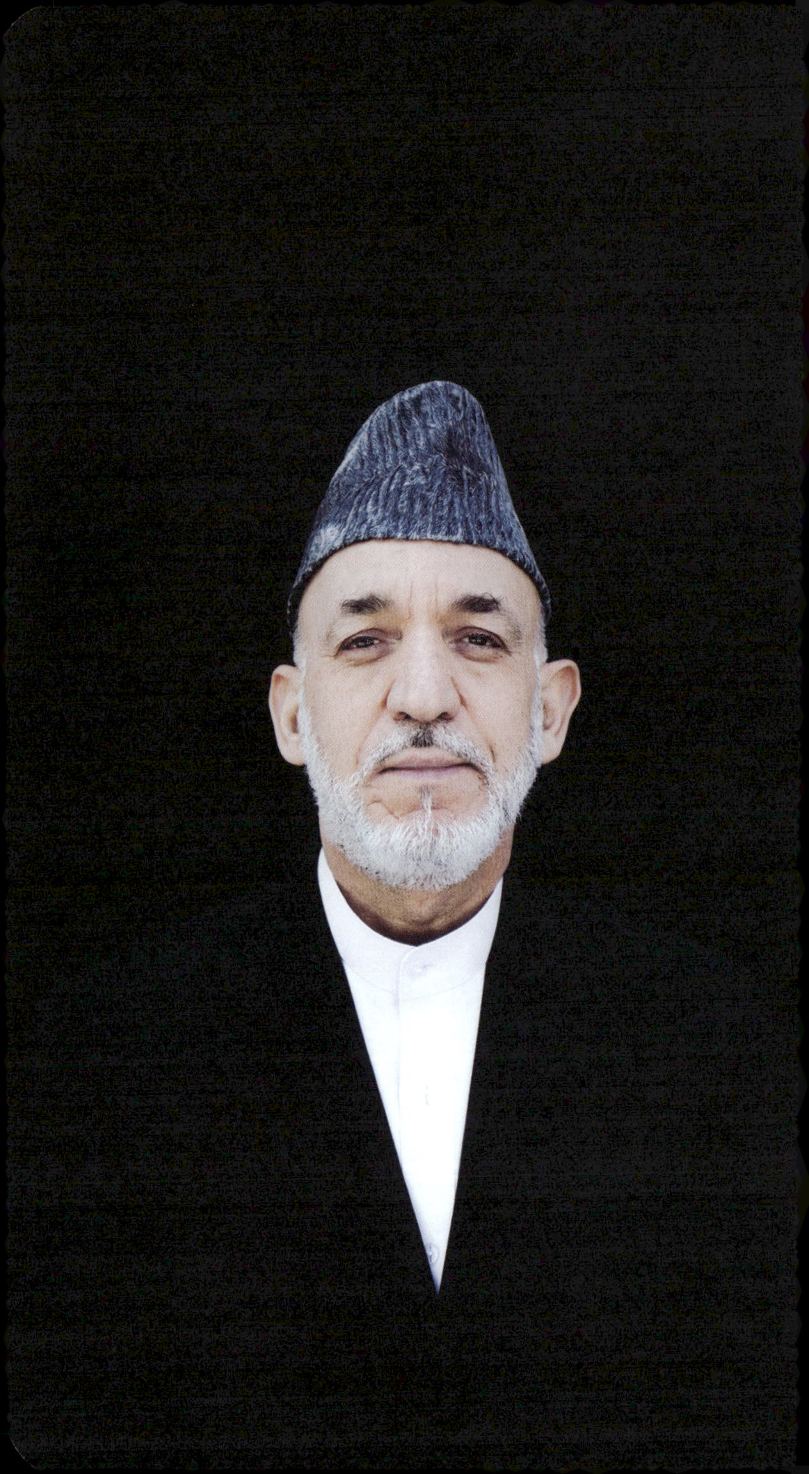

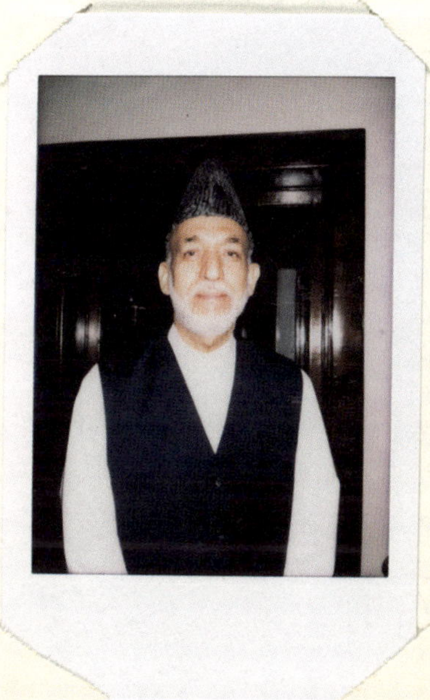

my hand. I mumble "it's an honor to meet you" and I mean it. First impression: What a friendly man!
He disappears again. Still no cameras and no William. Great.
~~We~~ Khwaja and I wait some more. William arrives, sweating, talking away. We are asked to go upstairs to the president's office. We are greeted again very warmly and the interview begins. I am allowed to photograph during the interview.
~~As~~ Once in a while Karzai tells me: "Sir, eat your biscuits!" or "Have some melon!"

He is in a good mood. Dips his bisquits into his coffee before eating it. He talks about his childhood and his time as a student in India. He loves India. Sometimes he falls back into "Mr. President"-mode. He goes on and on about how the Americans betrayed him. That they don't want a strong unified central government. He seems to believe in conspiracies. He thinks the Pakistanis *and* Americans are supporting the Taliban. He is right about the Pakistanis of course, but the Americans? I'm afraid the Americans are not sofisticated enough to play such elaborate double games. The Americans are straight. And terrible diplomats. They will never built a successful American empire. Those boys don't even learn the language of the nation that they are occupying. A hopelessly naive, black and white thinking bunch with the best intentions.

Before we leave I take a formal portrait. It's so bloody dark, I have to shoot with 32001501!! It's the disaster that I expected. What a defeat.

I go to bed late at night. Unhappy. Restless.

Only two days later I dare to look at the pictures. I run a test on one of the formal portraits and, tatah... it actually looks much better than I expected. I'm such an idiot. I'm beating myself up for days and in the end the pictures are fine. Pure Drama. I go to the palace two more times. On my second visit I talk to my friend Khwaja and tell him that I need to take another formal portrait of the President outside in the garden where the light is better. He promises to arrange it, but there is

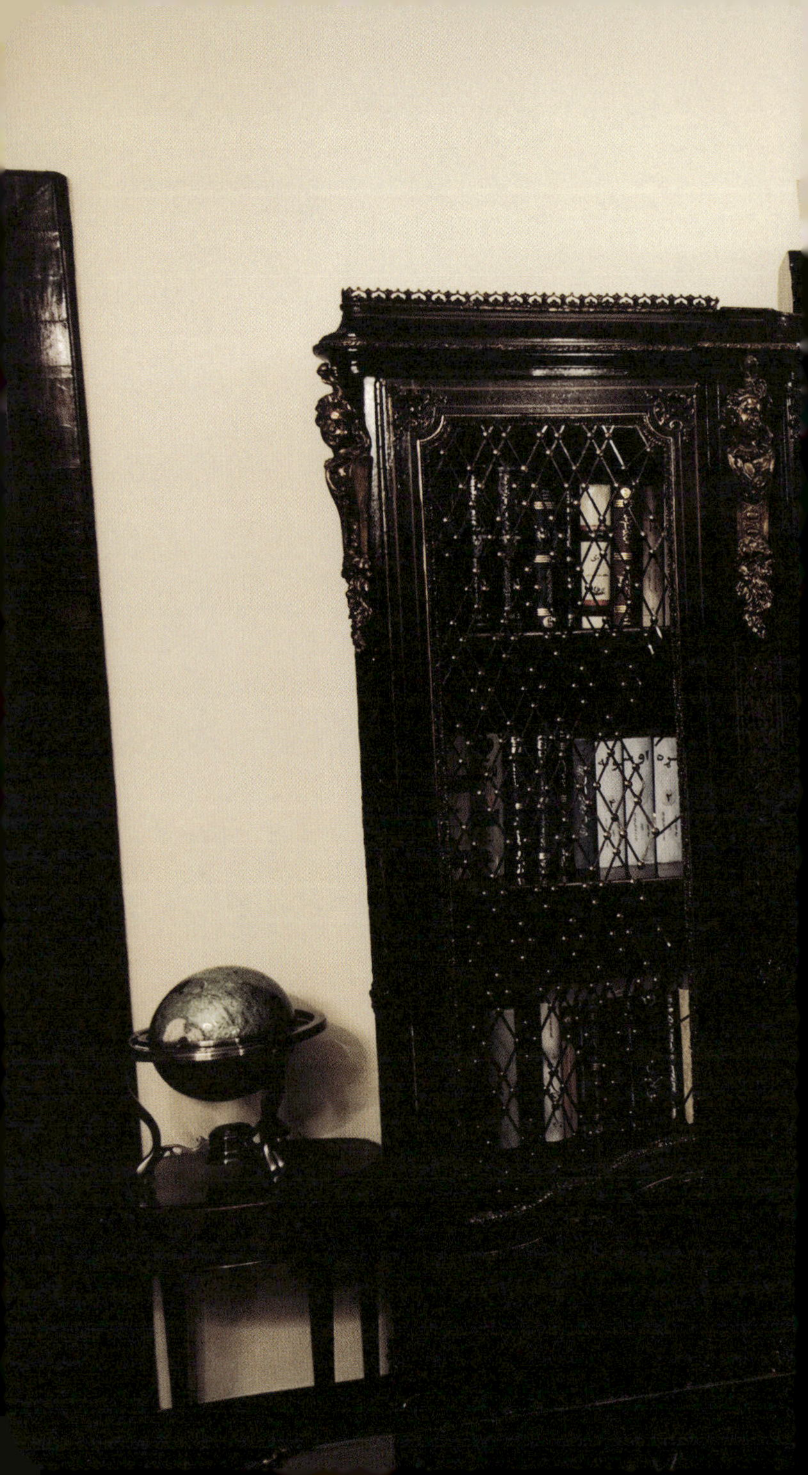

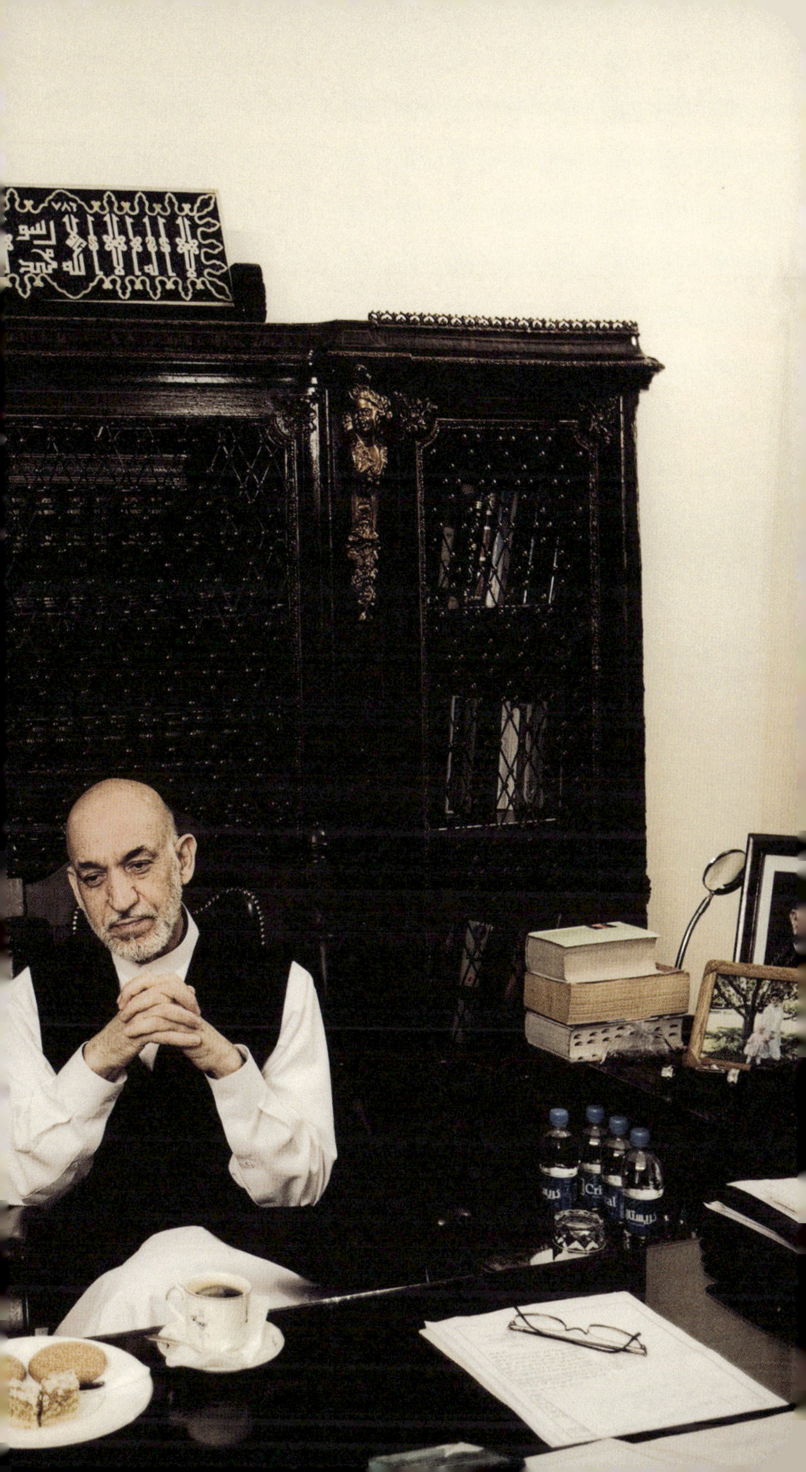

literally too scared to ask the president. I see everything slipping away and the shoot falling through, while I take all my courage and approach the president directly. There is a long silence after. The press people are mortified. The 20 or so bodyguards get all jumpy. Finally Karzai says: "Sure, let me just wash my face, I'll be right back." And he came back to the garden. I took a portrait in the entrance of the old king's palace and a few minutes later Karzai says:

"That's it." and the shoot is over. I thank him, shake his hand and he disappears with all his bodyguards and aides in tow. I made it. I got my portrait.

Karzai was the friendliest man in the entire palace. The rest people are completely useless. Incompetent. Khwaja is a coward. A friendly coward. None of them seem to understand the power of pictures. Few people actually get this, especially in the newspaper business, funny enough. They all think words are the most powerful thing. But they're not. Deeds are powerful. The things that people do. And what are pictures?

Pictures are the documentations, recordings and reflections on actions/deeds/events. It's the way we record events. And history. We remember in still pictures. Not words. Not moving images. Not sound.

DEEDS NOT WORDS!!

I'm on a trip with Sanjar, Azam and Kabir to Gardez (Paktia) and Khost. We're in Khost at the moment. Staying at the "Mility Guest House" Khost's best (and only) hotel. Kidnapping and targeted killings is a problem, so I stay most of the time in my room. I have palm trees.

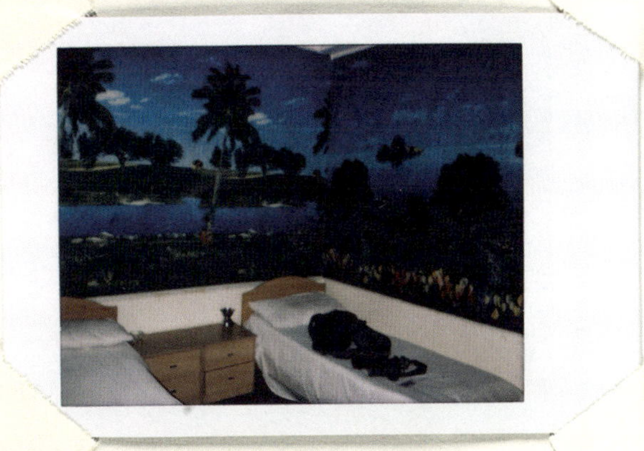

My room at the Utility Guest House.

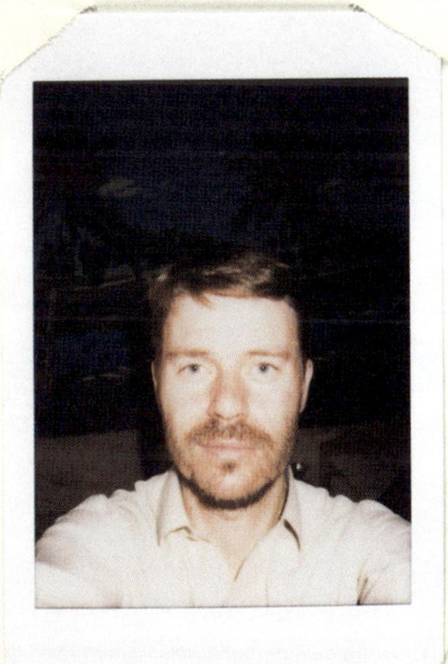

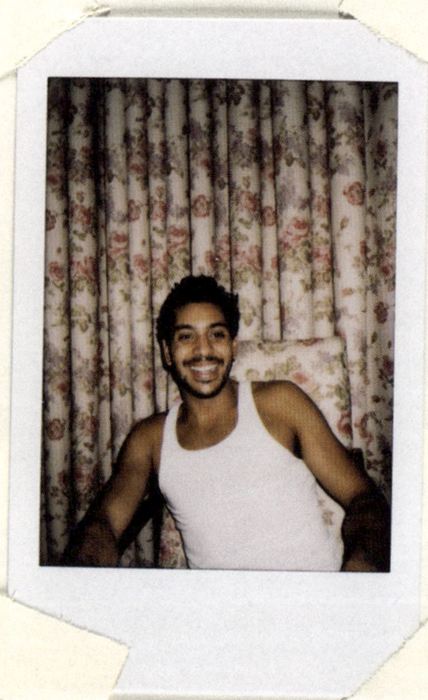

Azam with Laura Ashley / Martha Stewart
– background.

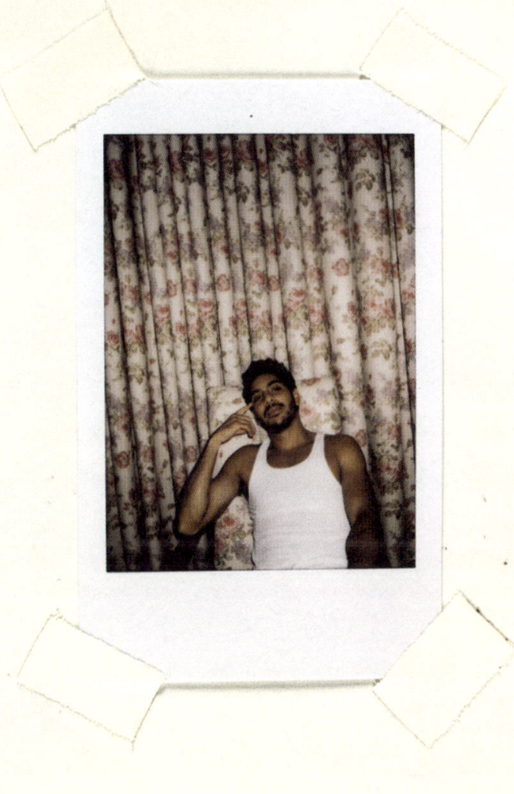

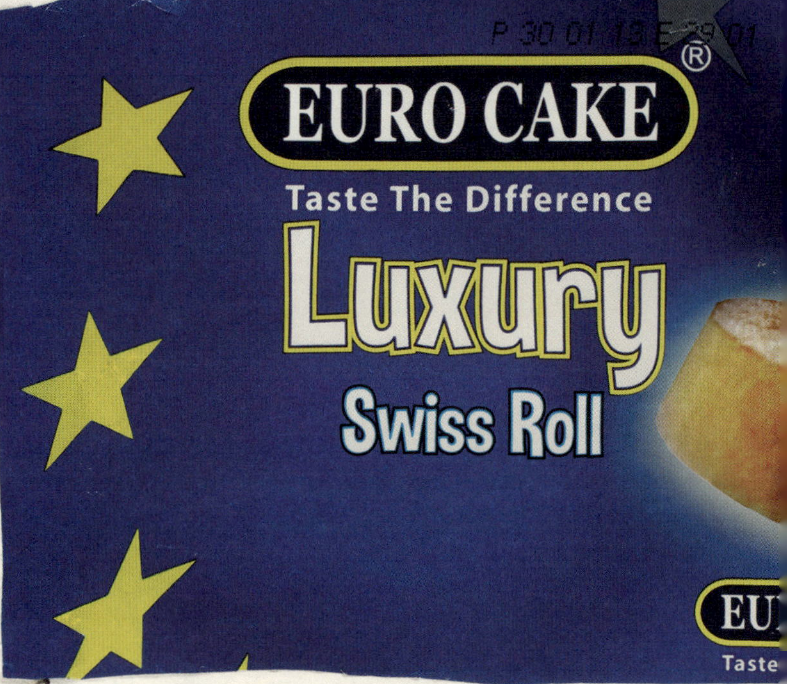

It's Ramadan and nobody is eating
or drinking during the day.
This is my lunch. Euro Cake. It
Thankyou Du
tastes like card board with sugar.
But I don't complain and am grateful
especially for the water that I am
allowed to drink (in secret in my room
during the day. ~~But~~ The weather is
very hot at the moment and everybody

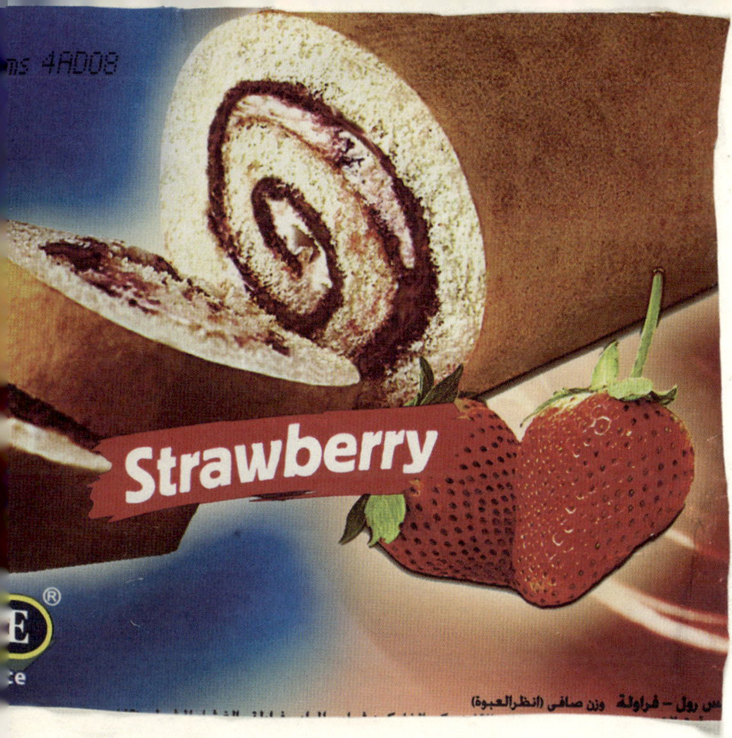

s basically constantly dehydrated and
hungry. I don't mind not eating.
specially because I've had diarrhea for
days now. But not drinking is hard.
If the Swiss knew that their "Swiss
Roll" is advertised as "Euro Cake"
with the European flag and all!
ean, Sangar, Kabir, Mangal (the local
kings) and I are breaking the fast together

every day at exactly 19:12 PM.
It's usually a feast with rice, beef, sheep/lamb, bread, chicken, vegetables and lots of water, sodas and tea.
The meal is called Iftar and it's not only a celebration of the breaking of the fast, but also a desperately longed for relief of awful thirst and overwhelming hunger.
But it's all worth it, because in the end what awaits us is: paradise!

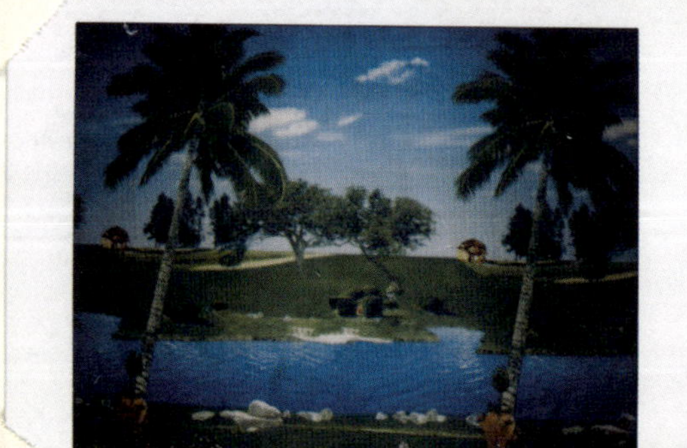

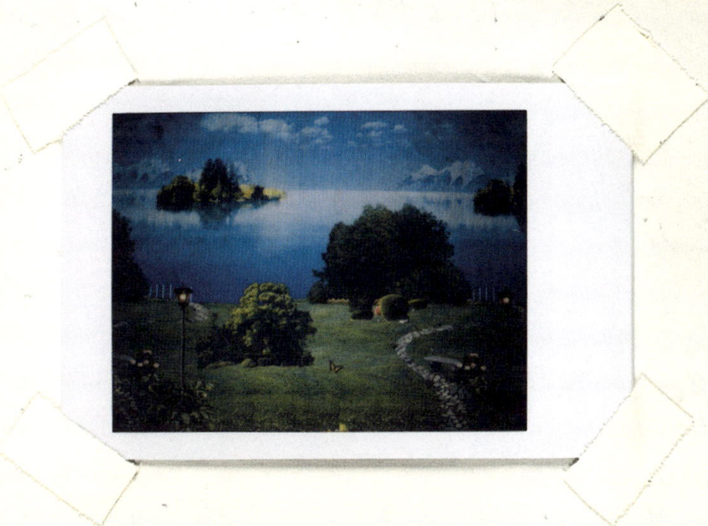

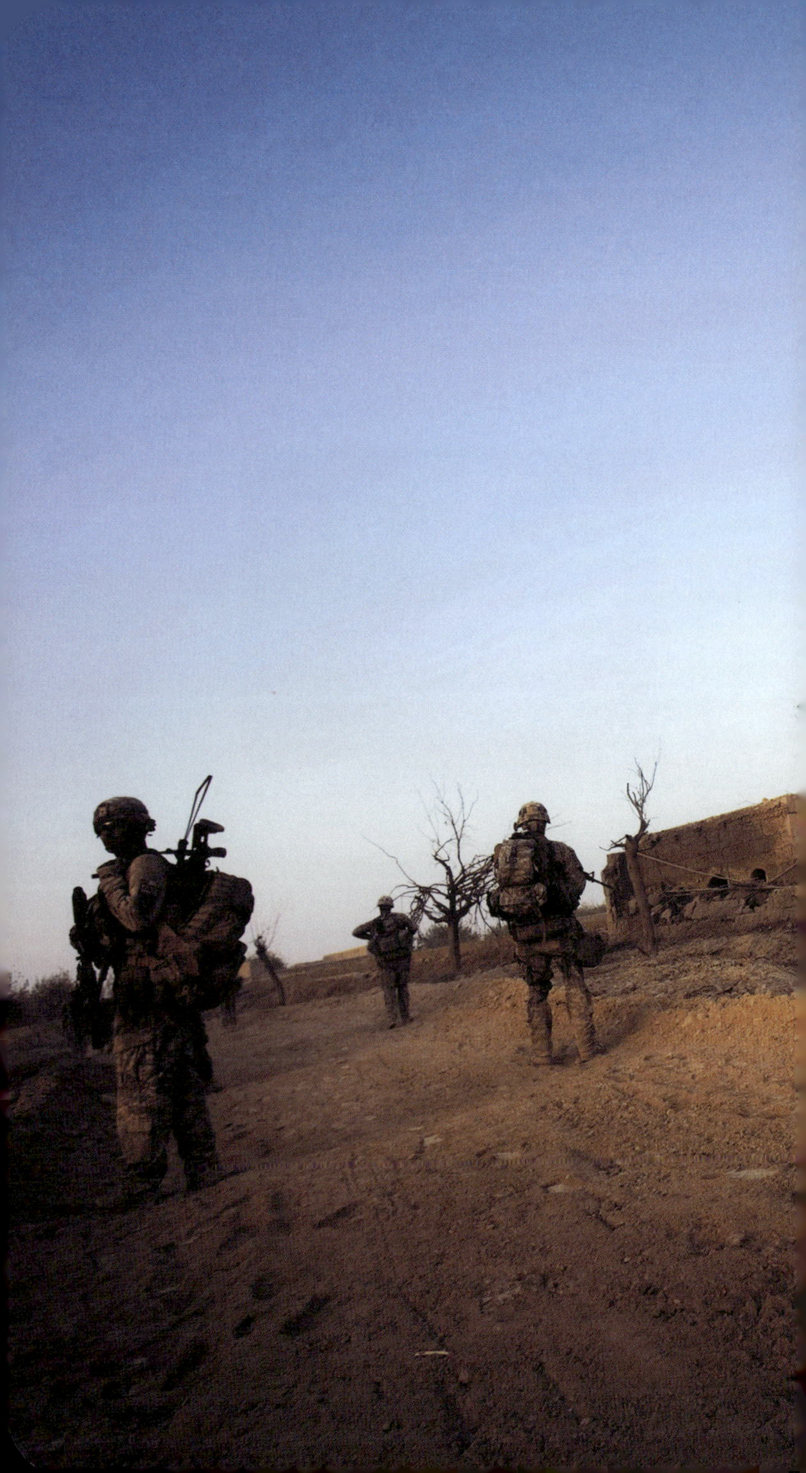

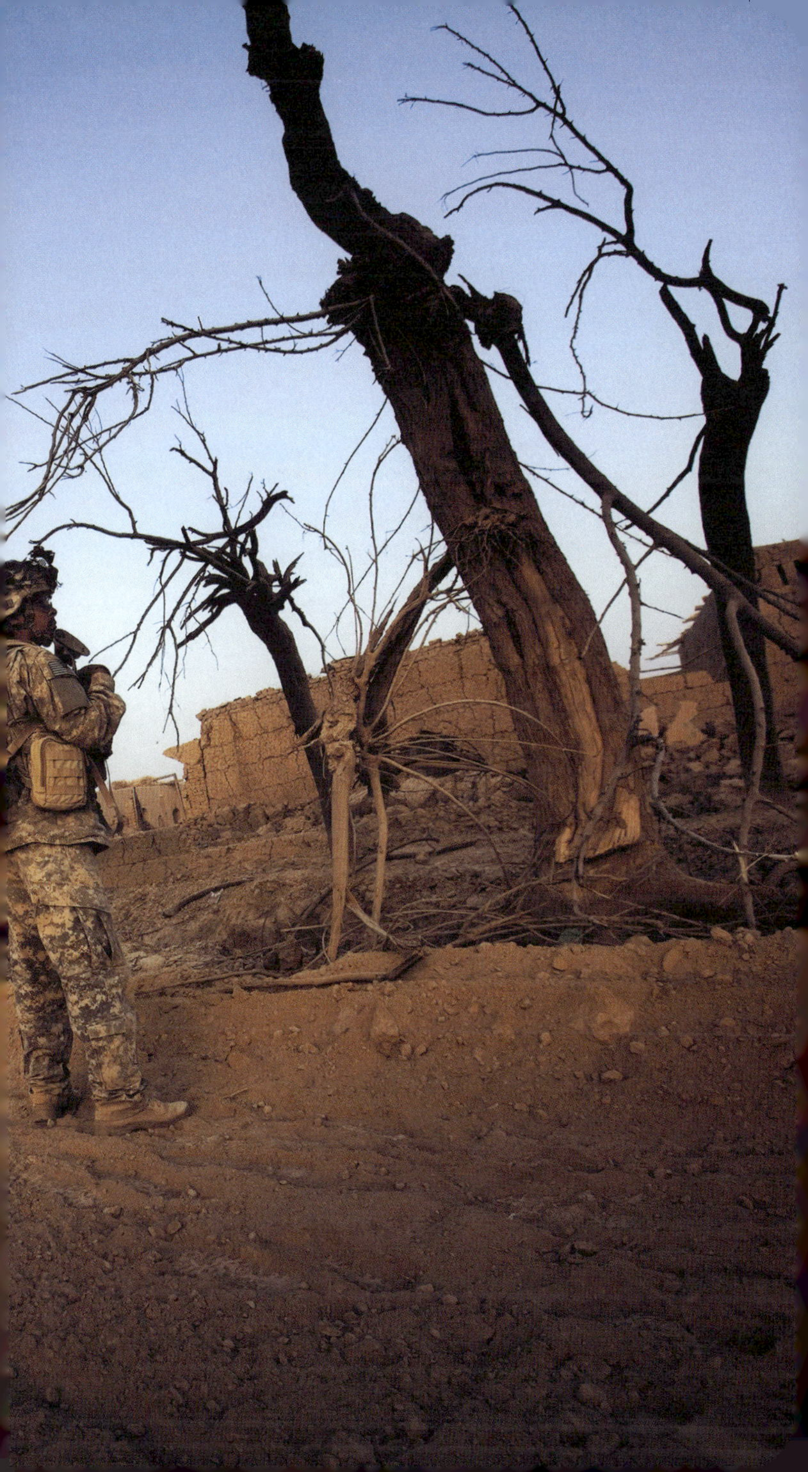

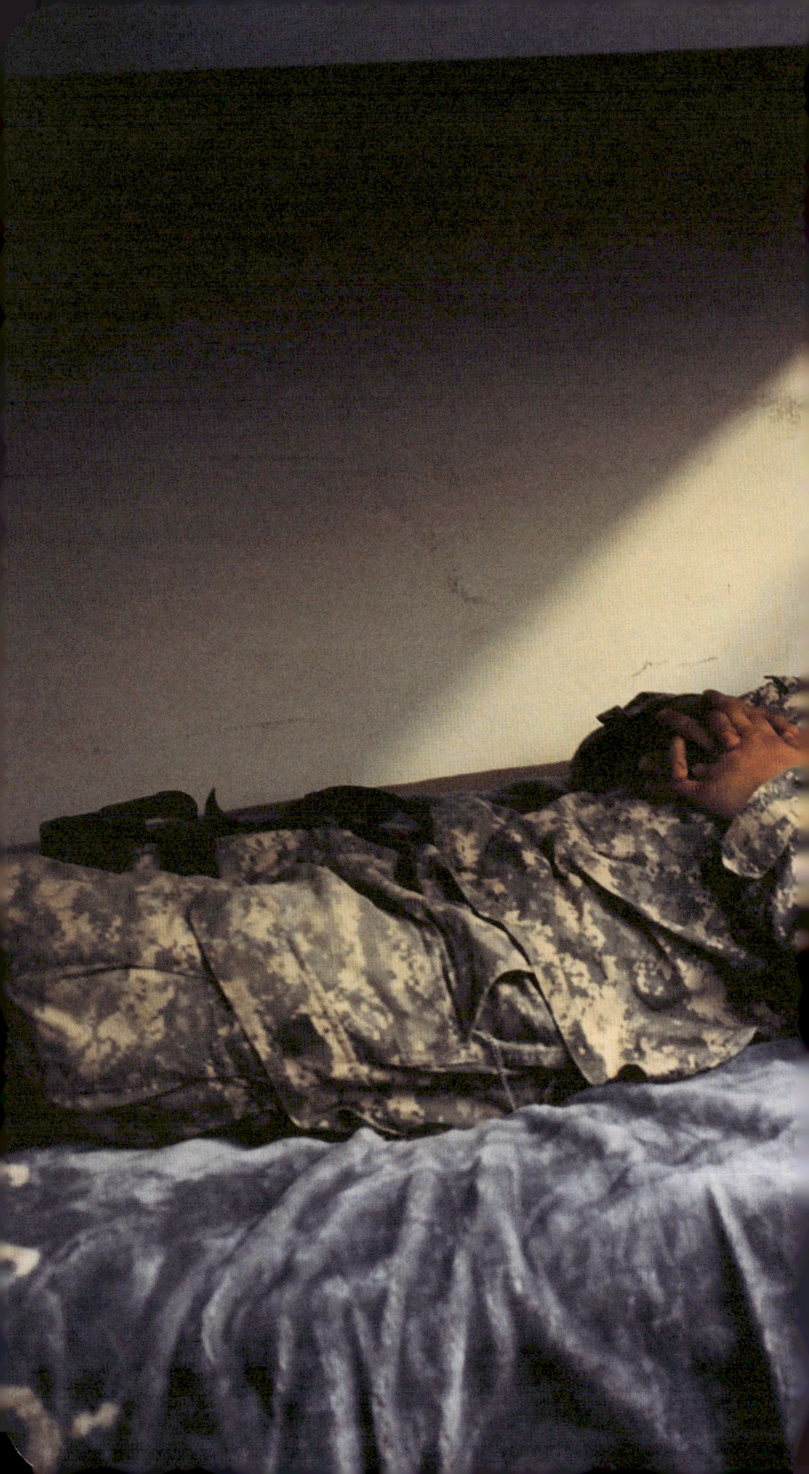

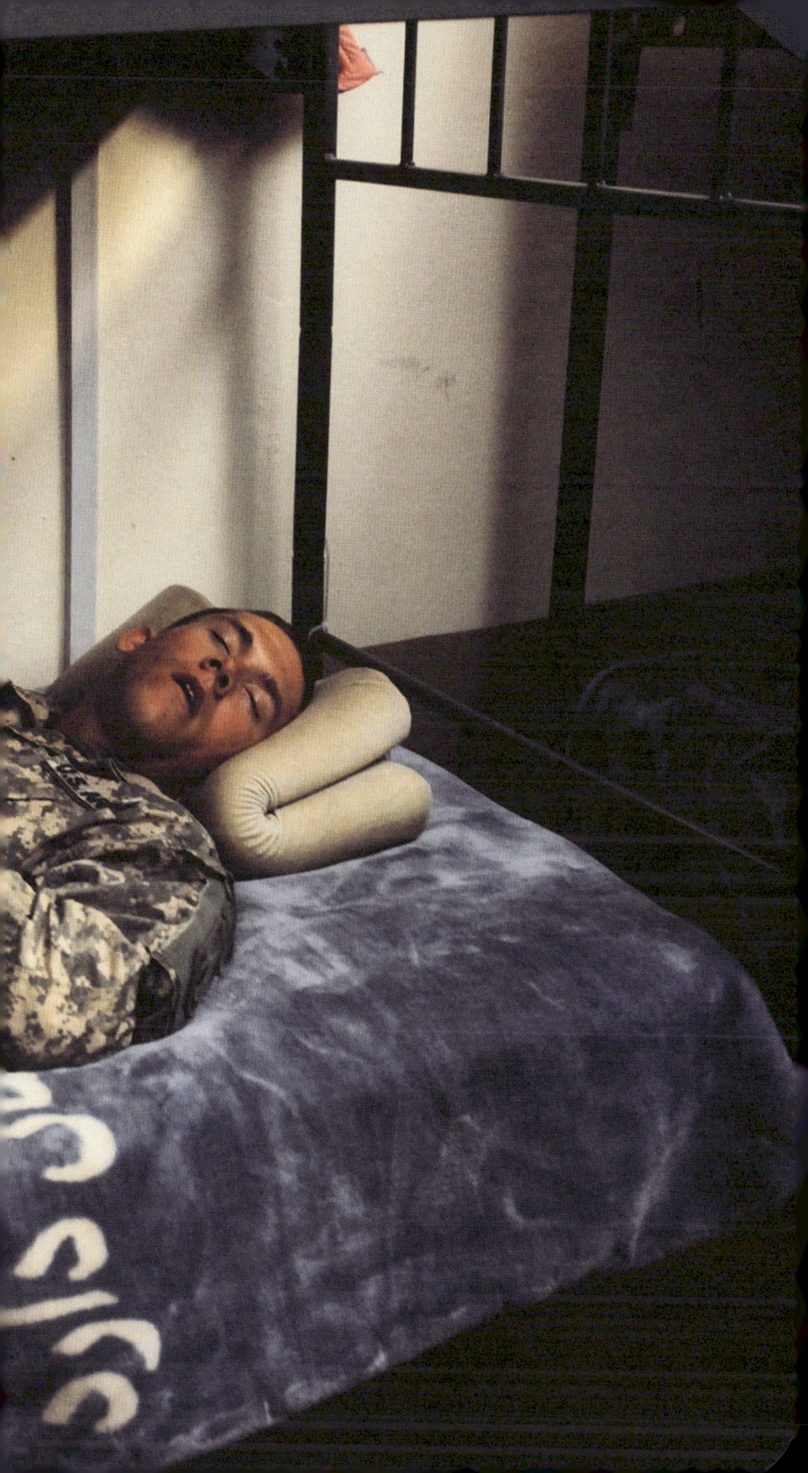

داسی خوک شتری دوو تابعیتم

وزیران ولو نشتی؟

دا بیت الحال به شش دو نیم لکه تنخواه درگیری

گرشا دیارسی بندل - جسن دجازتکلک

شتار تنخواه به خود زمرنبزه له هدونم دوحی

ر عالسن طلق بعجی جوابی به اوزه بیم که ریدان

شش لس طلن بحی نبود نقی شه تیلول کبری رودان

تا هدی به سر شش از زجاتد منع وامش لم لشی

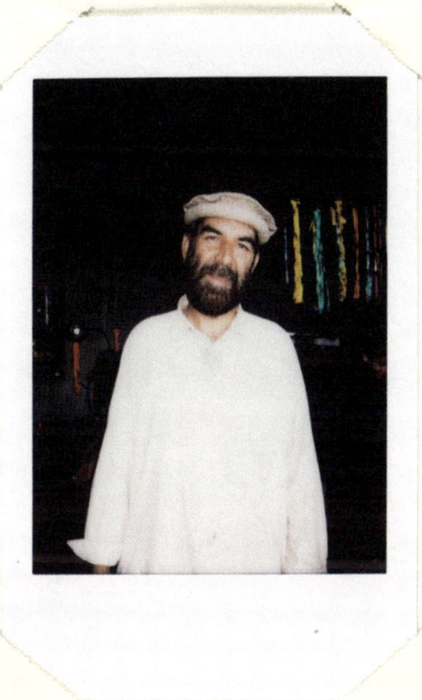

مطیع الله تراب

Afghanistan is producing nothing. Everything is imported from Pakistan, Dubai, India, Iran, Uzbekistan and China.

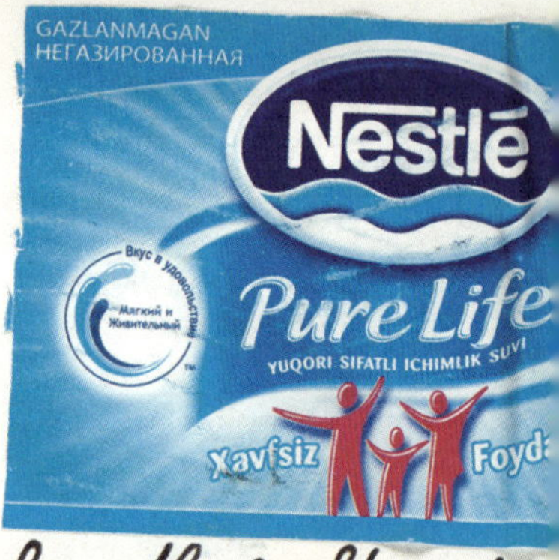

Thank you Nestlé for ruling the world and bringing bottled water to Afghanistan!

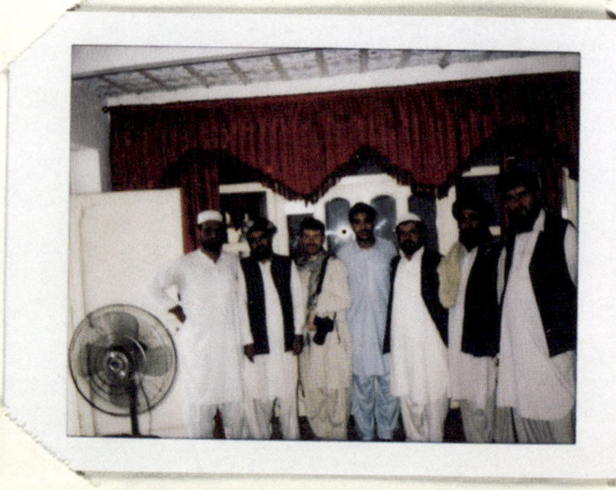

We meet some tribal elders. Big turbans, long beards. Proud pashtuns. They were absolutely convinced that America is playing a double game and are funding the Taliban through Pakistan and the ISI.

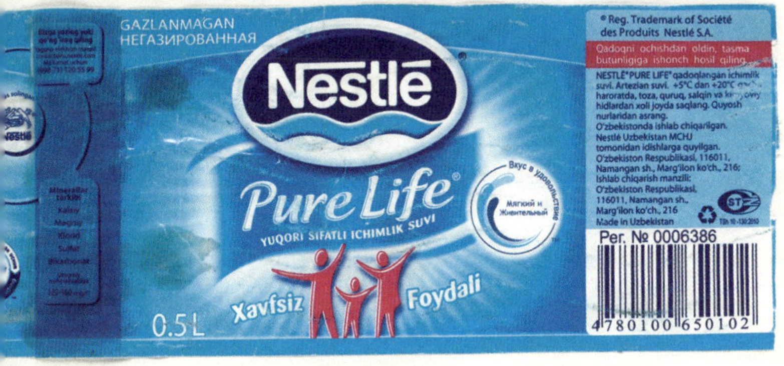

"America could end this war within two weeks if they just wanted to." They believe that the Americans are playing games and don't want Afghanistan to succeed. Pakistan is the devil and America is behind everything Pakistan does. Conspiracy. Conspiracy. Conspiracy. I'm afraid that America is not as sophisticated as these tribesmen believe it to be. Americans are lousy diplomats. Pakistan is constantly playing them and they just watch in awe.

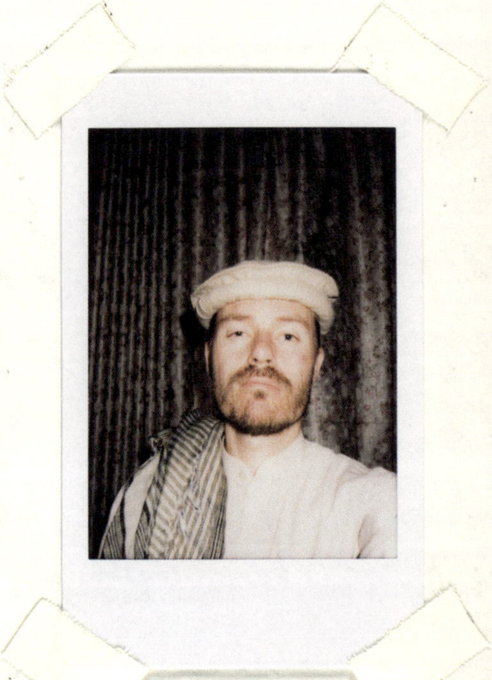

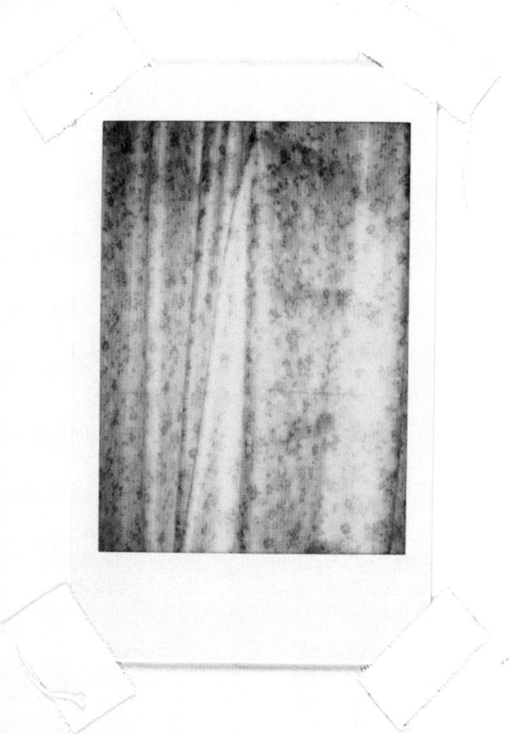

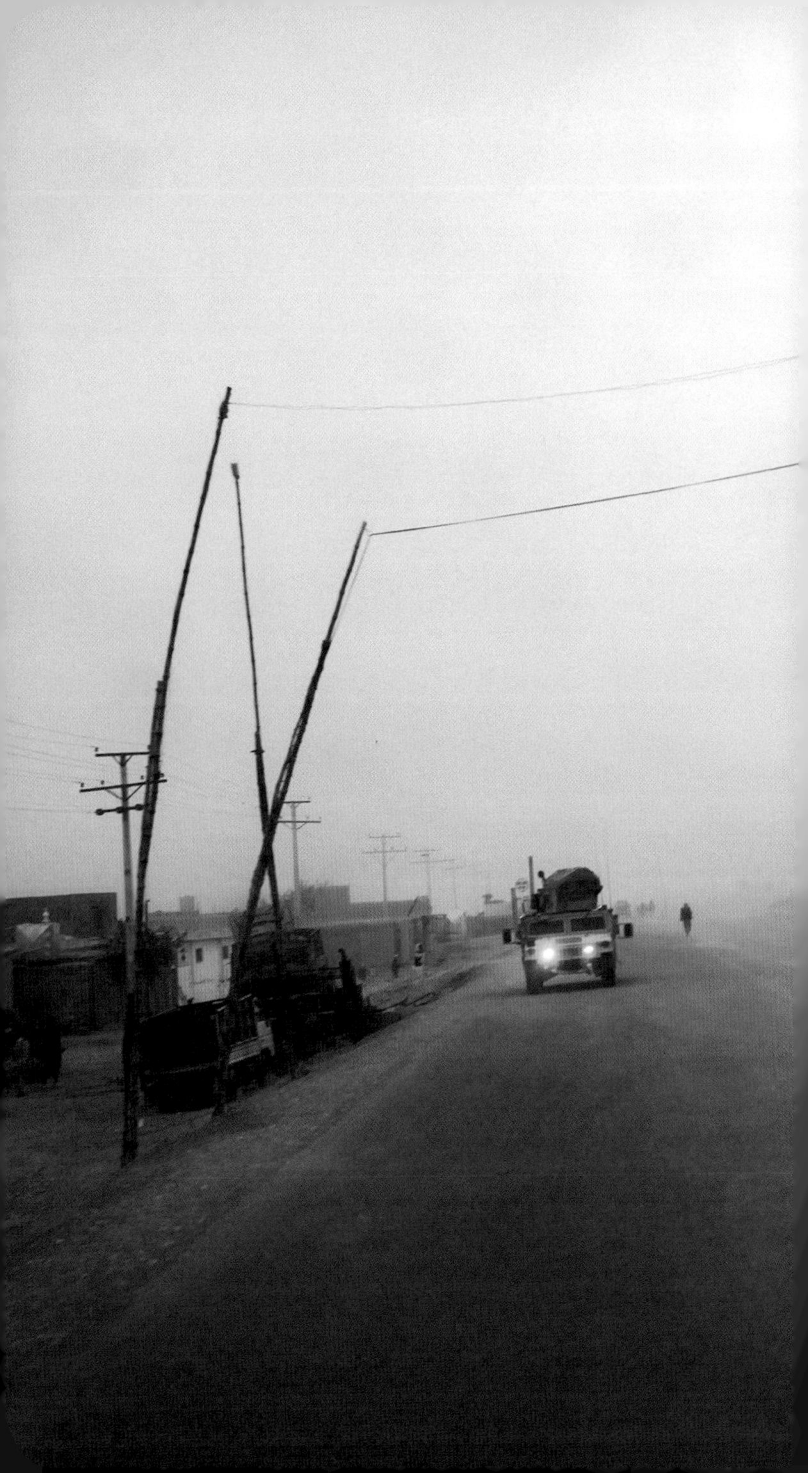

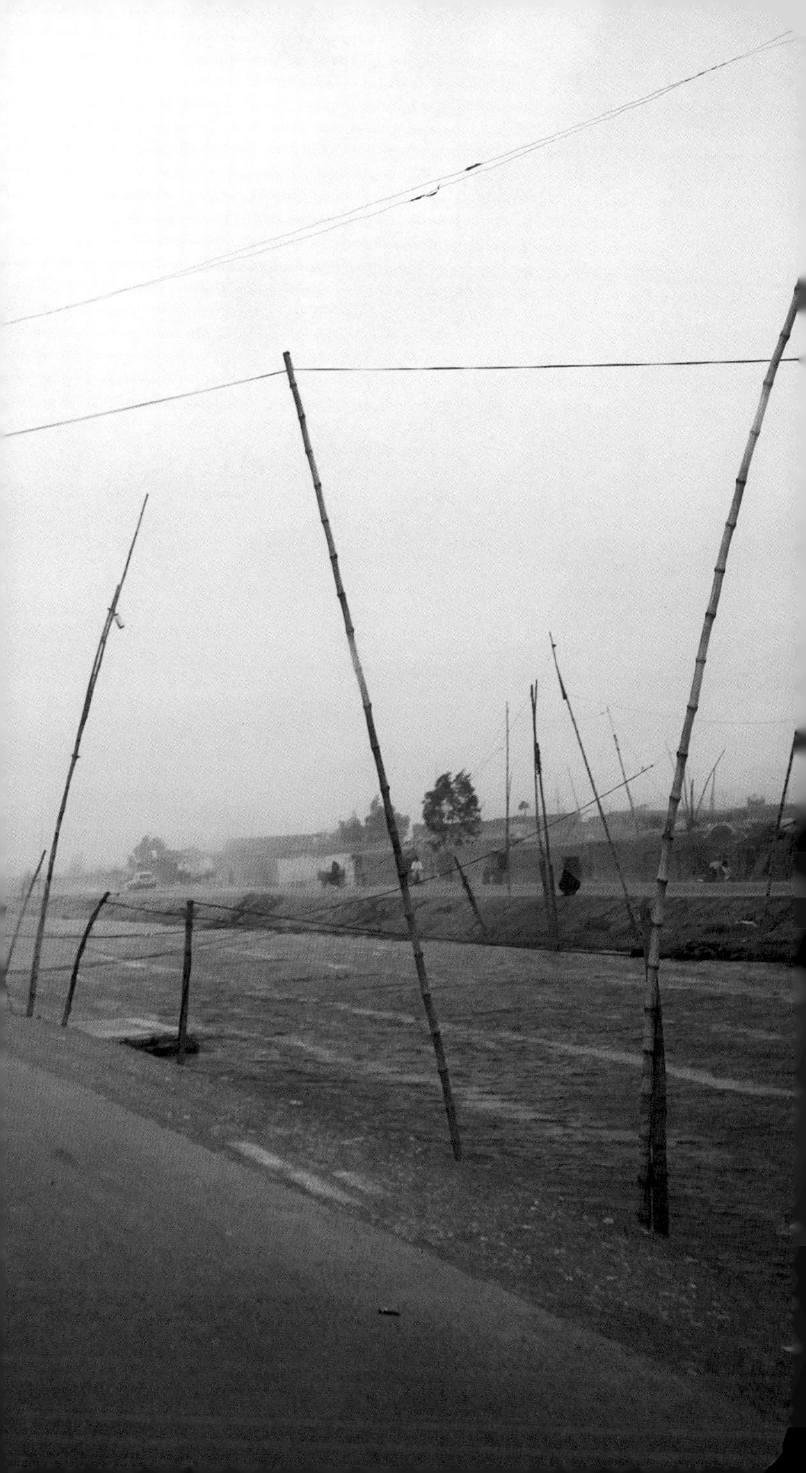

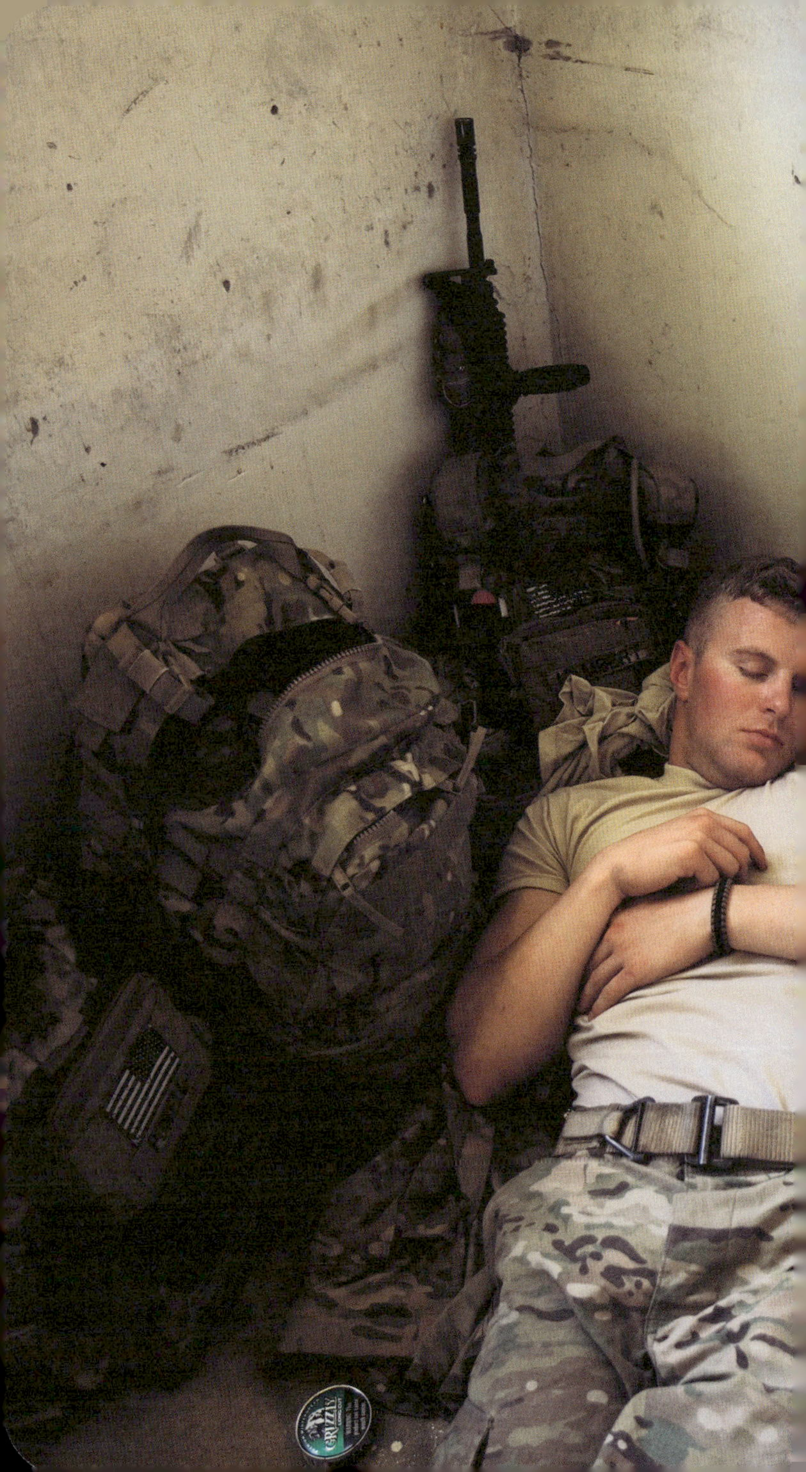

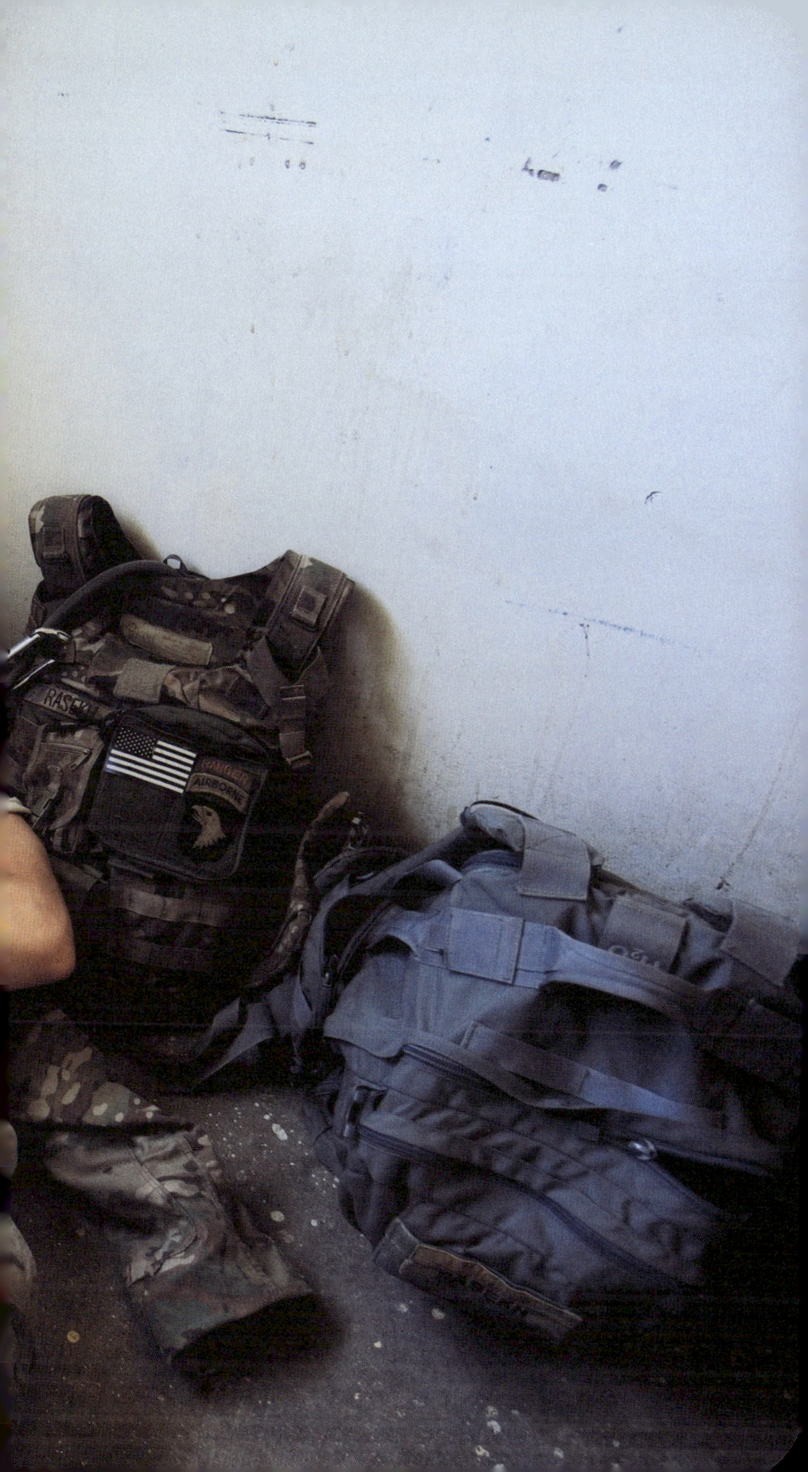
AIRBORNE

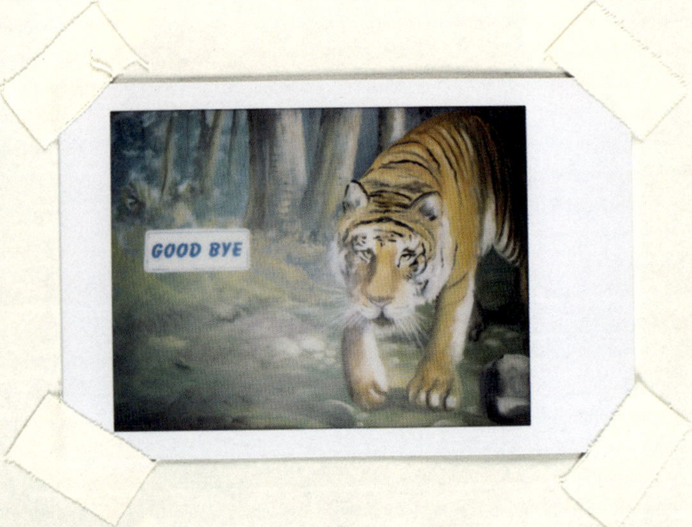

The good bye tiger.

Hungry. Waiting for Iftar. One hour and fourtytwo minutes to go. I'm in my room, writing, sleeping, thinking. This is not the kind of place where you can walk around as a white guy and take pictures in the streets. Despite my "sophisticated" disguise with Pakol, Shalwar-i-Kameez, scarf and leather shoes, I stand out in the crowd.

My skin is just too pink.

So I take it easy, because it's not worth it. The pictures I would take during a 15 minute push-and-rush-walk on the streets of Khost and are not worth the risk of getting kidnapped and spending three months in a dirt hole.

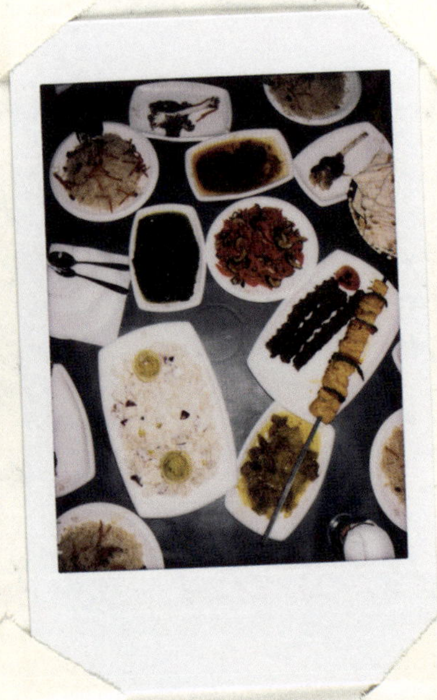

Iftar !!

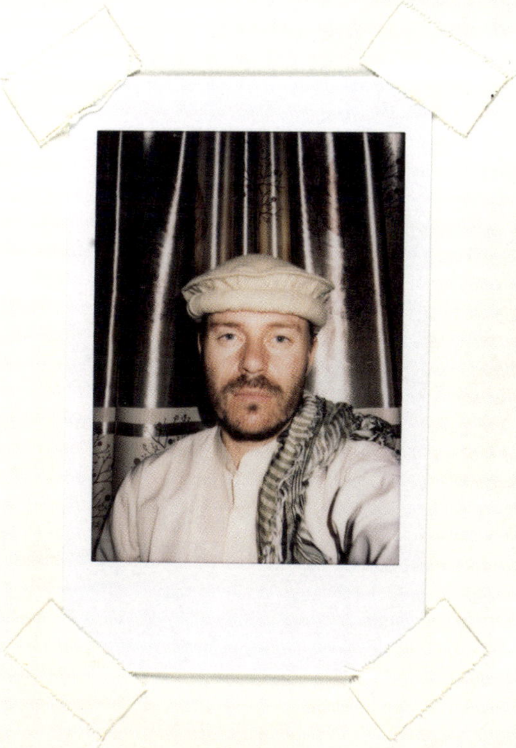

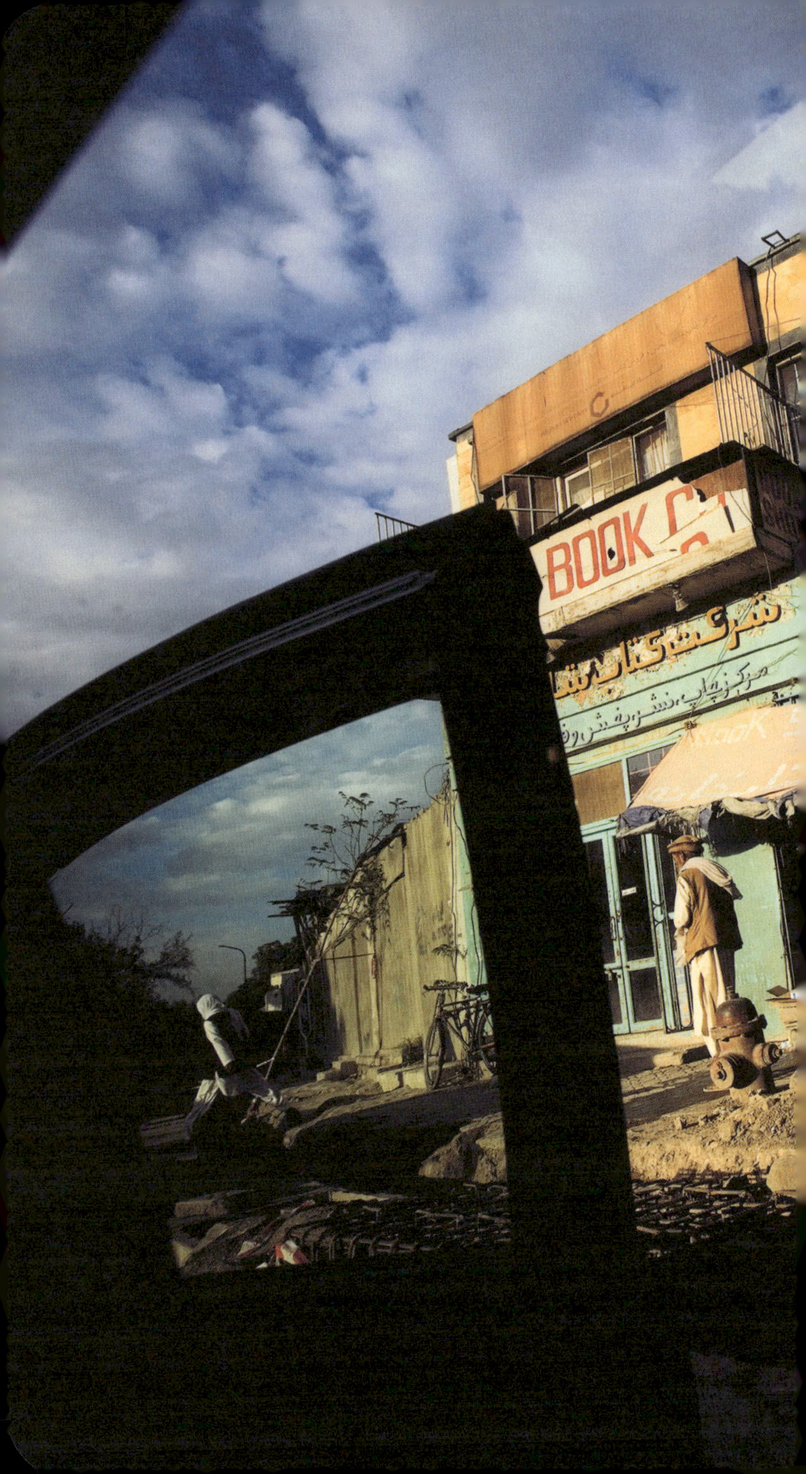
BOOK

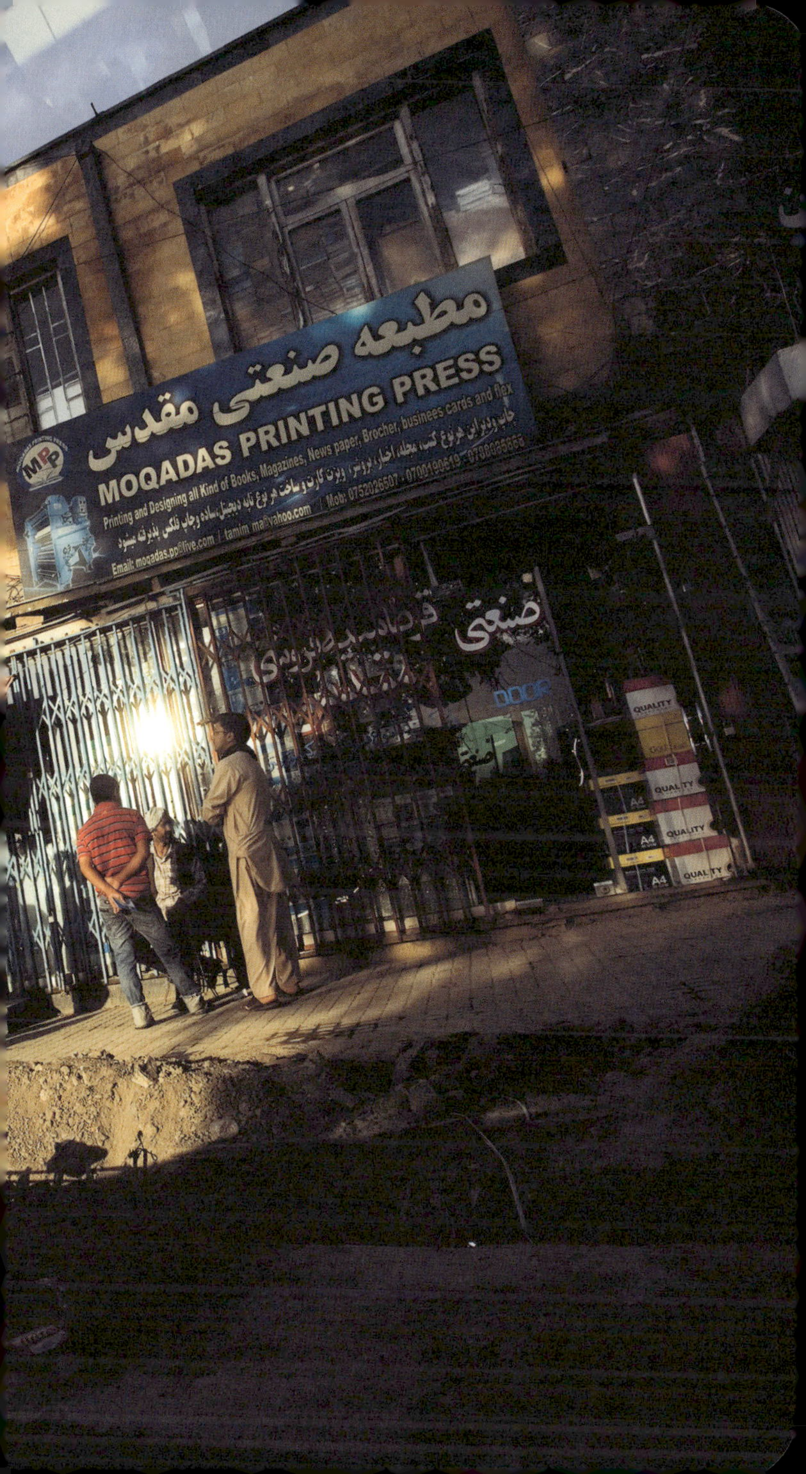
مطبعه صنعتی مقدس
MOQADAS PRINTING PRESS
Printing and Designing all Kind of Books, Magazines, News paper, Brocher, businees cards and flex
Email: moqadas.pp@live.com / tamim_ma@yahoo.com / Mob: 0752026507 - 0700190619 - 0788086860
صنعتی
QUALITY
A4

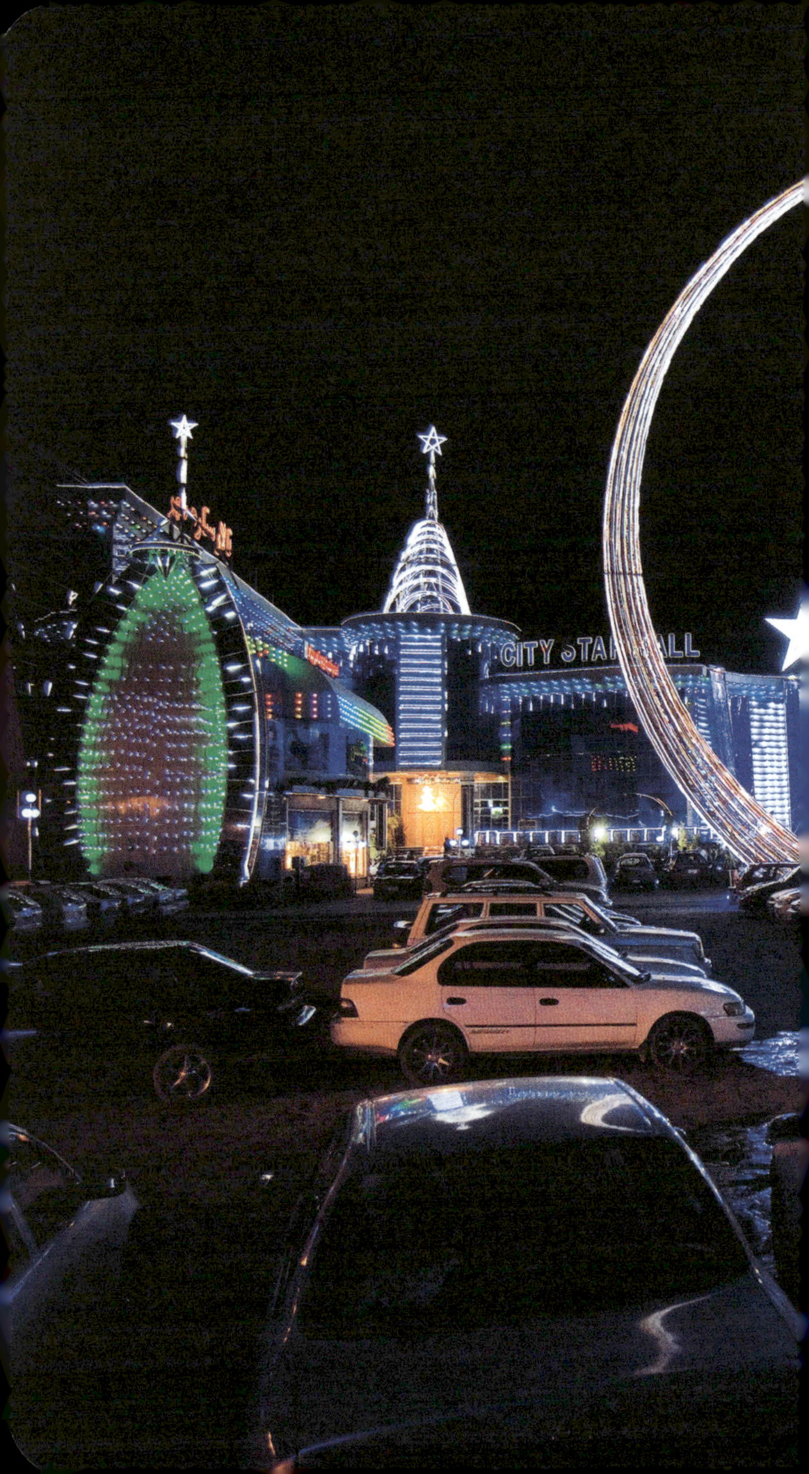

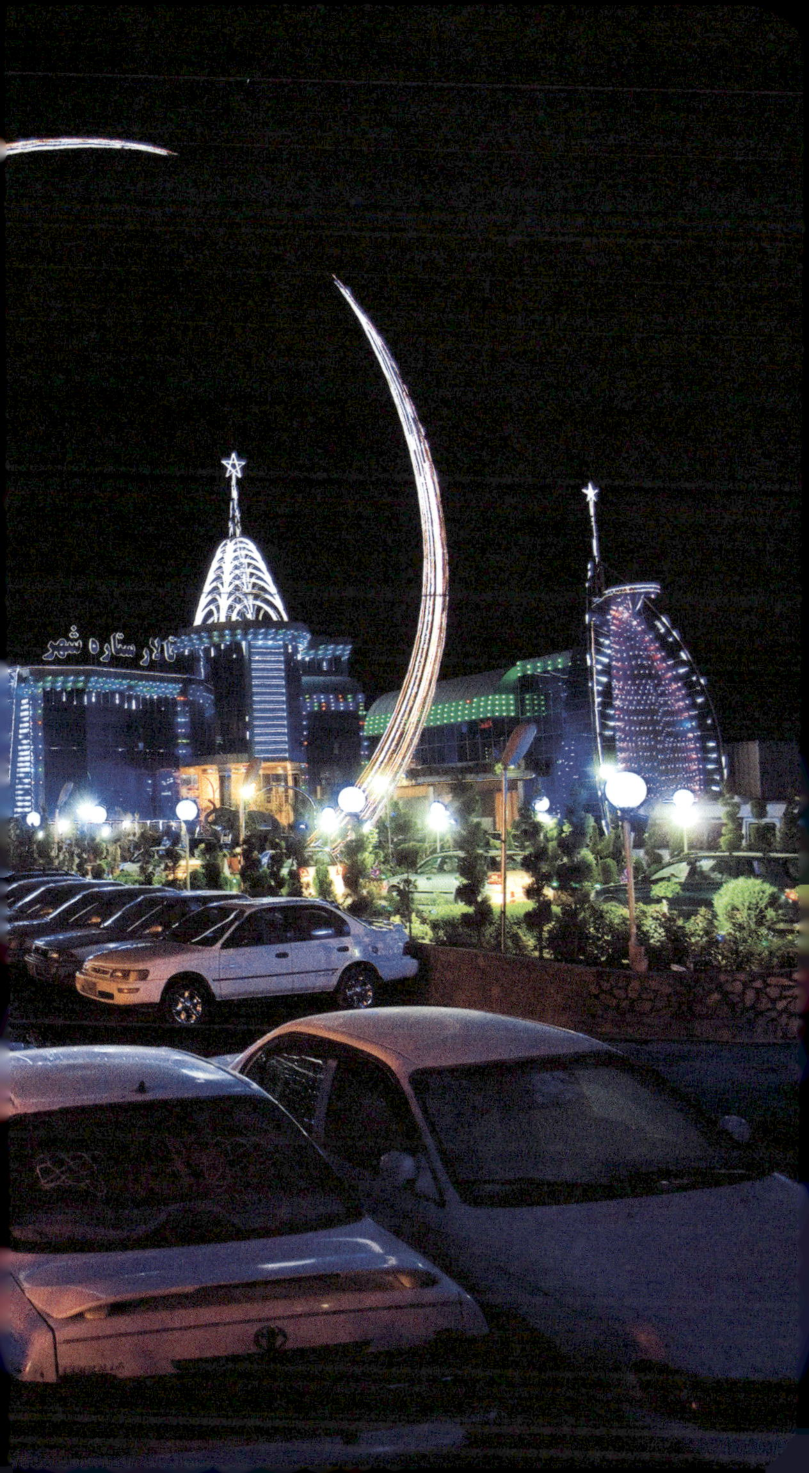
تالار ستاره شهر

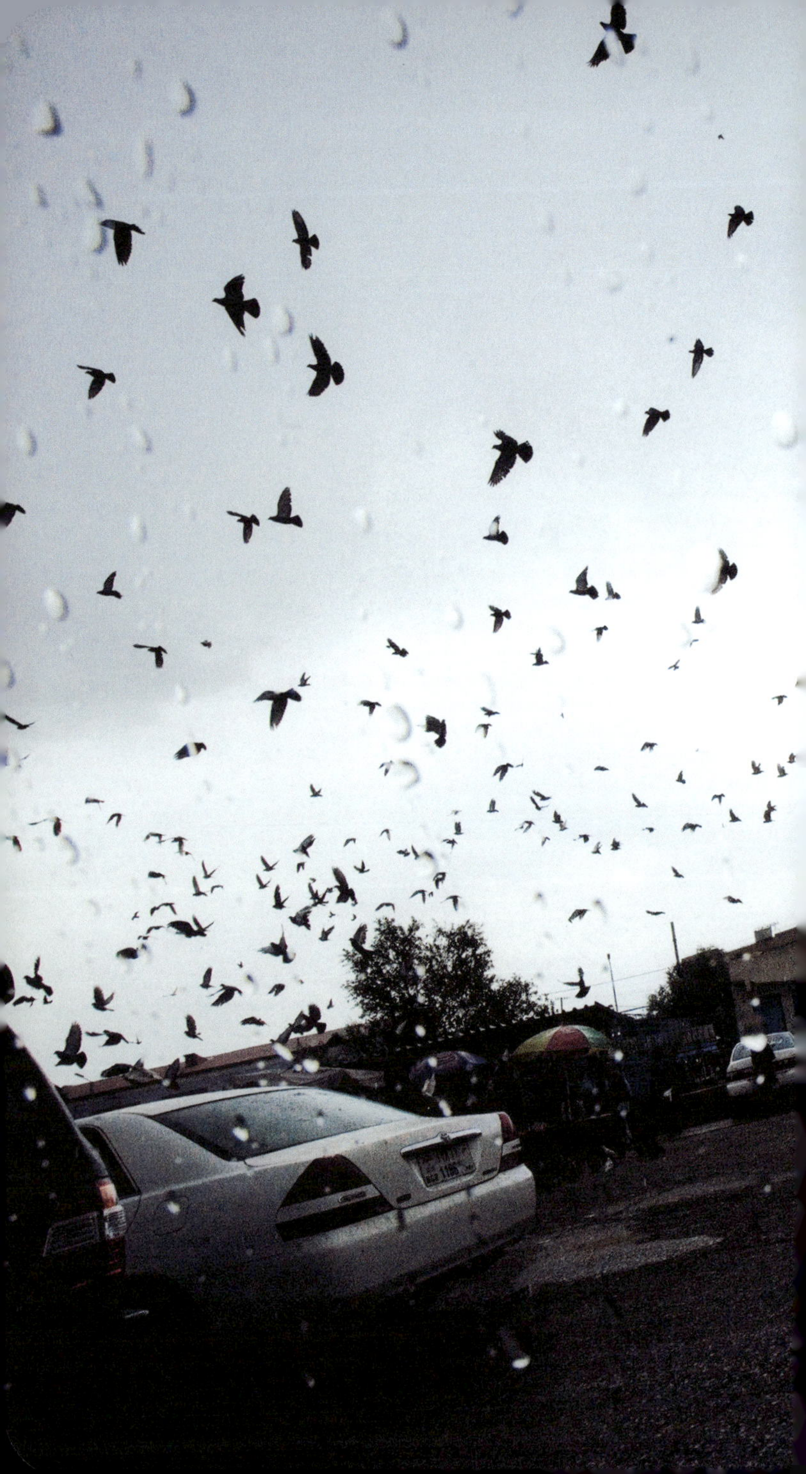

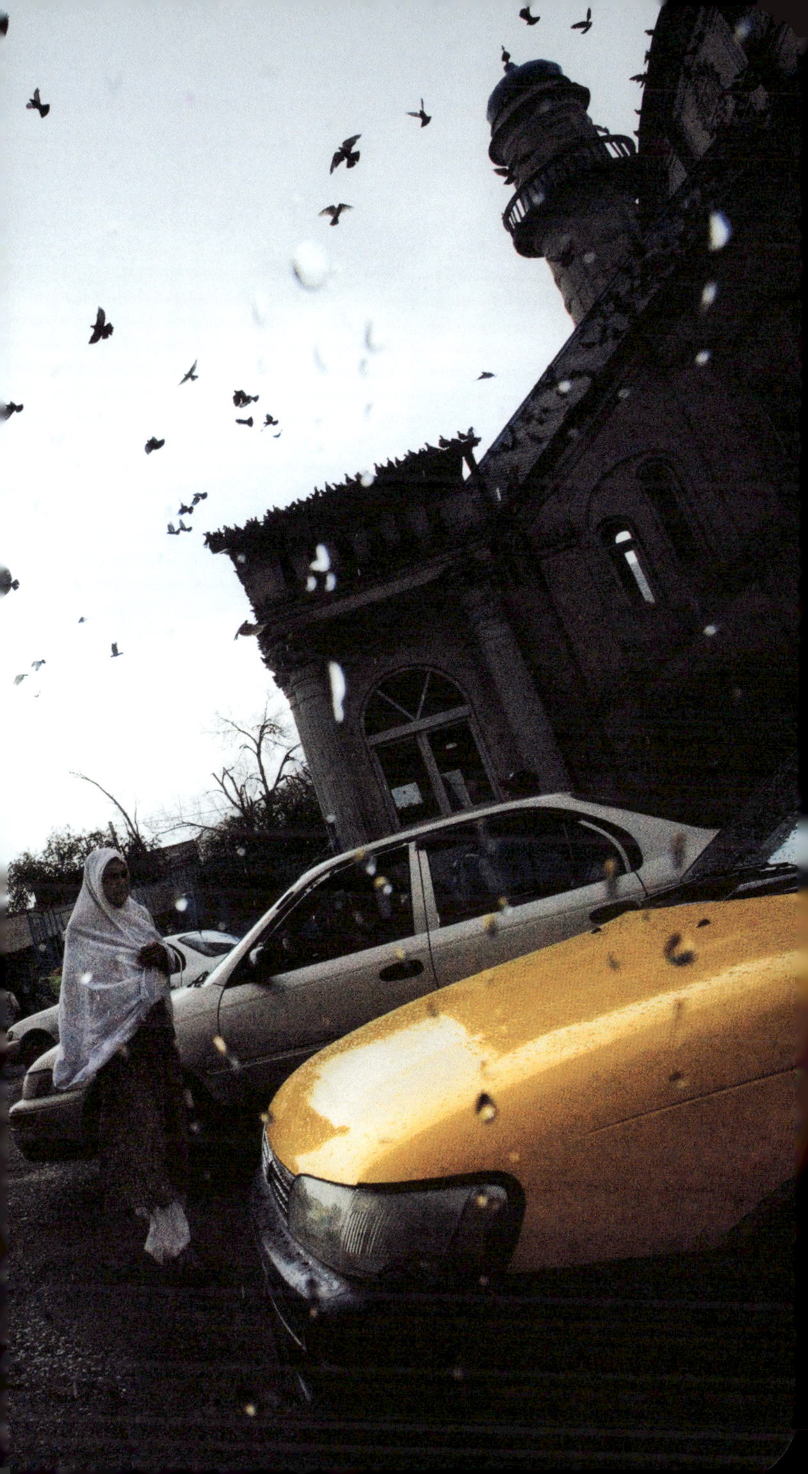

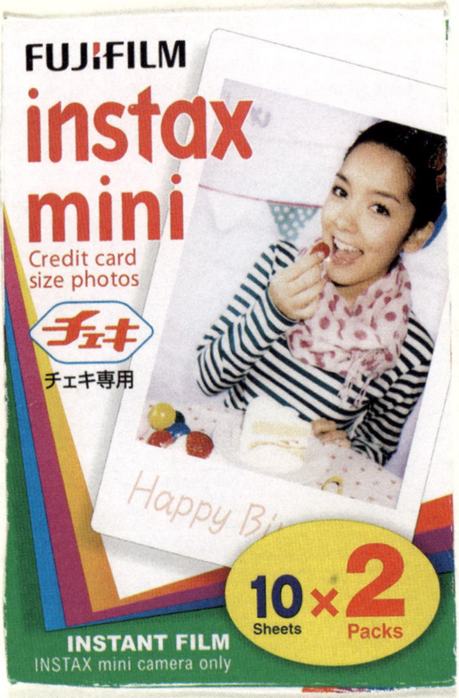
FUJIFILM
instax
mini
Credit card
size photos
チェキ
チェキ専用
Happy Bi
10 Sheets
× 2 Packs
INSTANT FILM
INSTAX mini camera only

Thank you Japan! Thank you, cute instax mini - girl for being my good friend. And for guiding me through my moments of insecurity and anxiety. What would I do in a place like this (Afghanistan) and a time like this time (July 2013 / now!) without a true friend? I would go insane, I guess. Completely mad. Of loneliness, boredom, fear and disgust. But you, cute (half-Japanese) instax mini - girl, are my savior from all this craziness and horror. I promise to protect you from dust, x-ray and overexposure. May our friendship last forever and be fruitful.

Love Christoph.

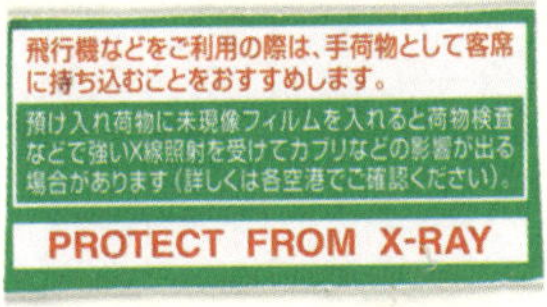

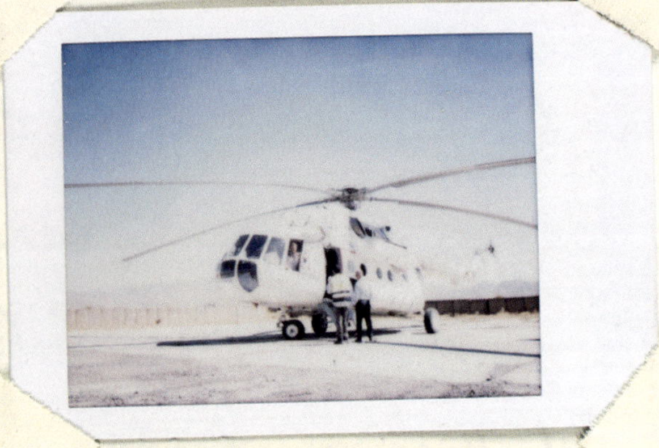

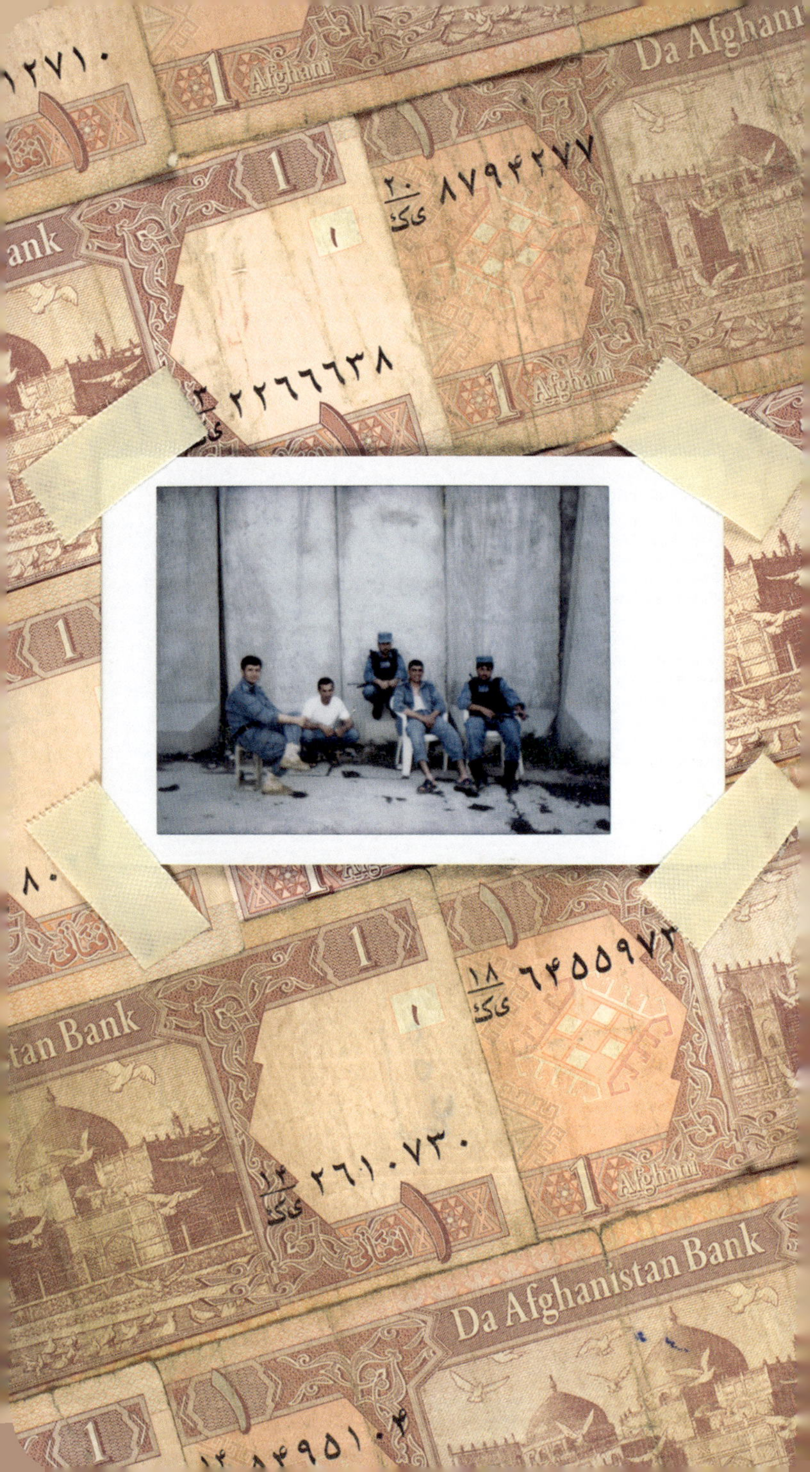
Da Afghanistan Bank
Afghani

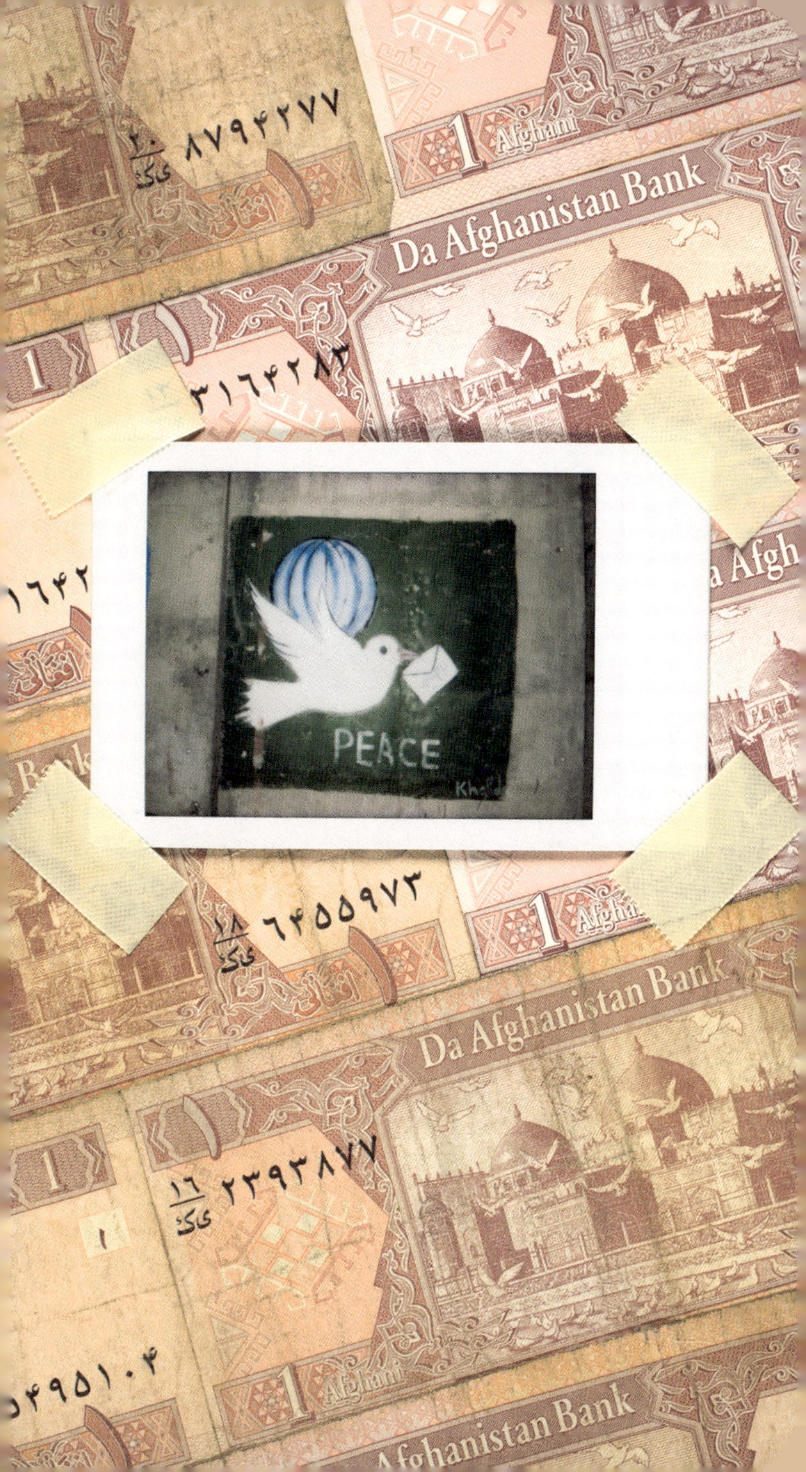
1 Afghani
Da Afghanistan Bank
PEACE
Da Afghanistan Bank

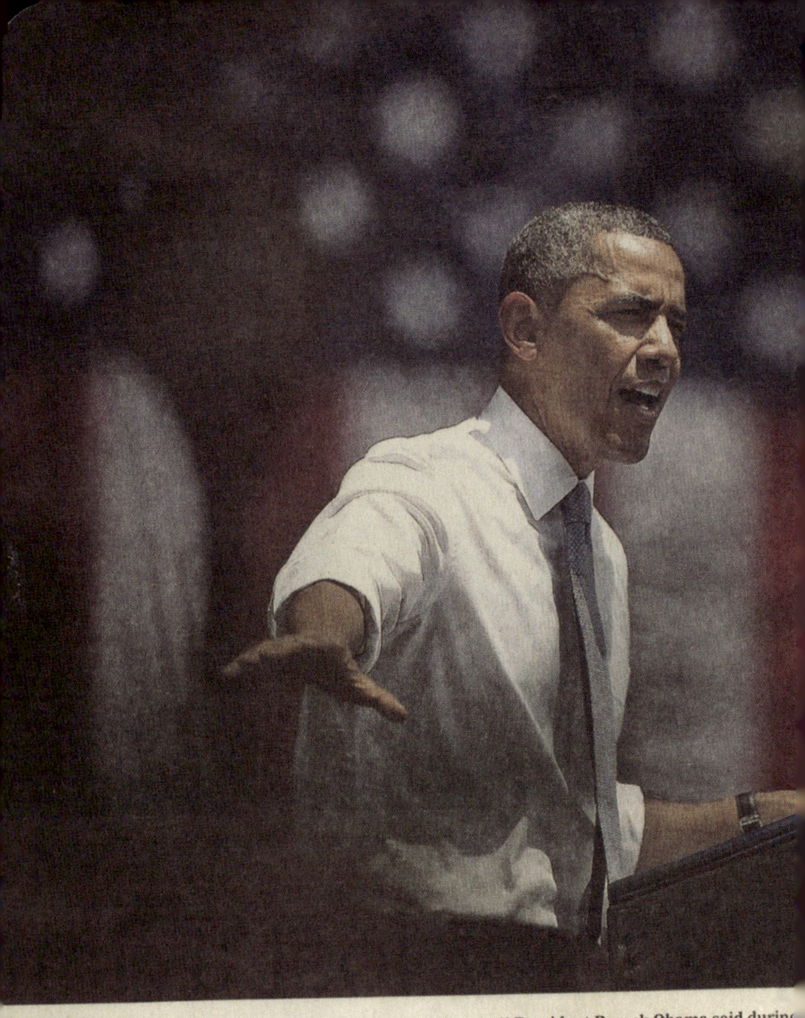

as a father, and as an American, I'm here to say, we need to act," President Barack Obama said during

Taliban attack heart of A

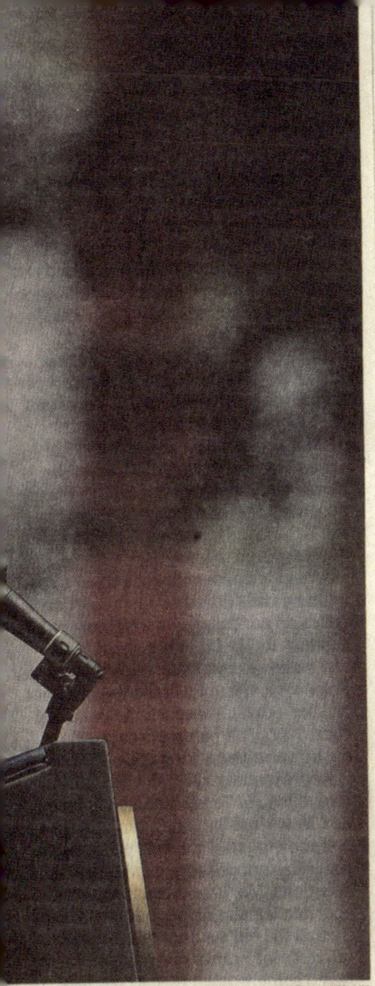

ALEX WONG/GETTY IMAGES-AFP

n Hikmatullah in Washington on Tuesday.

n government

STOCK INDEXES

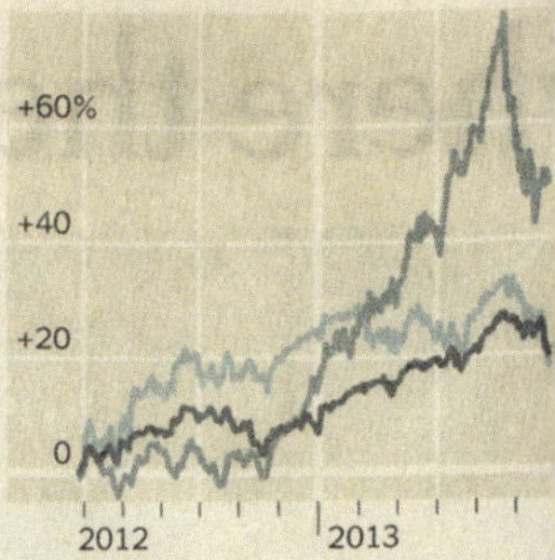

		52-week
UNITED STATES S&P 500		
1,587.13	+14.04	+18.9%
EUROPE DJ Stoxx 50		
2,543.37	+31.54	+16.3
JAPAN Nikkei 225		
12,969.34	−93.44	+47.4

CURRENCIES

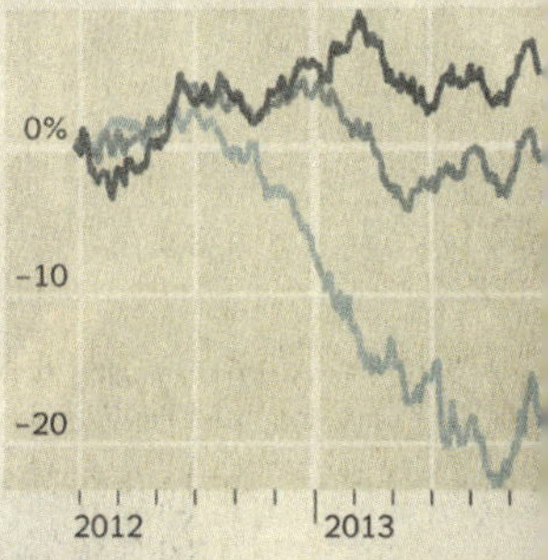

		52-week
EURO		
€1= $1.31	−0.002	+4.8%
YEN		
¥100= $1.02	flat	−18.5
POUND		
£1= $1.54	closed	−0.9

COMMODITIES

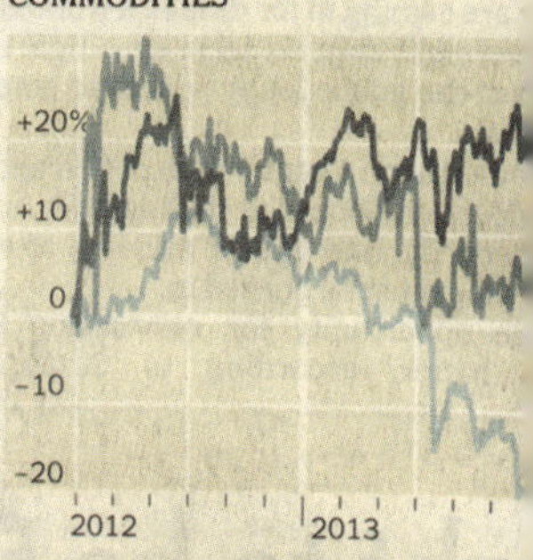

		52-week
OIL Nymex light sw. crude		
$95.37 a barrel	+0.19	+20.5%
GOLD New York		
$1,276.50 a tr. oz.	+0.40	−19.5

a wo

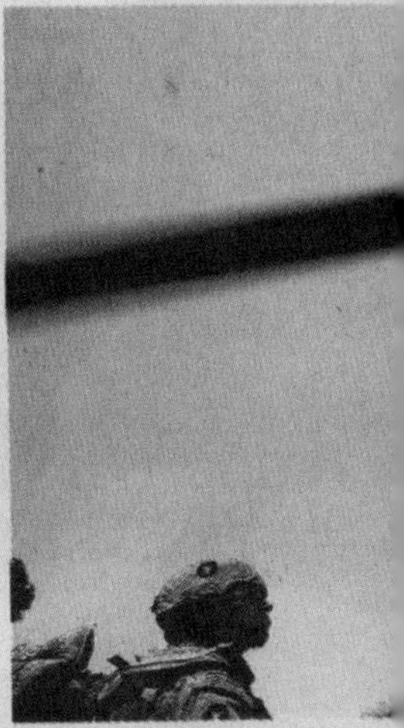

U.S. MILITARY Mitt Romney has

Afghanistan fighting

# of possibilities

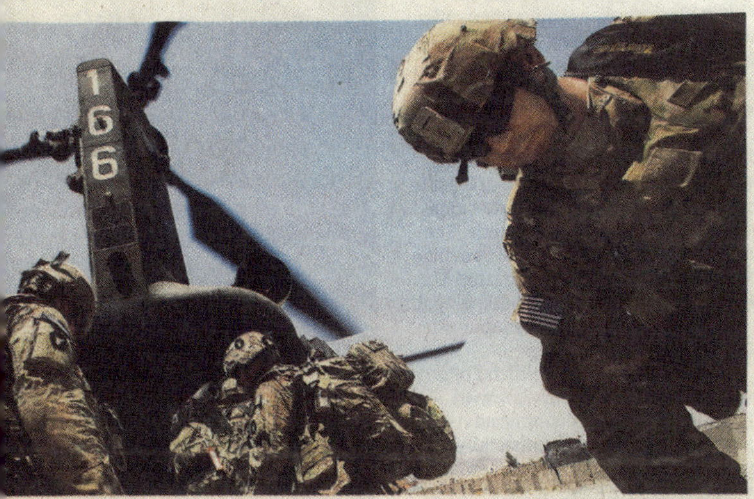

CHRISTOPH BANGERT FOR THE NEW YORK TIMES

cuts in the military budget mandated by legislation supported by lawmakers in both parties.

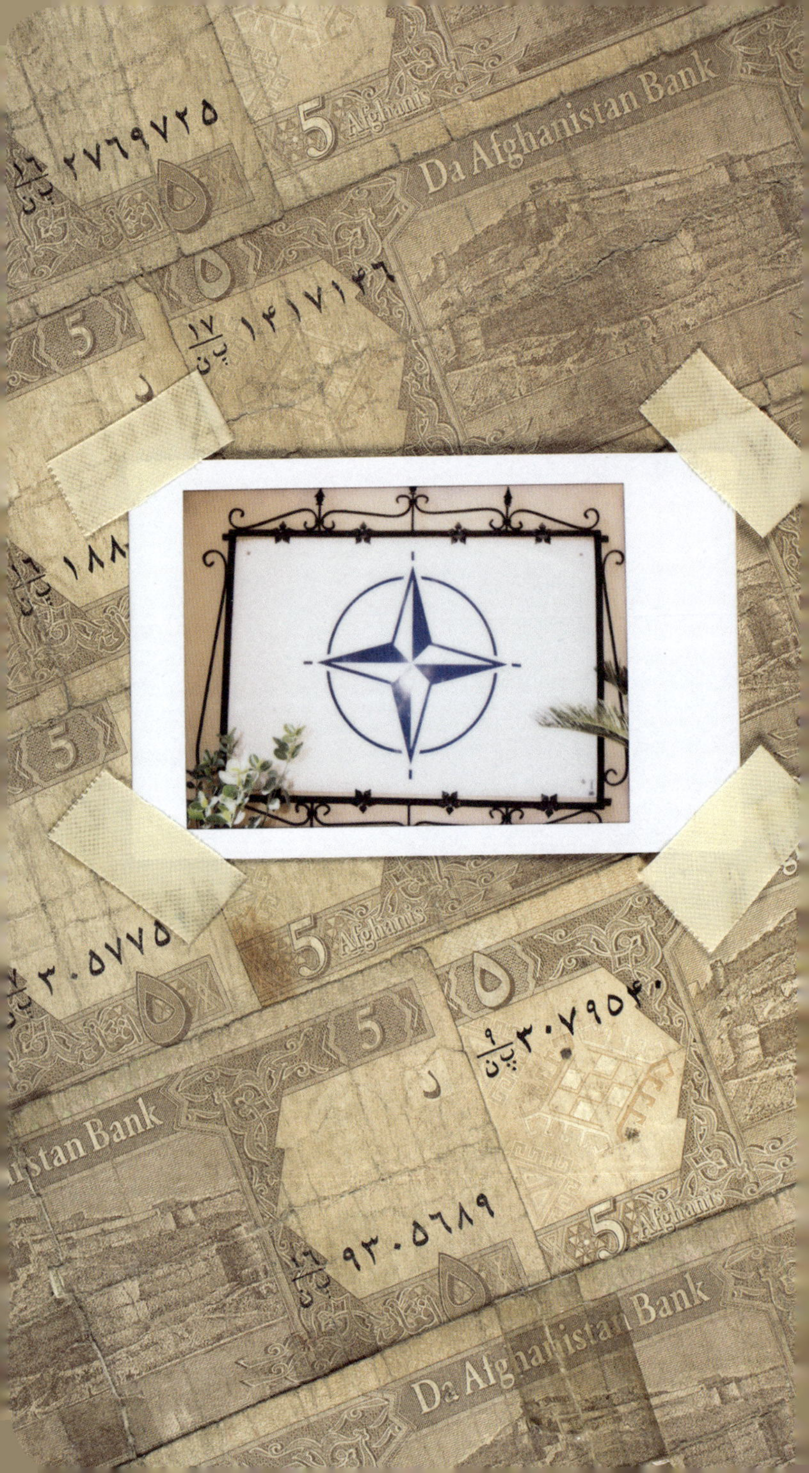
Da Afghanistan Bank
5 Afghanis

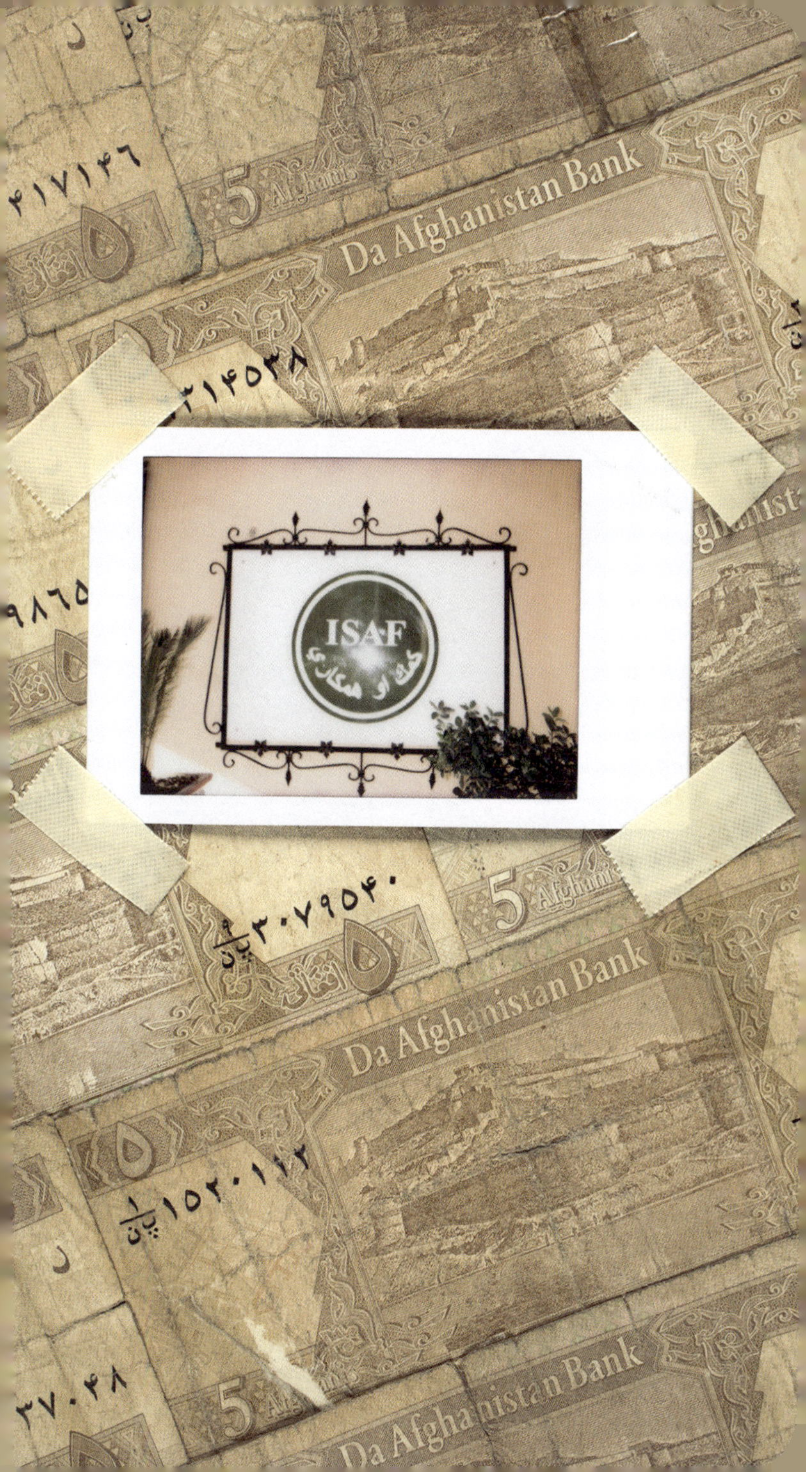
Da Afghanistan Bank
5 Afghanis
ISAF

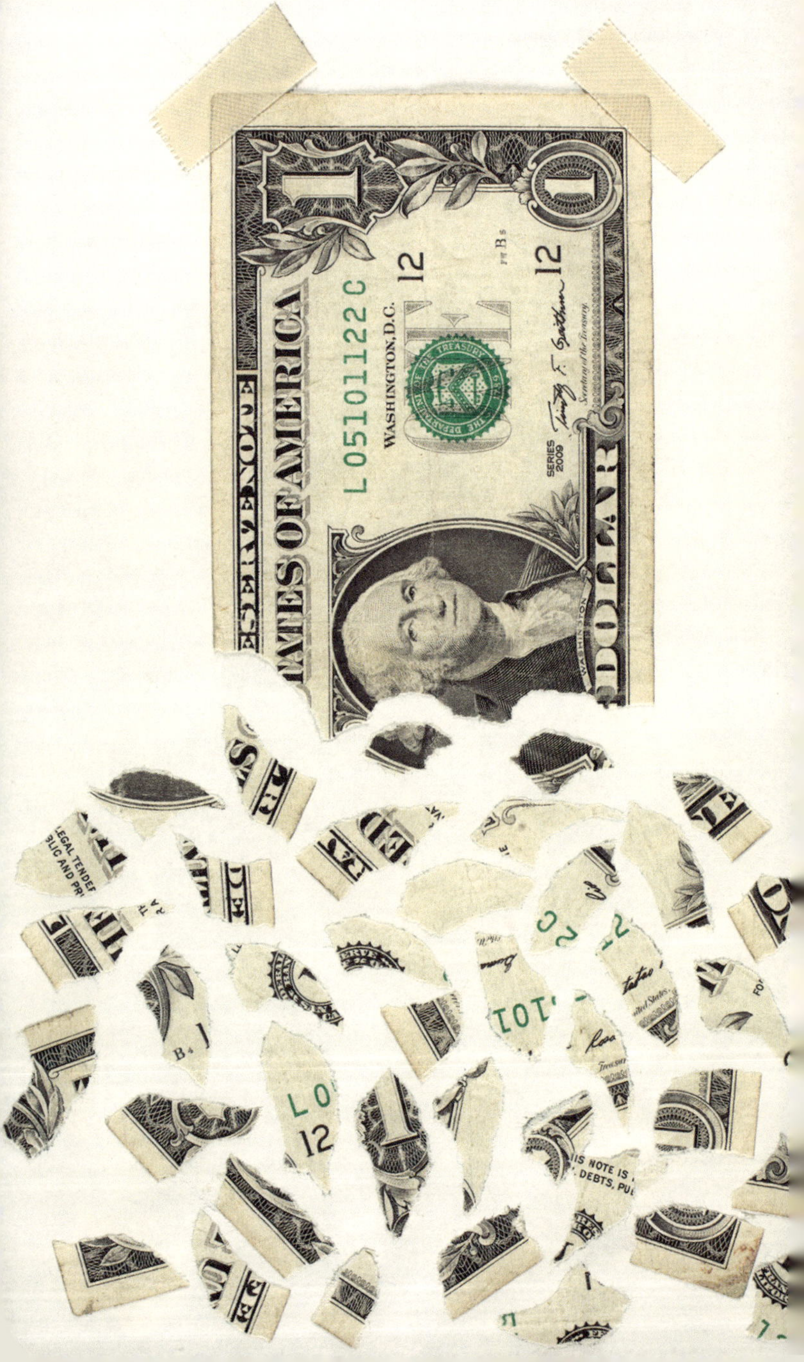

STATES OF AMERICA
L 05101122 C
WASHINGTON, D.C.
SERIES 2009

USAID
FROM THE AMERICAN PEOPLE

USAID
FROM THE AMERICAN PEOPLE

USAID
FROM THE AMERICAN PEOPLE

USAID
FROM THE AMERICAN PEOPLE

USAID
FROM THE AMERICAN PEOPLE

USAID
FROM THE AMERICAN PEOPLE

USAID
FROM THE AMERICAN PEOPLE

USAID
FROM THE AMERICAN PEOPLE

USAID
FROM THE AMERICAN PEOPLE

USAID
FROM THE AMERICAN PEOPLE

USAID
FROM THE AMERICAN PEOPLE

USAID
FROM THE AMERICAN PEOPLE

USAID
FROM THE AMERICAN PEOPLE

USAID
FROM THE AMERICAN PEOPLE

USAID
FROM THE AMERICAN PEOPLE

USAID
FROM THE AMERICAN PEOPLE

USAID
FROM THE AMERICAN PEOPLE

USAID
FROM THE AMERICAN PEOPLE

USAID
FROM THE AMERICAN PEOPLE

USAID
FROM THE AMERICAN PEOPLE

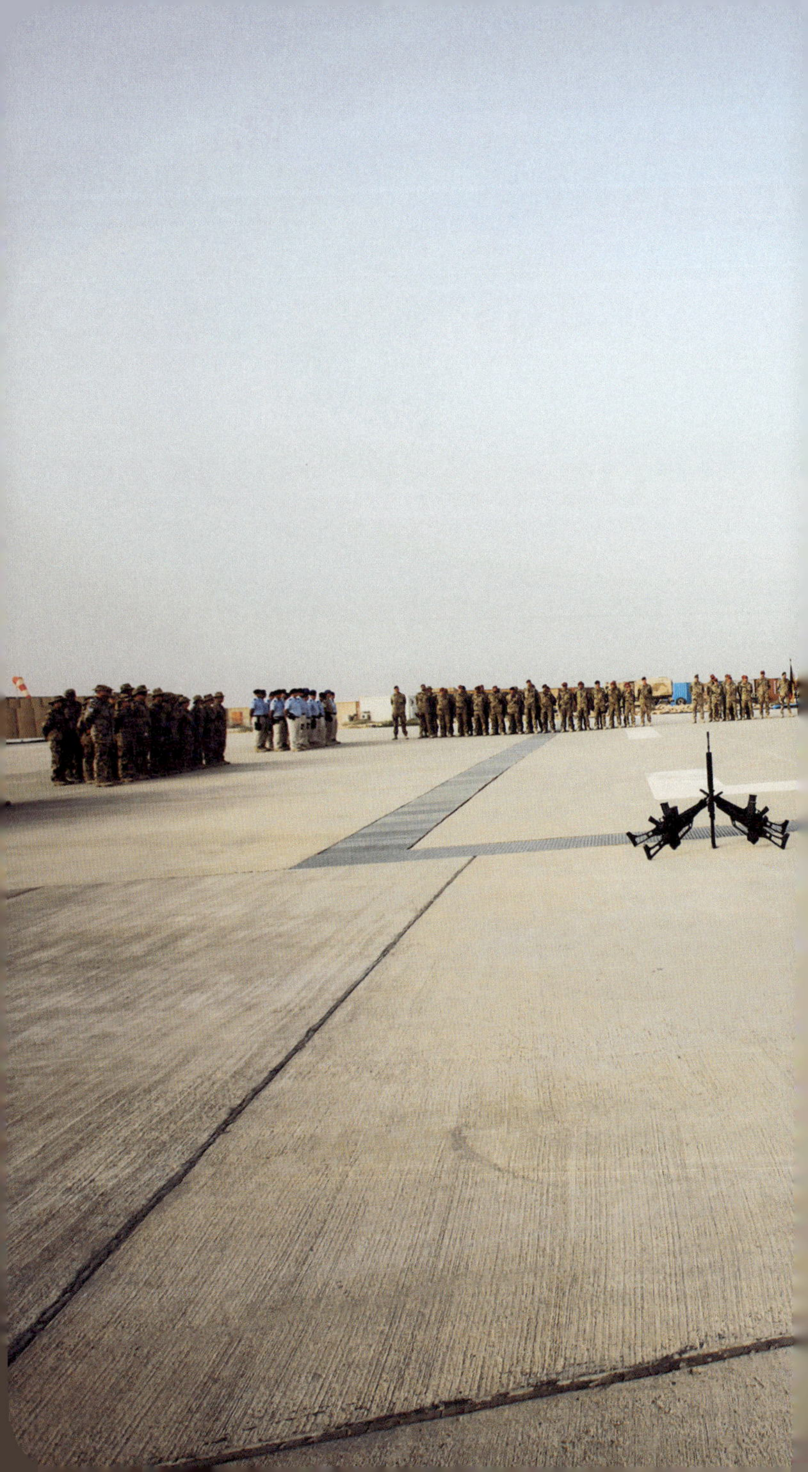

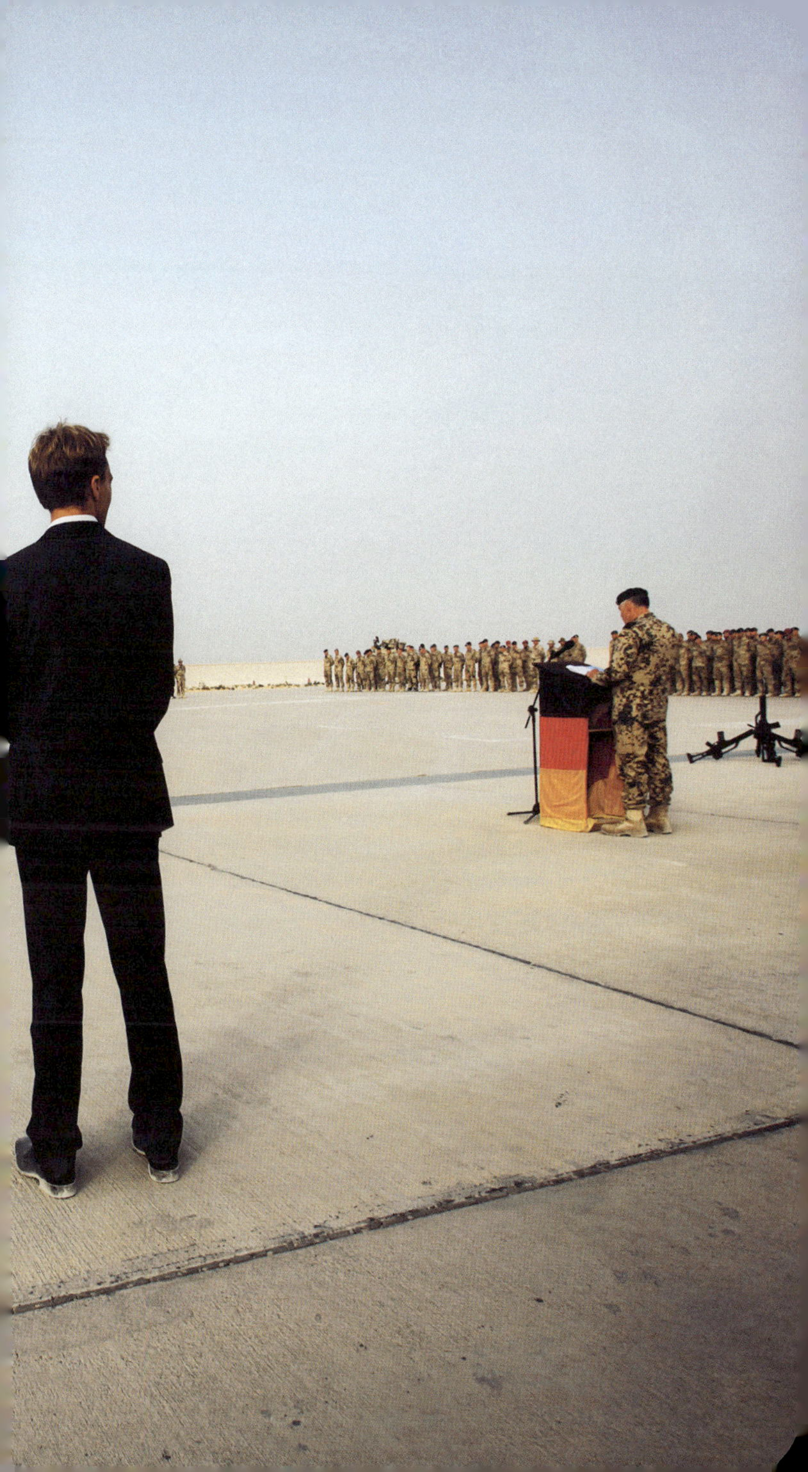

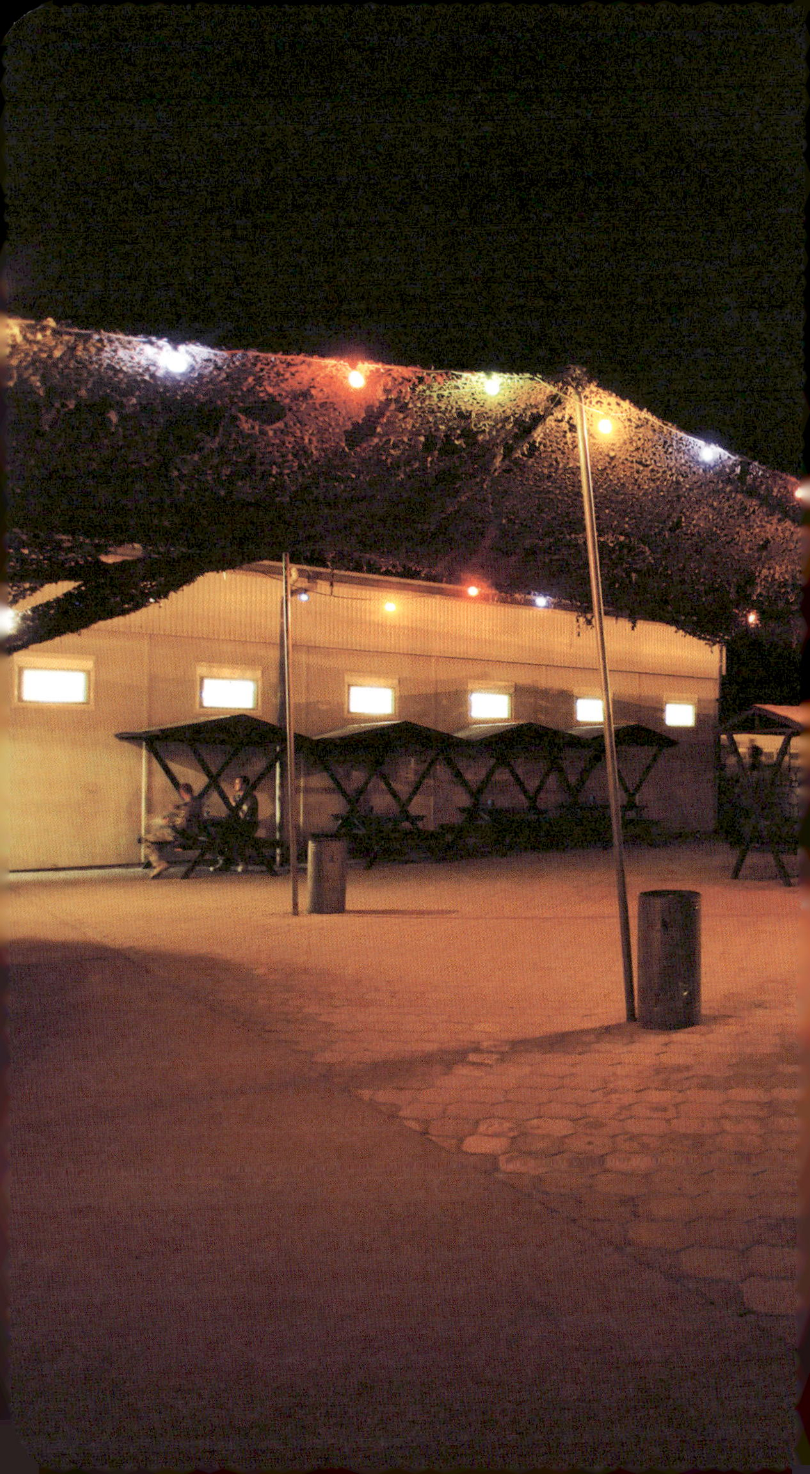

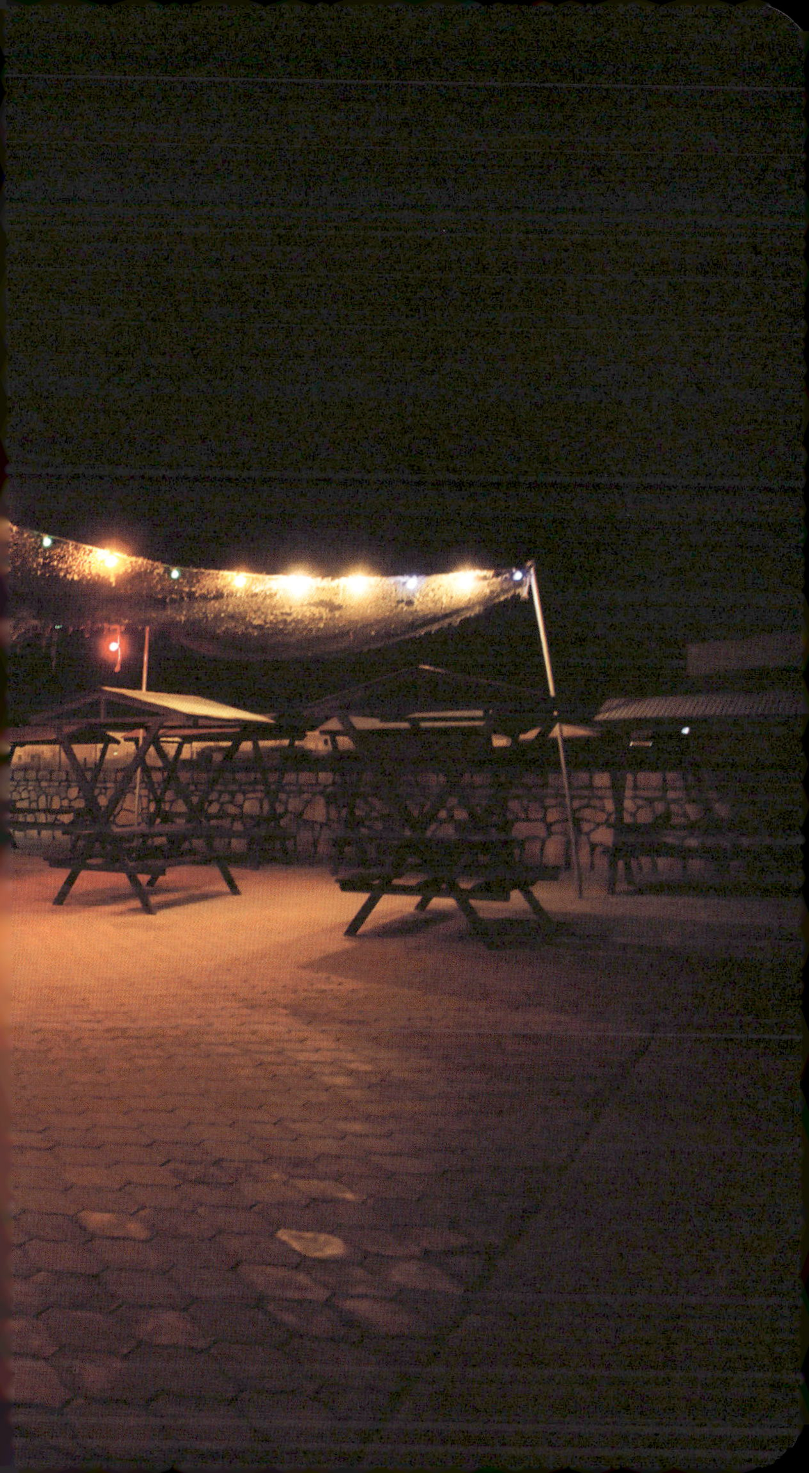

25-are you married? ۲۵- آیا شما ازدواج کرده اید؟

آز یُو مَرِید؟

26-No, I'm not married. ۲۶- نه. من ازدواج نکرده ام.

نُ ، آیم نات مَرِید.

27-you're very beautiful. ۲۷- شما خیلی زیبا هستید.

یُور وِری بیُ یُو تیُ فول.

28-what's it to you?

واتس ایت تو یُو؟

۲۸- به شما چه ربطی دارد؟ (به شما چه؟)

29-you are very handsome.

یُو آز وِری هَندسام.

۲۹- شما خیلی خوش تیپ هستید.

30-really? ری یِلی؟ ۳۰- واقعا؟

31-well.It was nice meeting you.

وِلْ. ایت واز نایس میتینگ یُو.

۳۱- خوب. از دیدار با شما لذت بردم .

32-I have to go now. bye.

آی هَف تو گُ نو . بای

۳۲- من مجبور هستم حالا بروم. خدا حافظ.

33-It was nice meeting you. ۳۳- از دیدار با شما لذت بردم.

ایت واز نایس میتینگ یُو

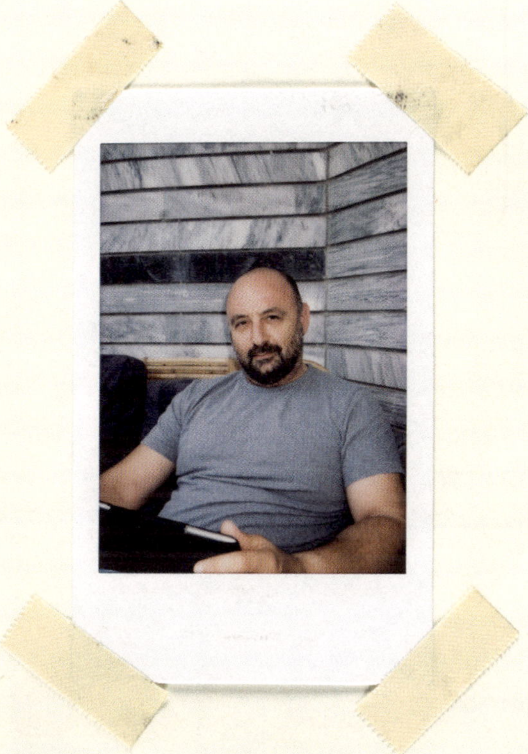

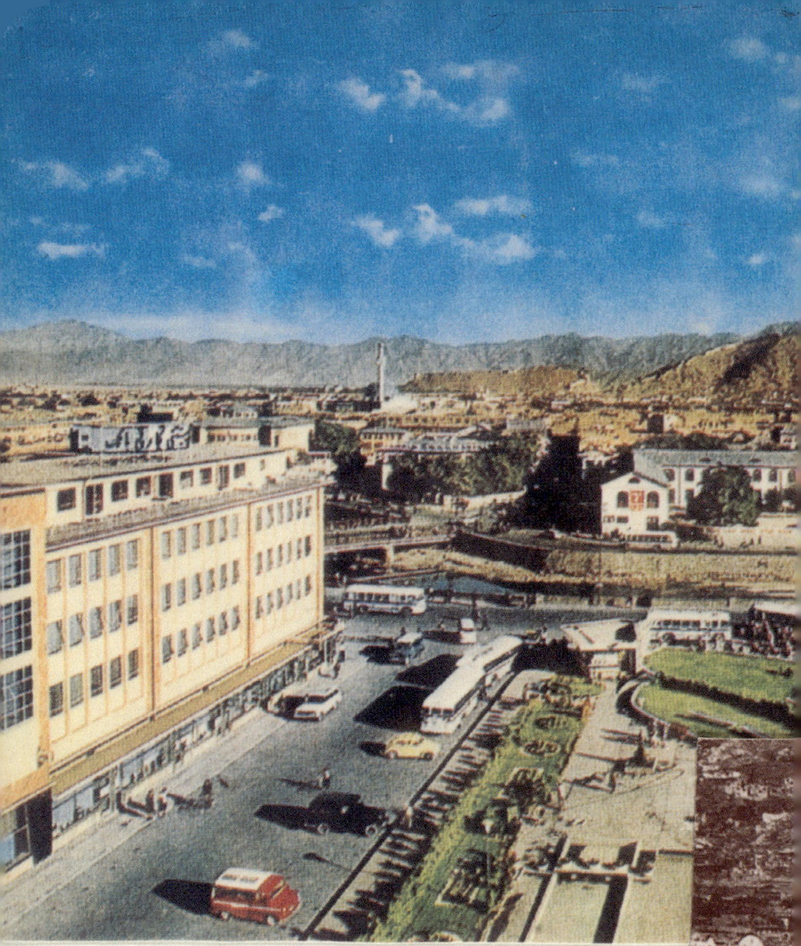

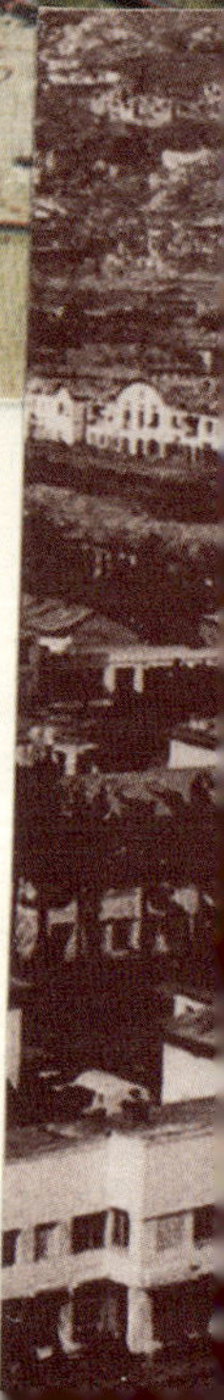

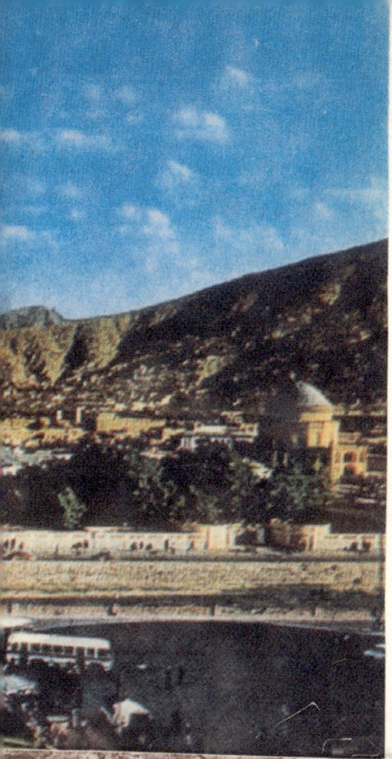

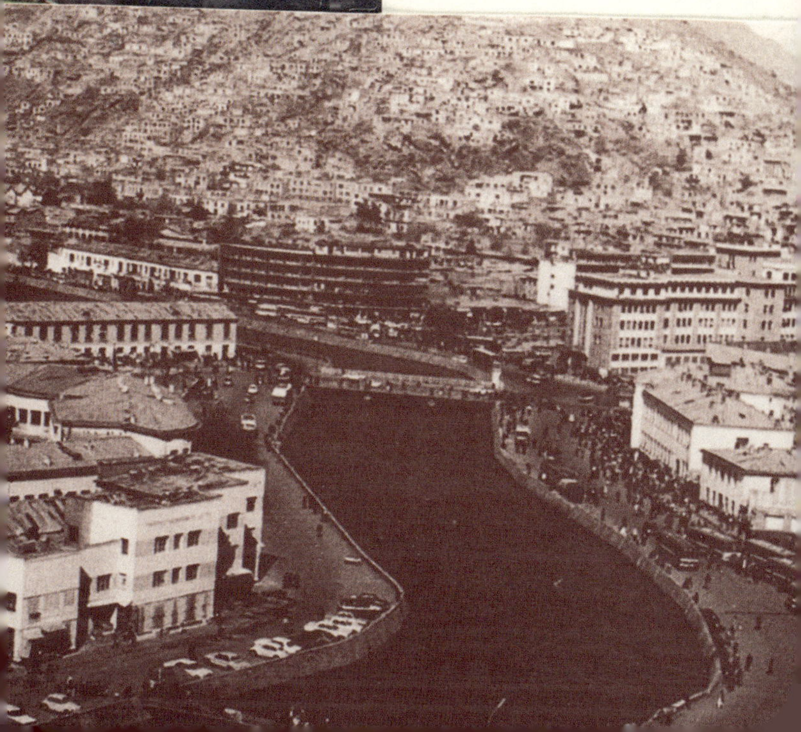

The New York Times

no pain no gain

نَ پِینْ نَ گِینْ

نابرده رنج گنج میسر نمی شود

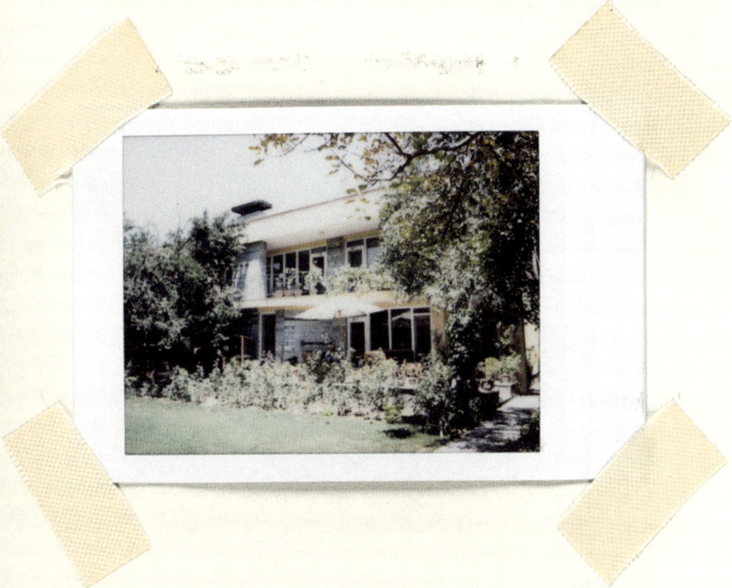

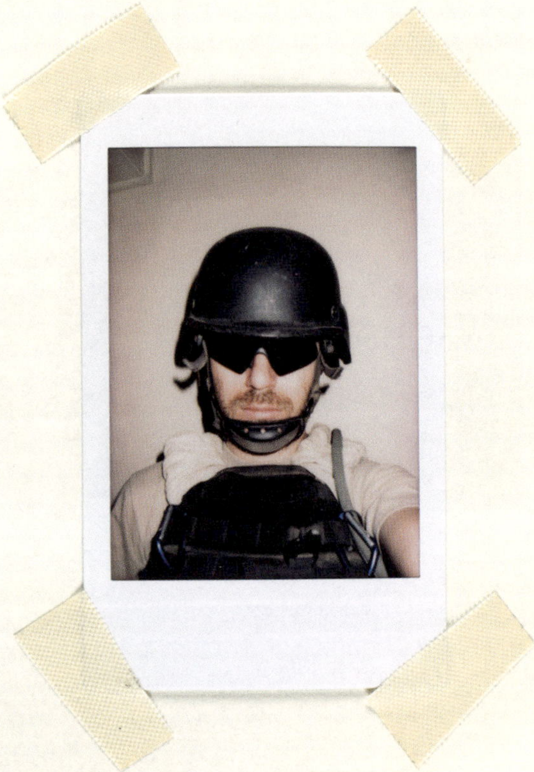

Christoph Bangert. Photographer. Author. Rally driver. Adventurer. Tough as hell German.

Flashback! the day I left home.

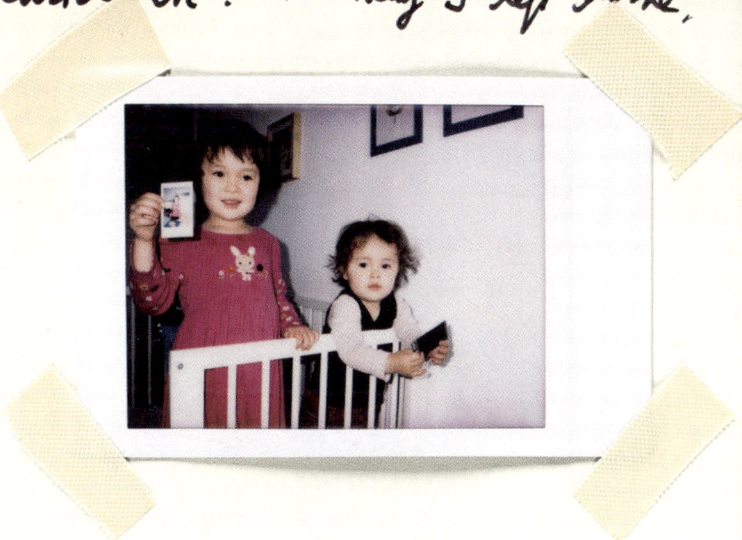

Four more days. I'm tired and I just want to go home. I'm pacing up and down in my room. I miss Anna, Lilli and Chiho. I'm restless and not very productive. I'm working on the computer mainly, editing pictures and photoshopping them. I've been there many times before. This is more or less what insanity must feel like. Four more days.

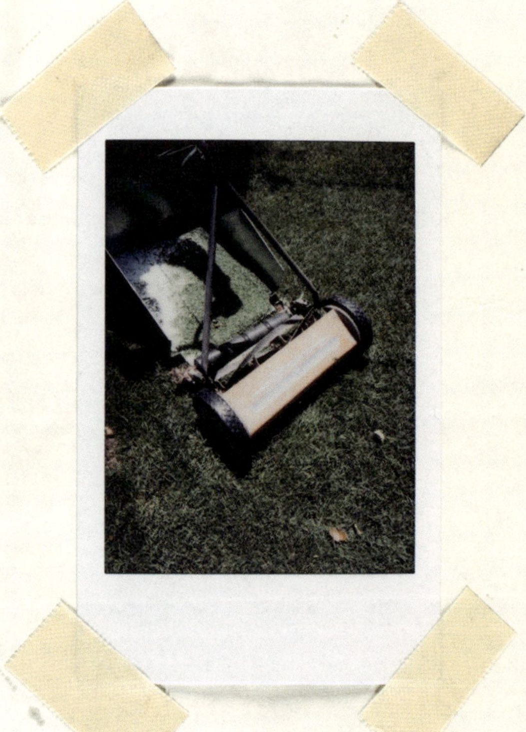

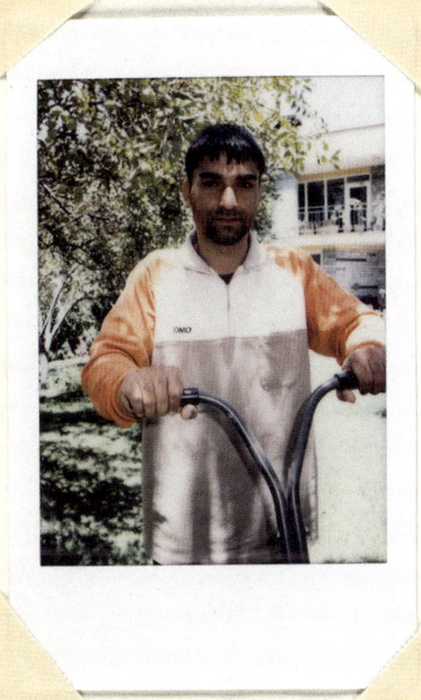

This is Zamir Ahmad. He's 25 years old and he's the gardener. I like Zamir.

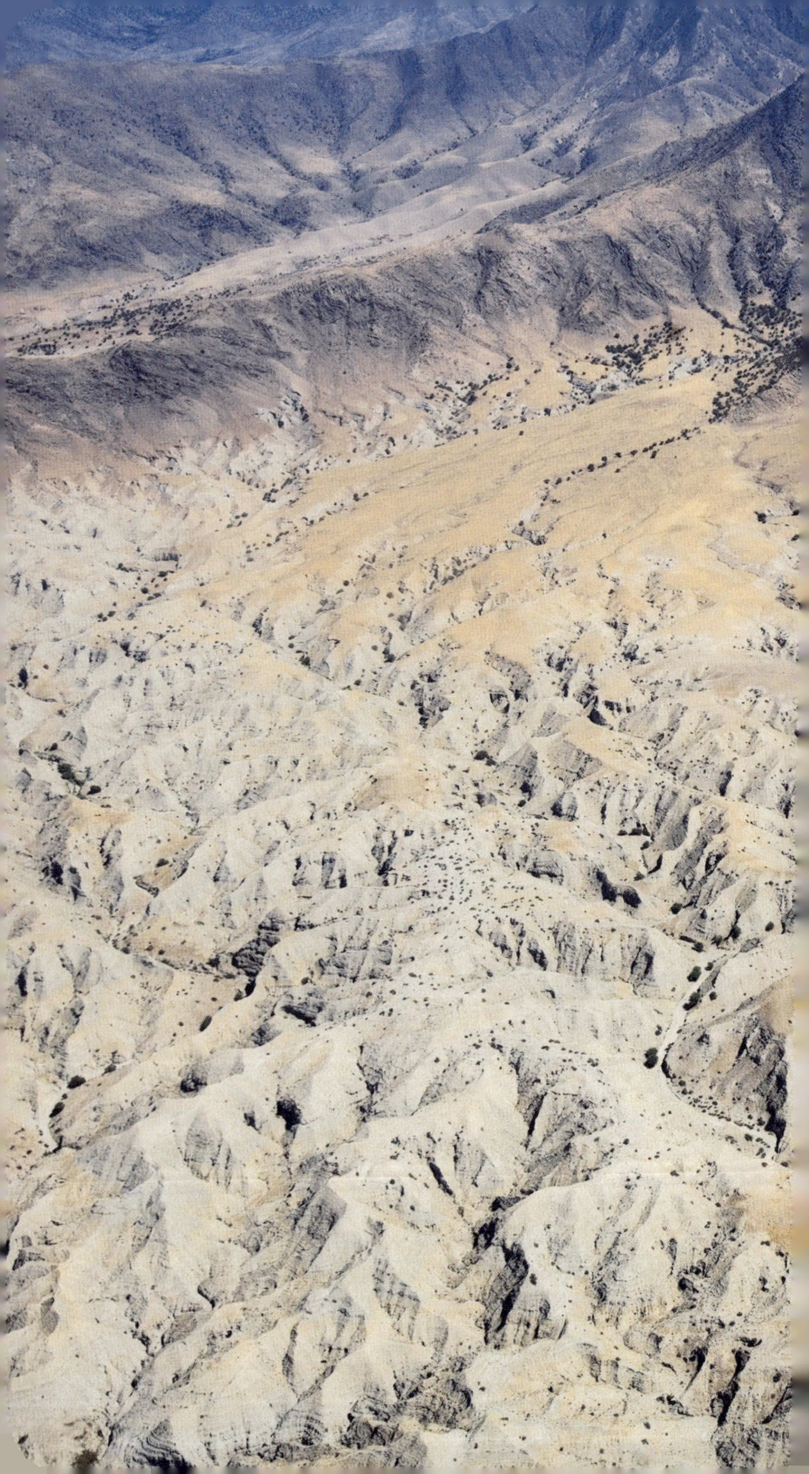

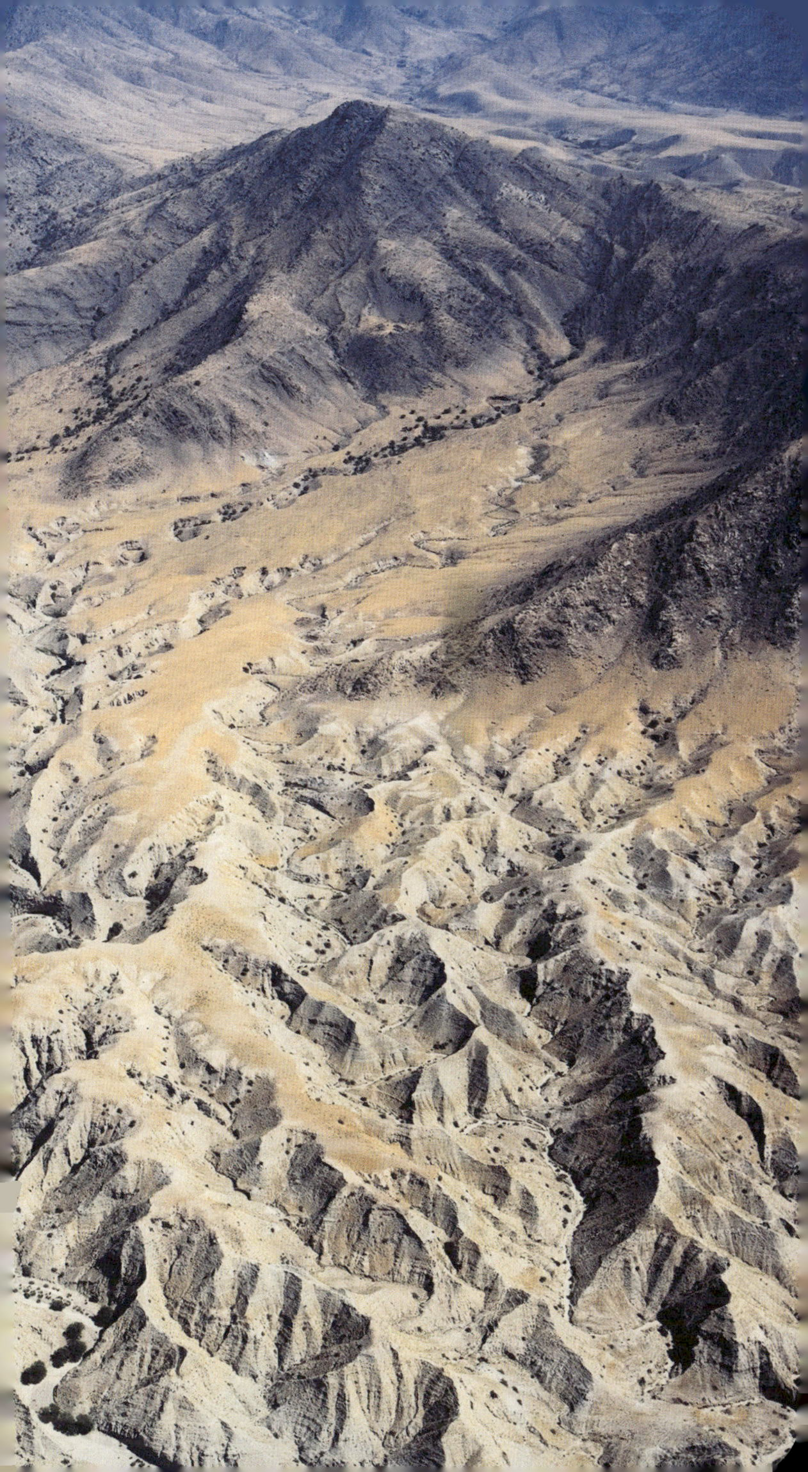

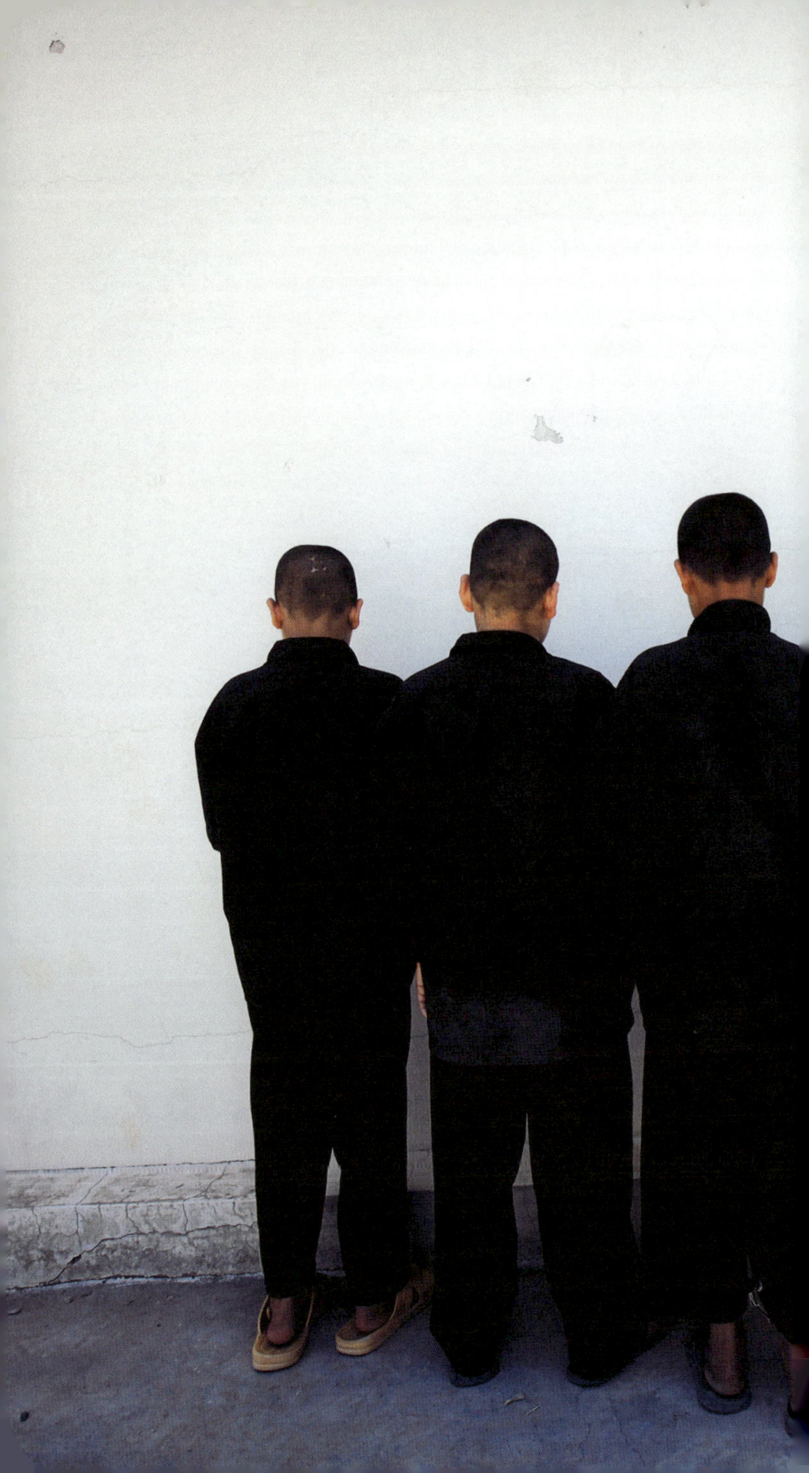

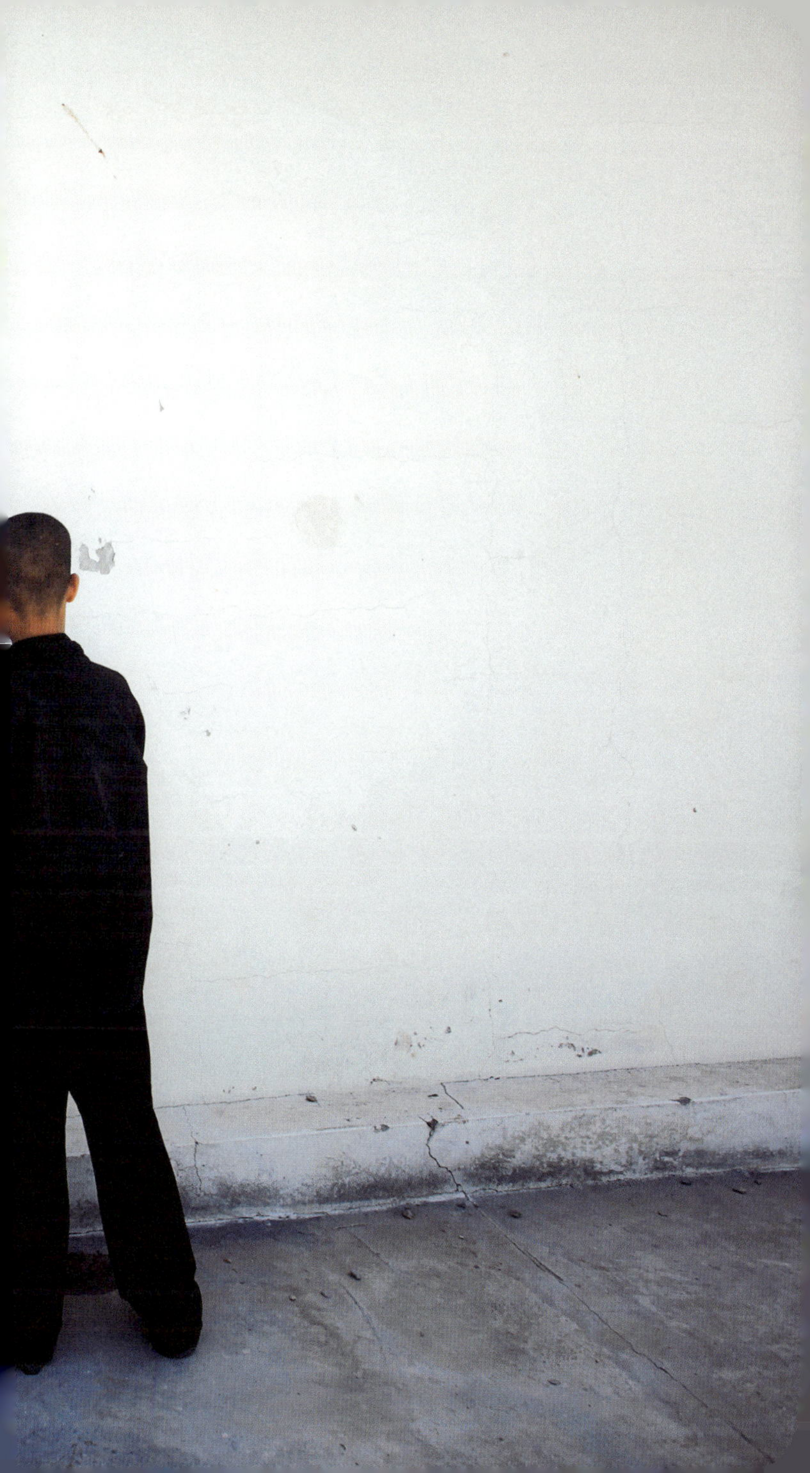

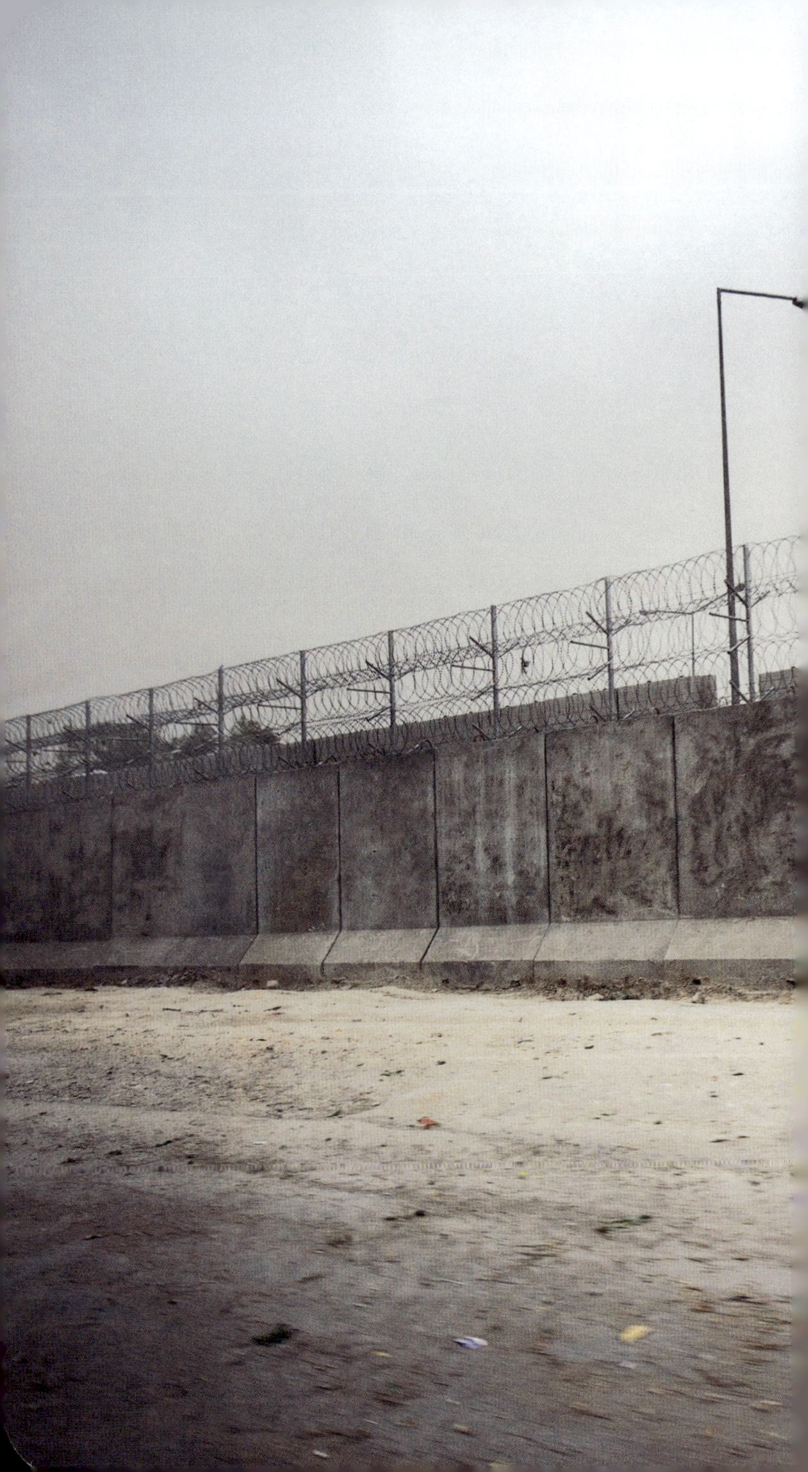

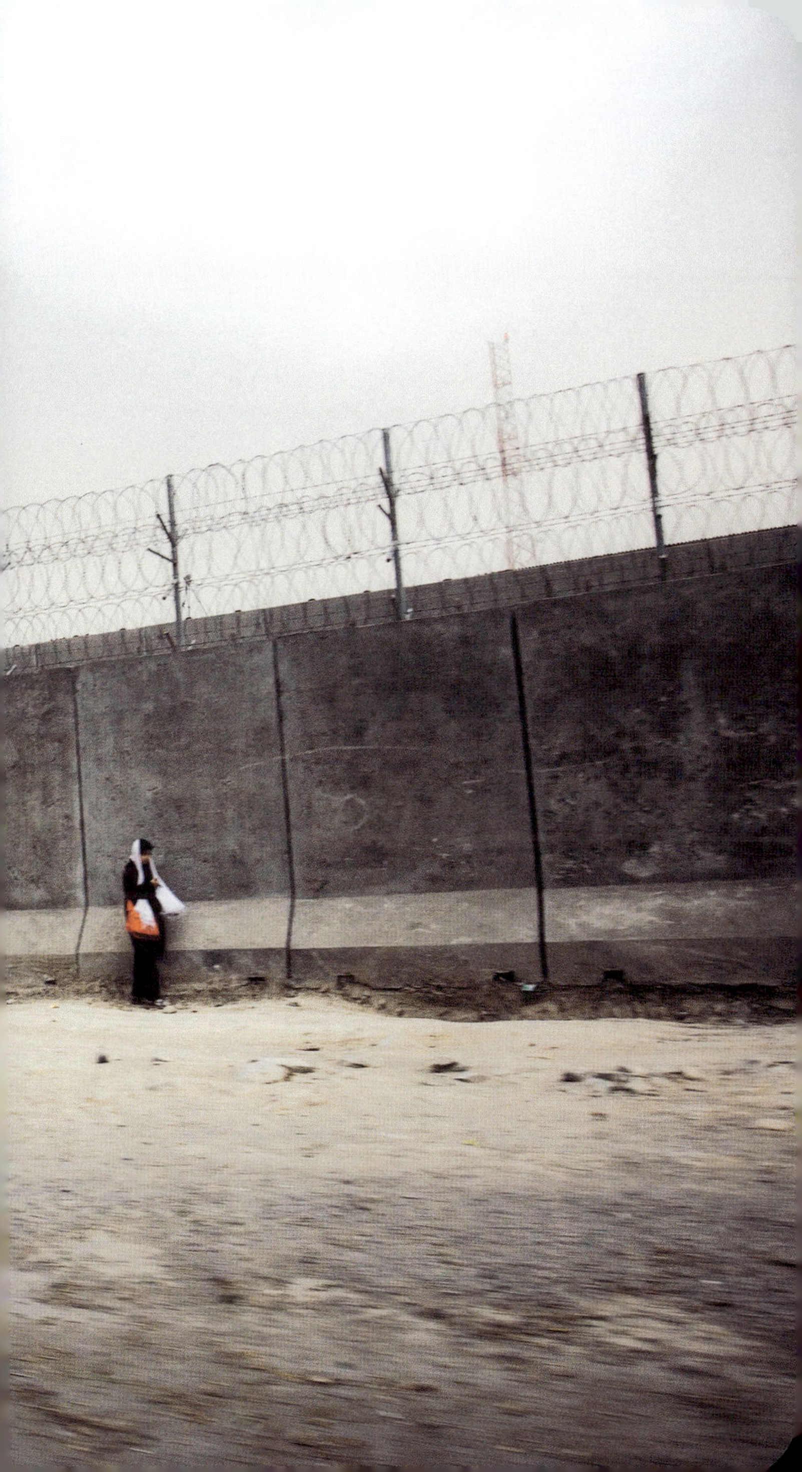

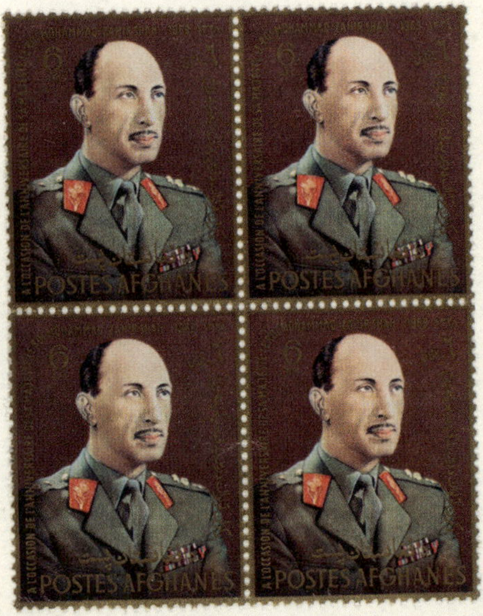
POSTES AFGHANES
POSTES AFGHANES
POSTES AFGHANES
POSTES AFGHANES

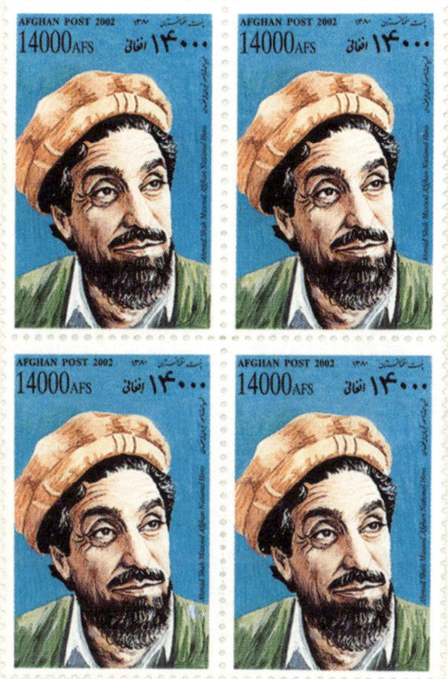
AFGHAN POST 2002
14000AFS
۱۴۰۰۰ افغانی

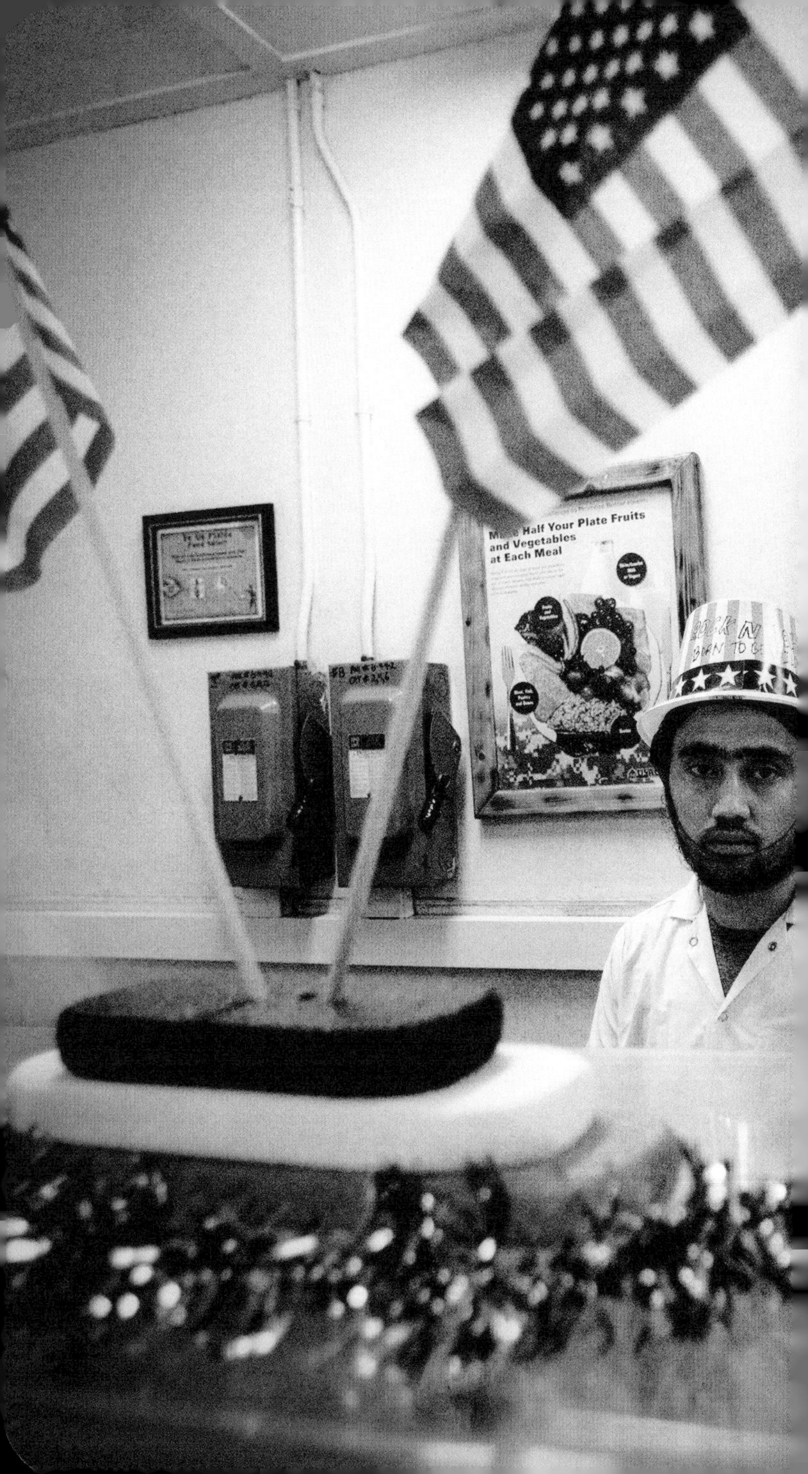
Half Your Plate Fruits
and Vegetables
at Each Meal

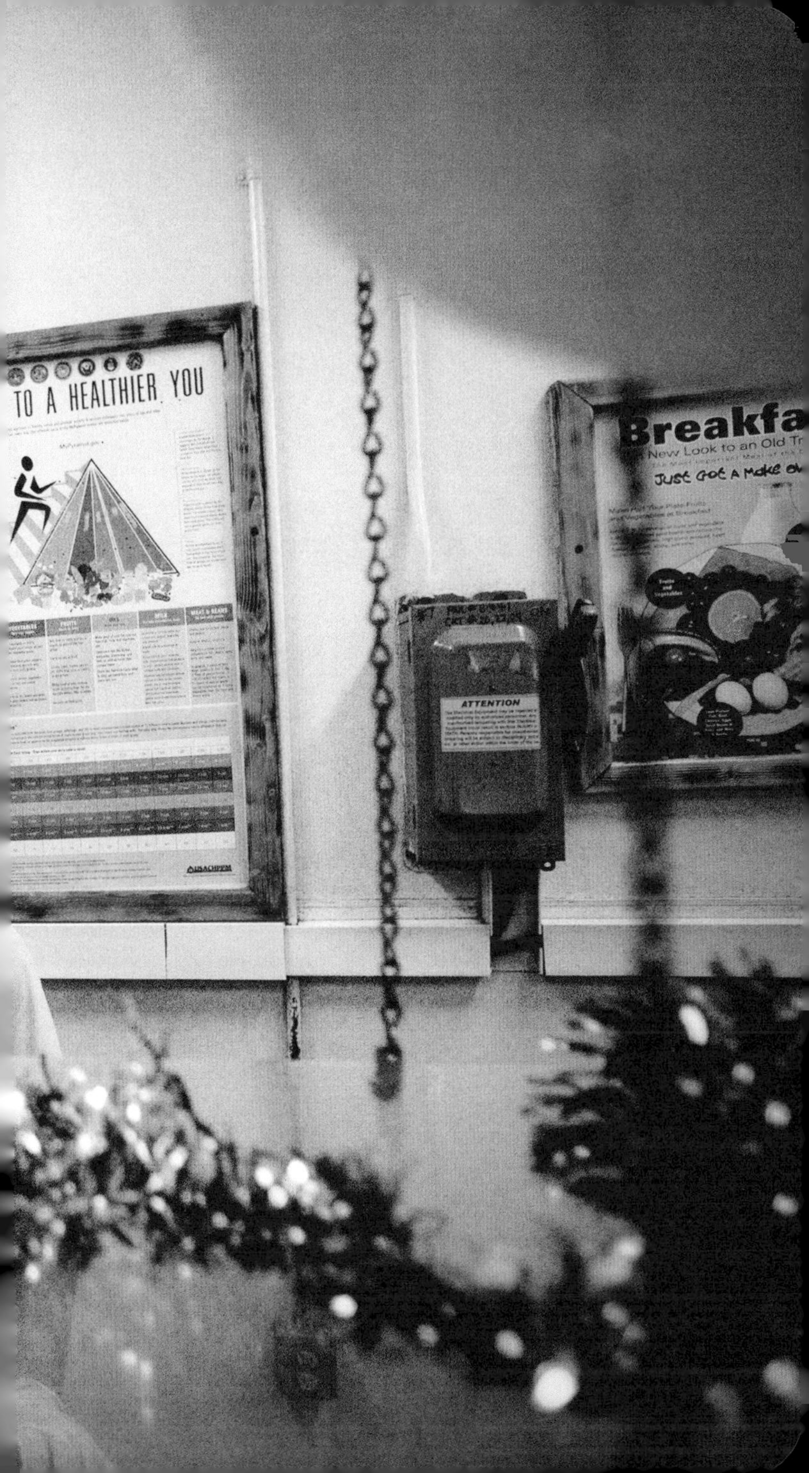
TO A HEALTHIER YOU
Breakfa
New Look to an Old Tr
Just Got A Make
ATTENTION

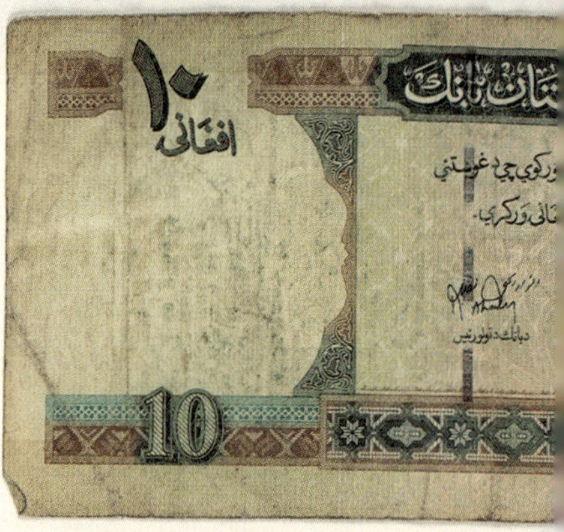
۱۰
افغانی
10

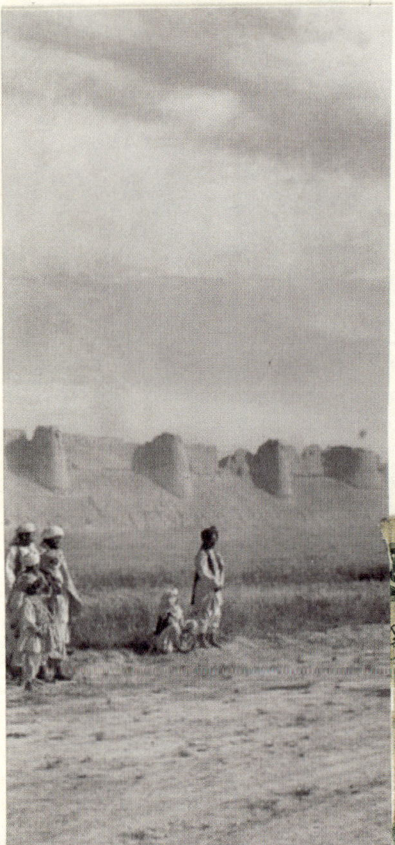

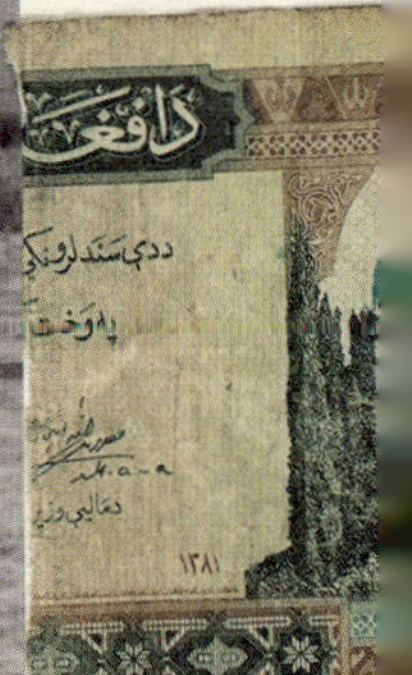
۱۳۸۱

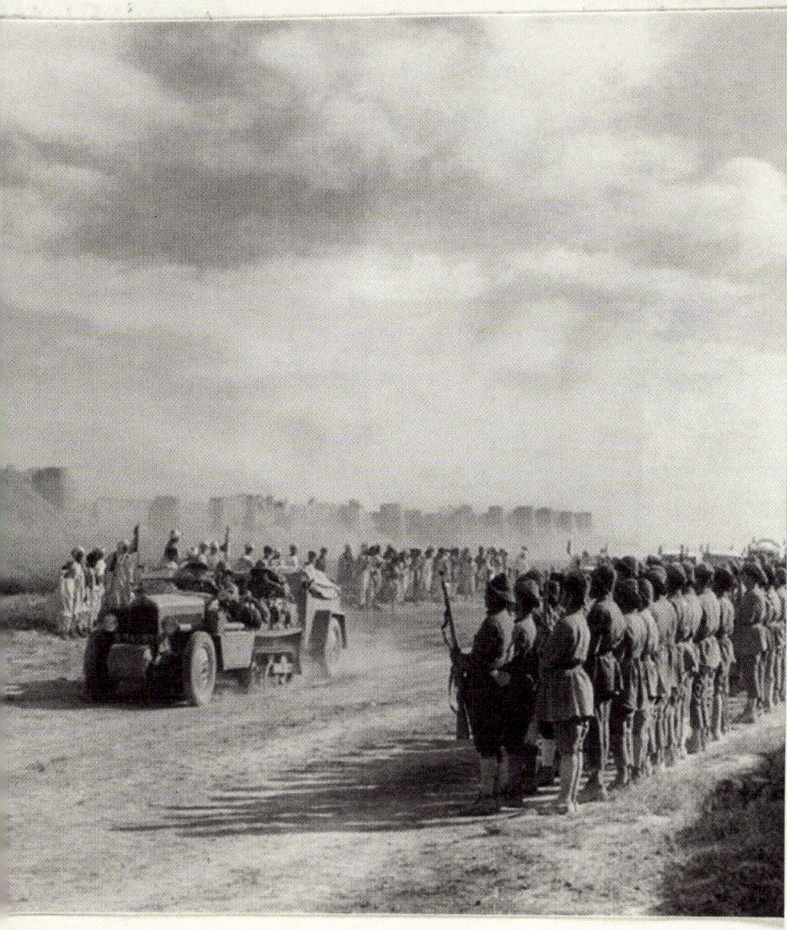

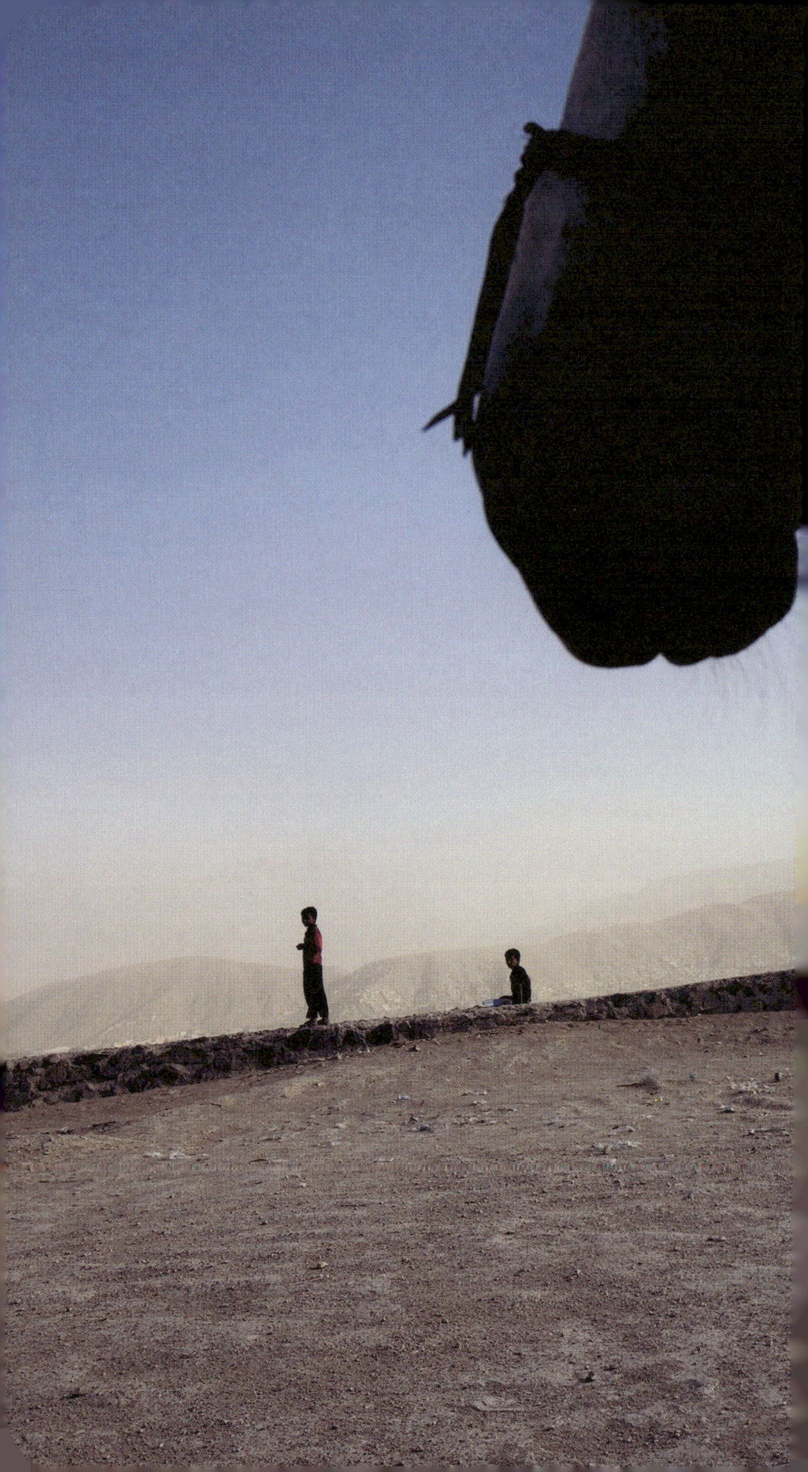

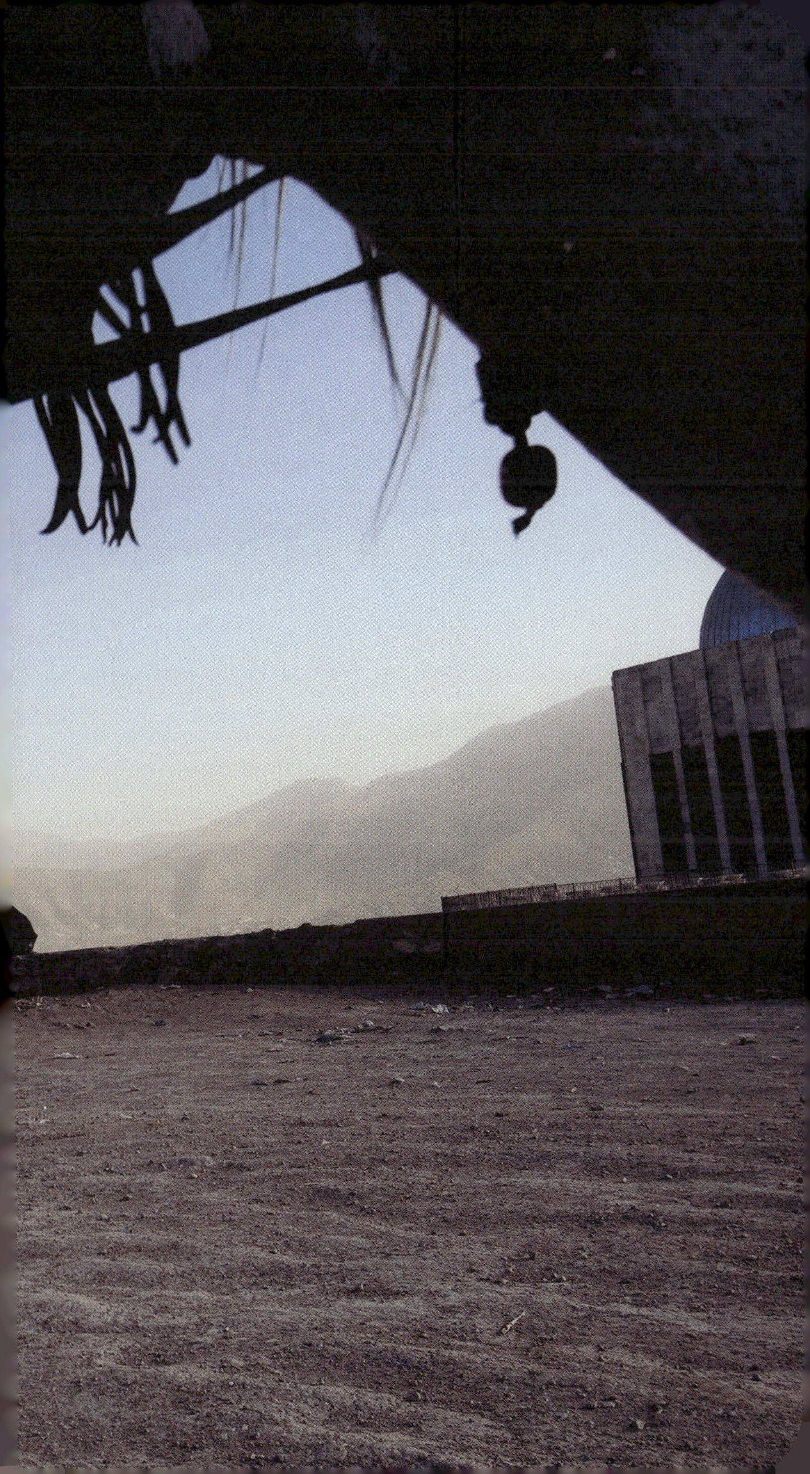

BECOME AN AMERICAN (OR W-EUROPE
IN 4 SIMPLE STEPS:
STEP (1): GET YOURSELF INTO THE COUNTR

Immigration and Customs* مهاجرت و گمرک**

ایمیگ رِیشِن آند کاستمز

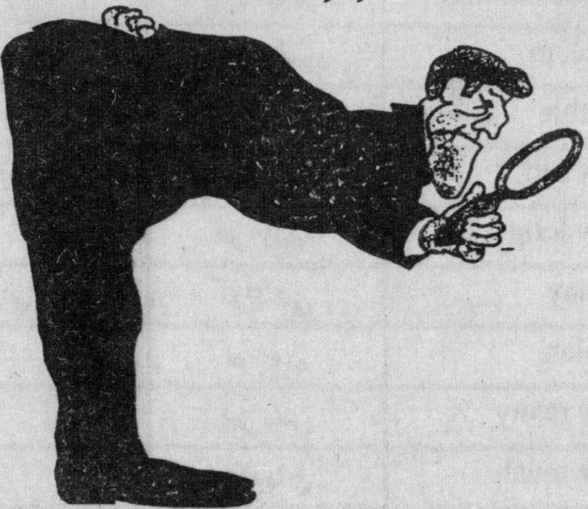

173-good afternoon. may I see your passport, please?

گود آفترنون. می آی سی یُر پسپورت .پیلیز؟

۱۷۳- بعدازظهر بخیر.آیا ممکن است پاسپورت شما را ببینم ,لطفاً؟

174-Yes, here it is. and here's my visa.

یس. هییر ایت ایز آند هییرز مای ویزا.

۱۷۴- بله. بفرمایید بگیرید. و این هم ویزای من است.

175-thank you. You have a tourist visa for three months.

تنکی یو.یو هو ا توریستن ویزا فر ثیری مانث.

۱۷۵- متشکرم. شما یک ویزای توریستی بمدت سه ماه دارید.

176-Yes, that's right. ۱۷۶- بله.درست است.

یس. دتس رایت.

STEP ②: FIND A GOOD LAWYER!

Meeting an attorney ملاقات یک وکیل

میتینگ اَن اَترنی

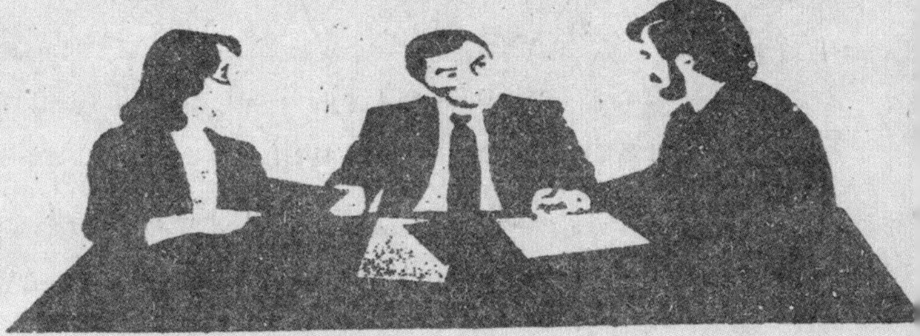

STEP ③: GET A CREDIT CARD!

Applying for a credit card

اَپلا اینگ فُر اِ کرِدیت کارد

تقاضای کارت اعتباری کردن

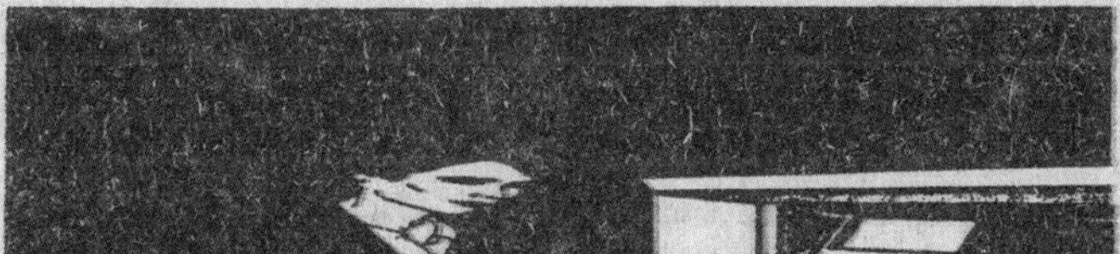

535-are you applying for a charge account?

آر یو اَپلا اینگ فُر اِ چارج اَکونت؟

۵۳۵- آیا شما تقاضای حساب جاری دارید؟

536-Yes. How long will it take for approval?

یس .هو لانگ ویل ایت تیک فُر اَپرووال

۵۳۶- بله. چه مدت برای موافقت طول خواهد کشید؟

STEP ④: GO SHOPPING!!
(AND CREATE A HUGE DEBT...)

shopping at the Mall * خرید از فروشگاه مال**

شاپینگ اَت دِ مال

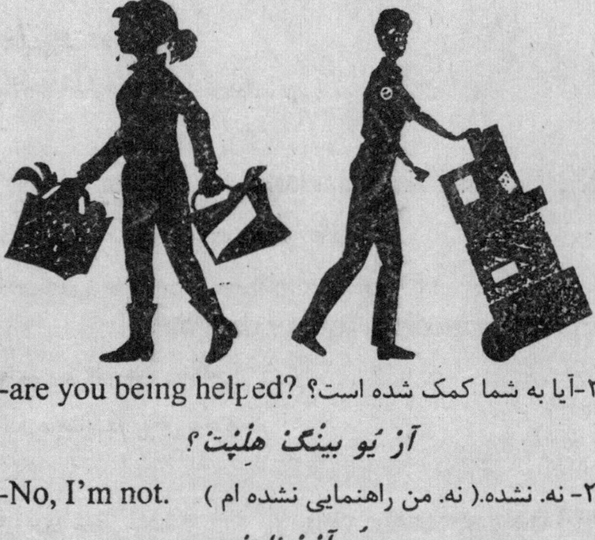

224-are you being helped? ۲۲۴-آیا به شما کمک شده است؟

آز یُو بینگ هِلپت؟

225-No, I'm not. ۲۲۵- نه. نشده.(نه. من راهنمایی نشده ام)

نَ. آیم نات.

226-I'm looking for gifts for my children.

یم لوکینگ فُر گیفتس فُر مای چیلدرن.

۲۲۶- من دارم دنبال هدایایی برای بچه هایم میگردم.

227-possibly T-shirts. ۲۲۷- احتمالاً تی شرت.

پاسیبلی تی شرتس.

... or a girl or a boy? ۲۲۸- برای دختر یا پسر؟

فُر اِ گرل آز اِ بی؟

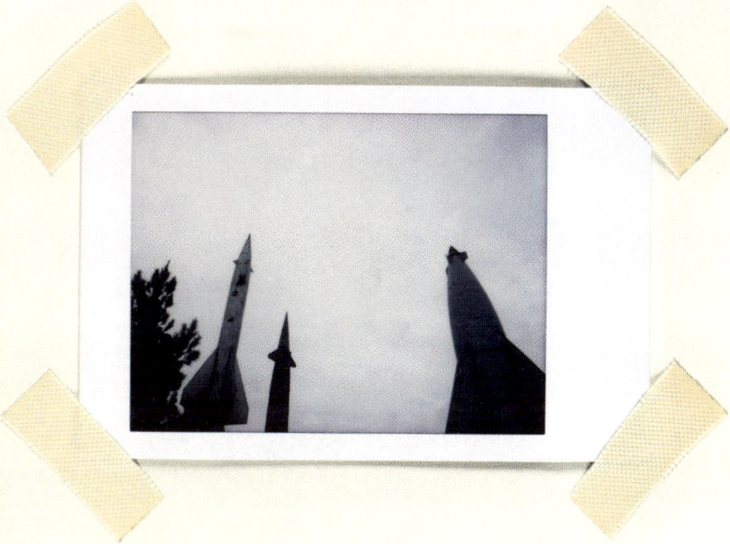

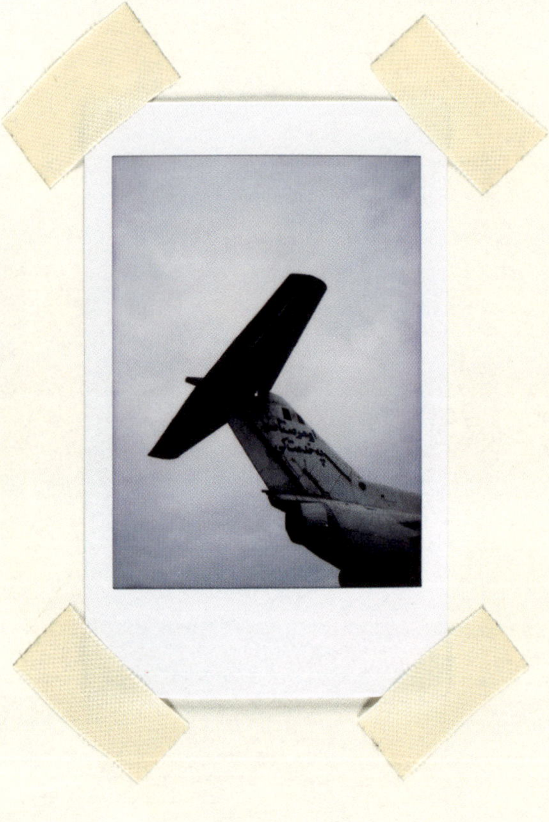

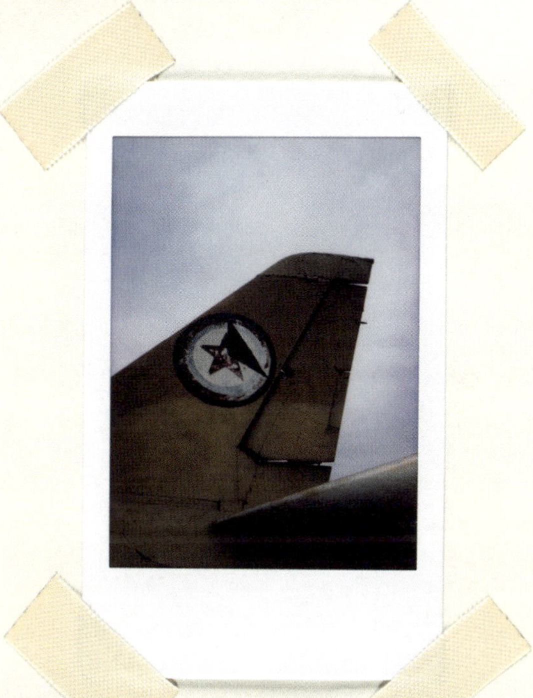

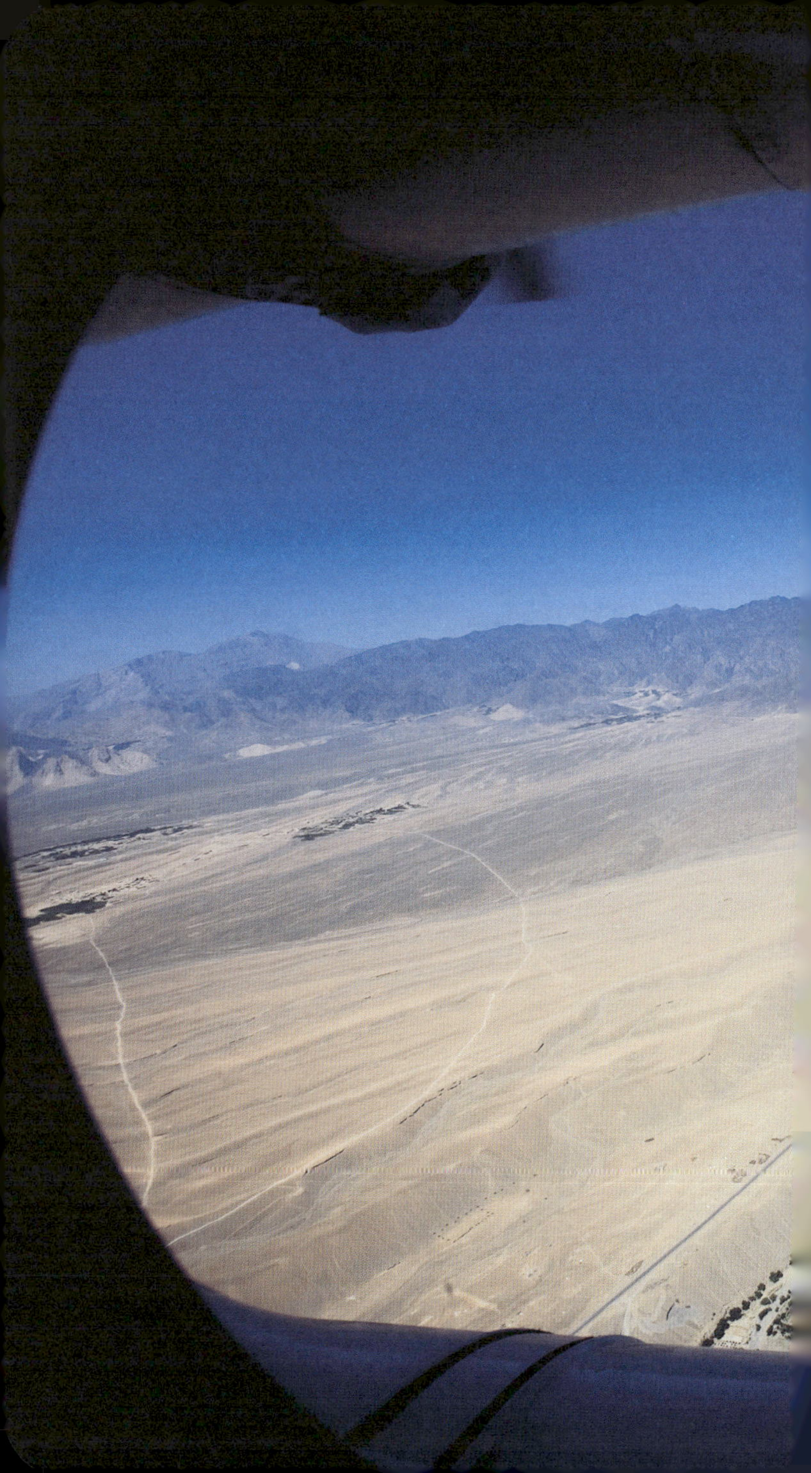

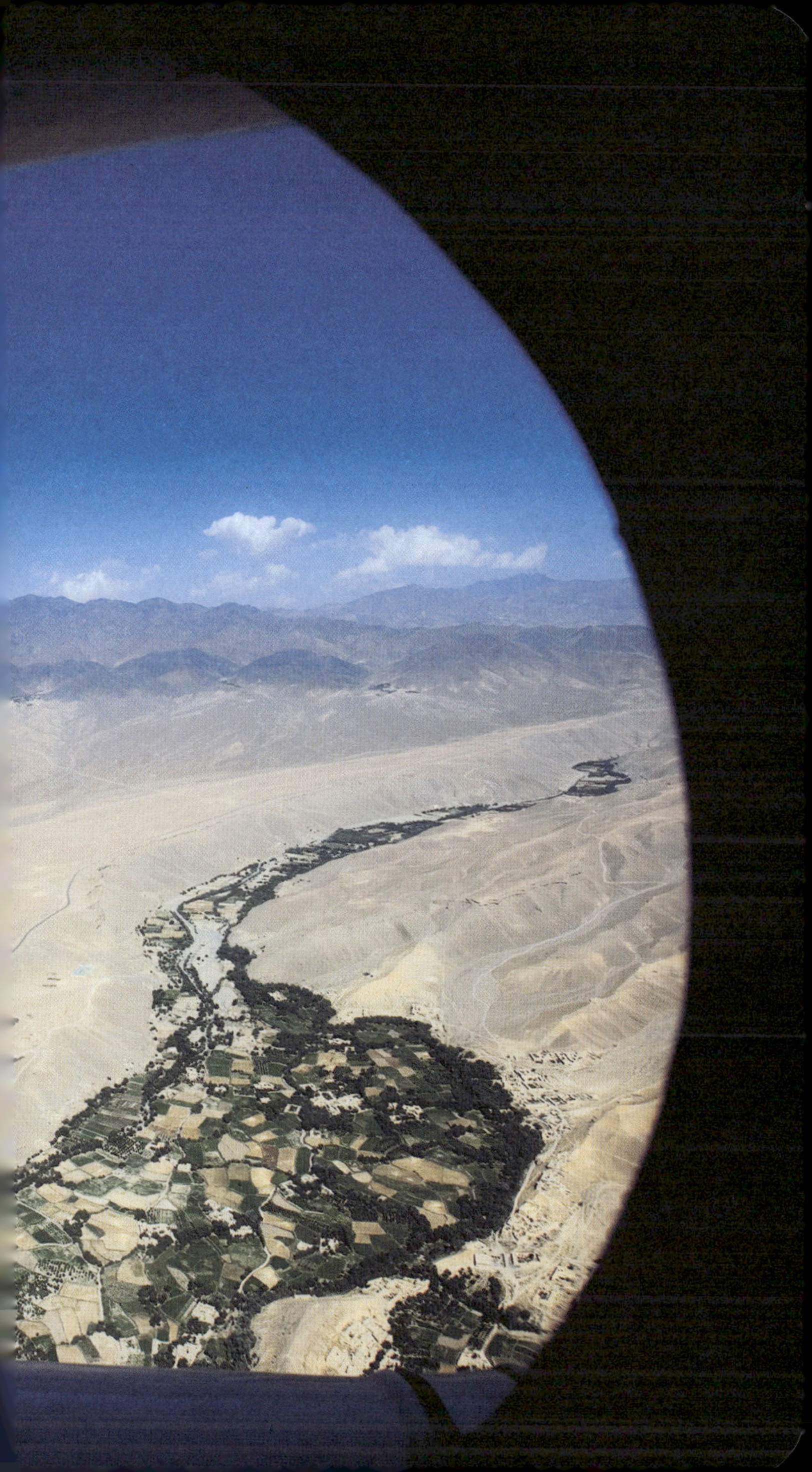

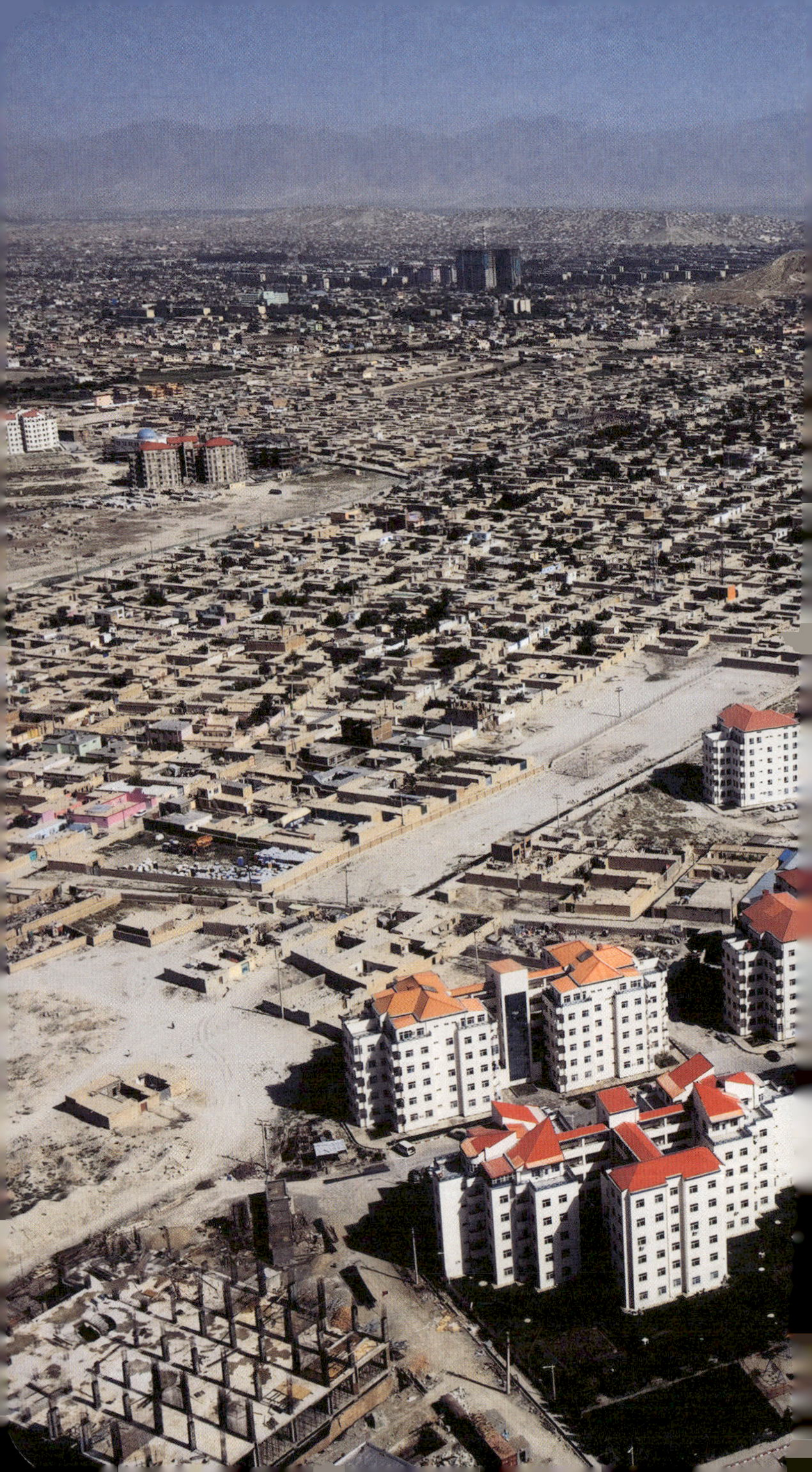

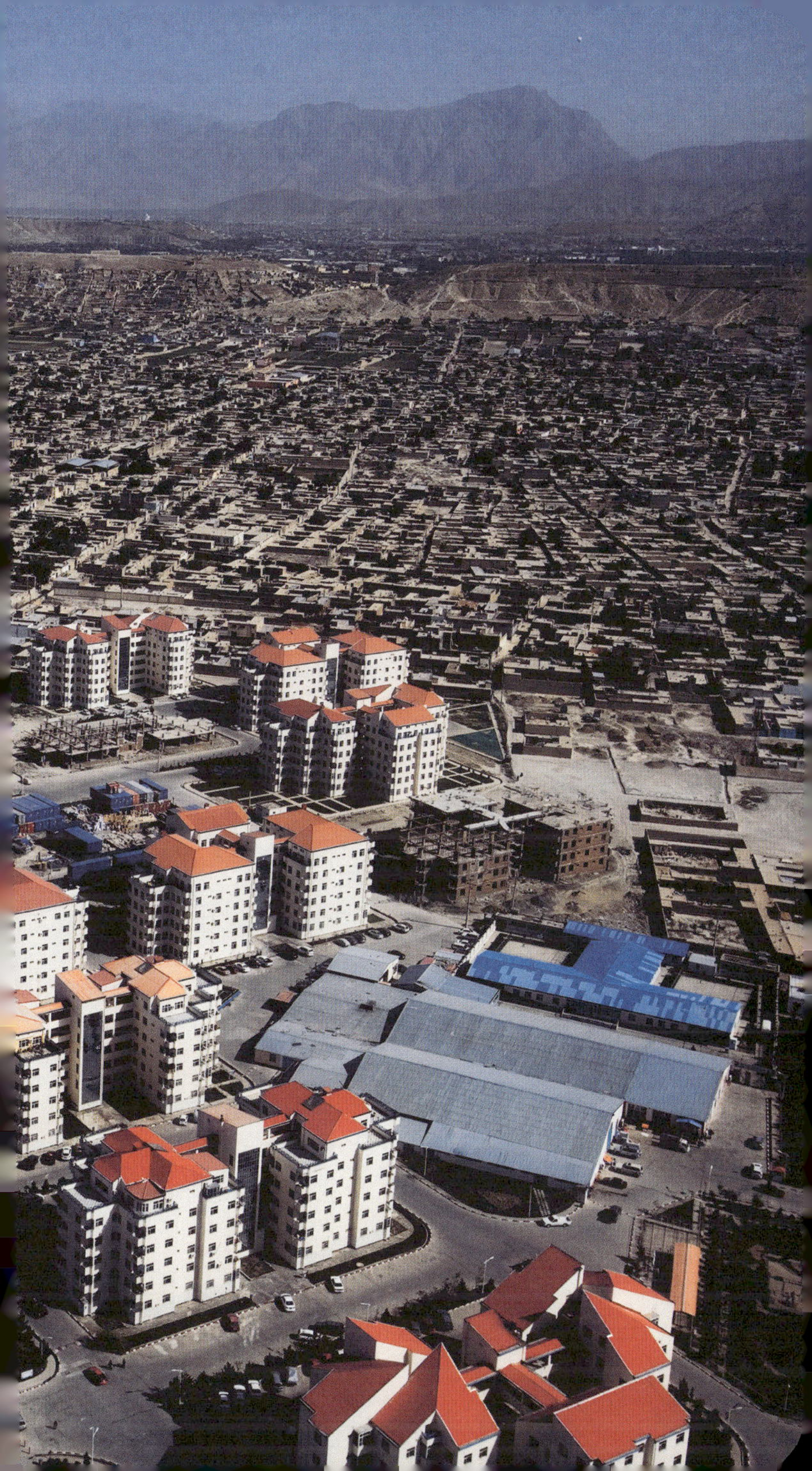

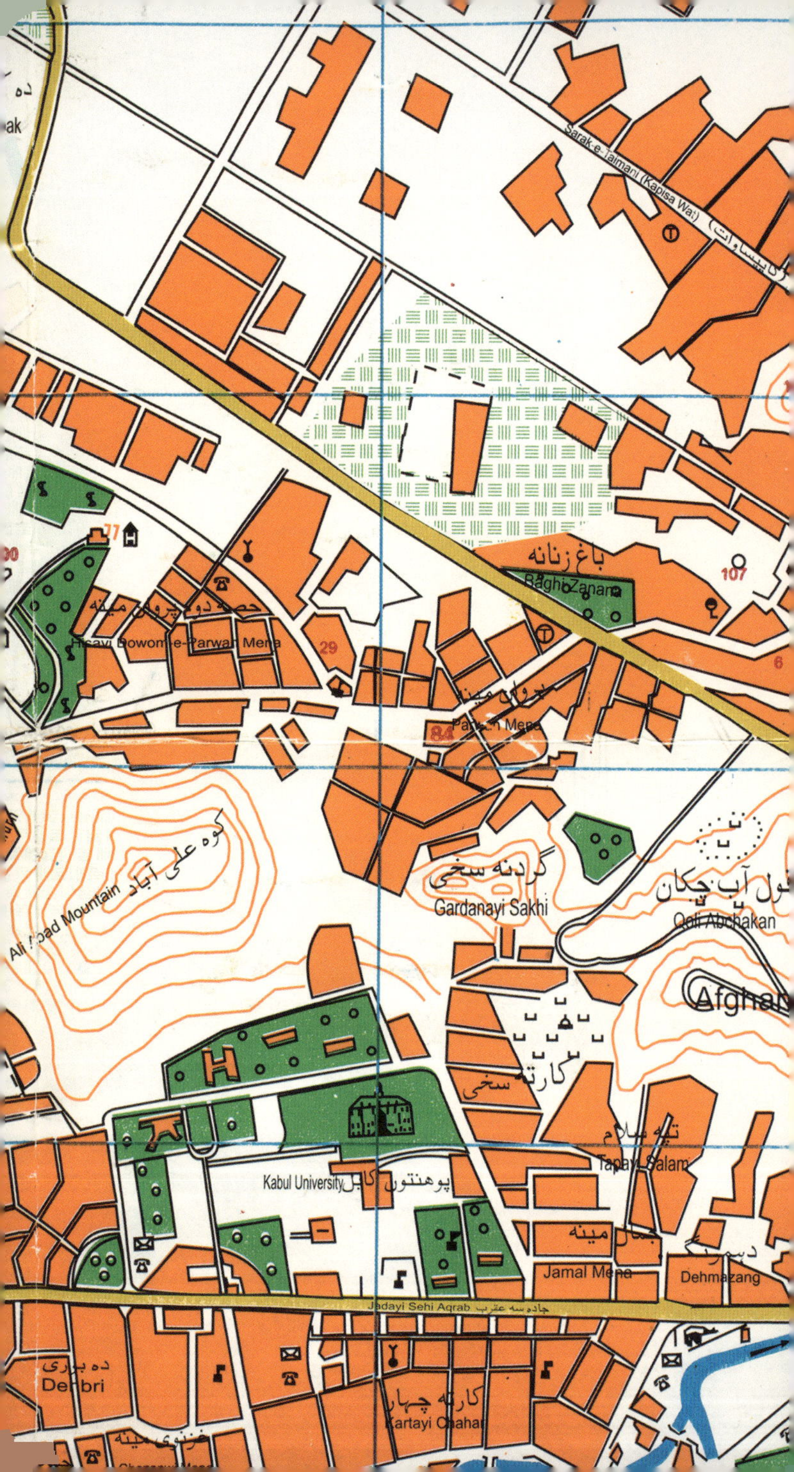

Sarak-e-Taimani (Kapisa Wat)
باغ زنانه
Baghi Zanana
107
Hisayi Dowom-e-Parwan Mena
29
Parwan Mena
84
کوه علی آباد
Ali Abad Mountain
گردنه سخی
Gardanayi Sakhi
Qoli Abchakan
کارته سخی
Tapayi Salam
Kabul University
پوهنتون کابل
Jamal Mena
Dehmazang
Jadayi Sehi Aqrab
کارته چهار
Kartayi Chahar

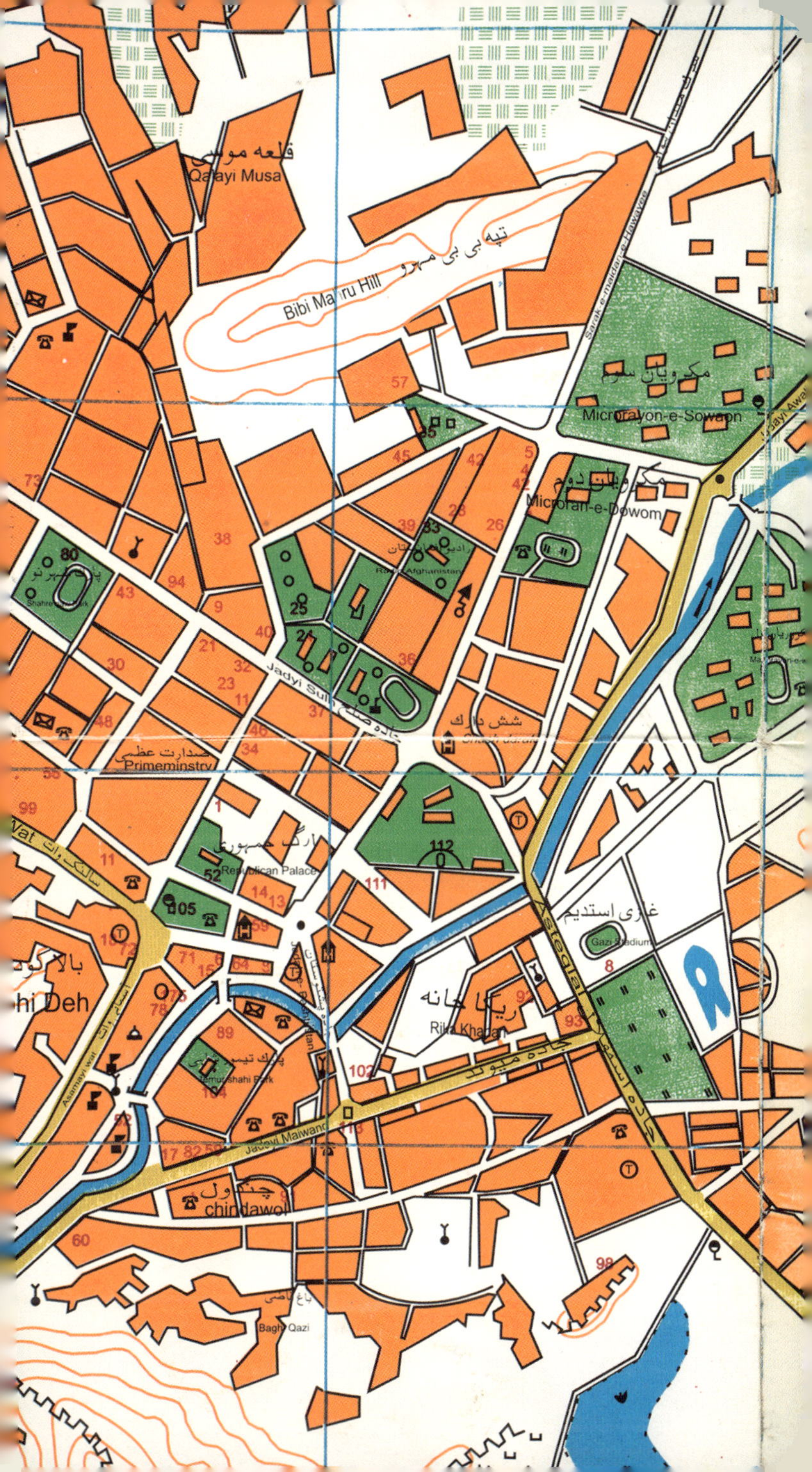
قلعه موسی
Qalayi Musa
تپه بی بی مهرو
Bibi Mahru Hill
مکرویان سوم
Microrayon-e-Sowom
مکرویان دوم
Microrayon-e-Dowom
Radio Afghanistan
Shahre-nau Park
شش درک
Shash darak
صدارت عظمی
Primeminstry
ارگ جمهوری
Republican Palace
غازی استدیم
Gazi Stadium
ریکا خانه
Rika Khana
جاده میوند
Jadayi Maiwand
Timur Shahi Park
چنداول
chindawol
باغ قاضی
Bagh Qazi
Asamayi wat

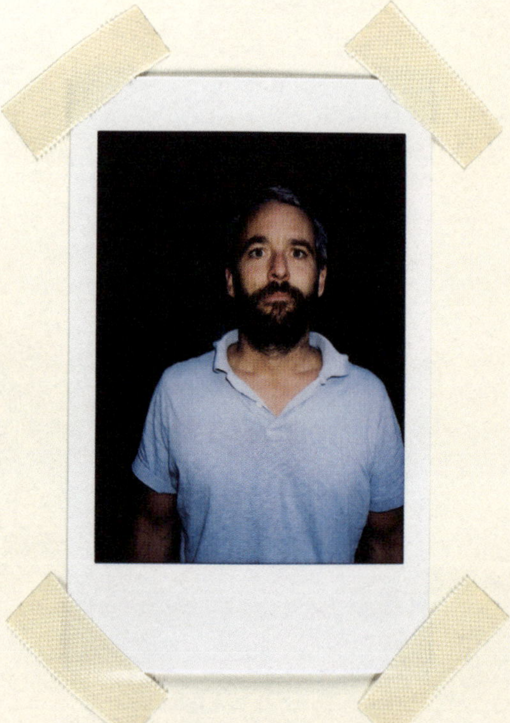

Tyler.

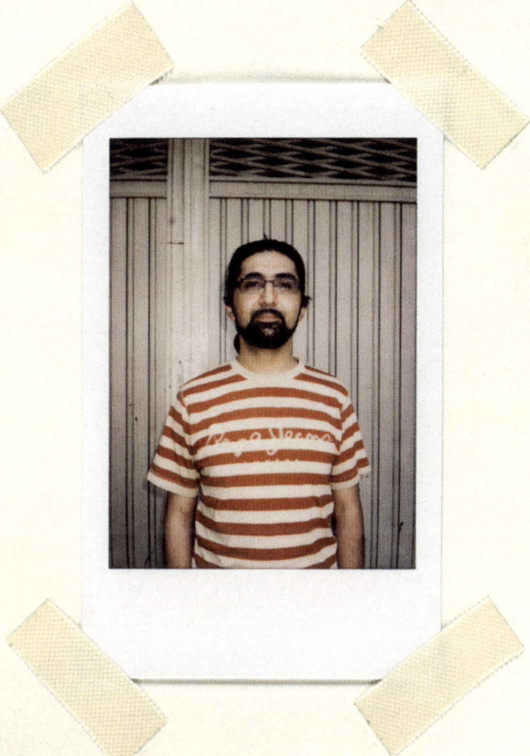

Massoud.

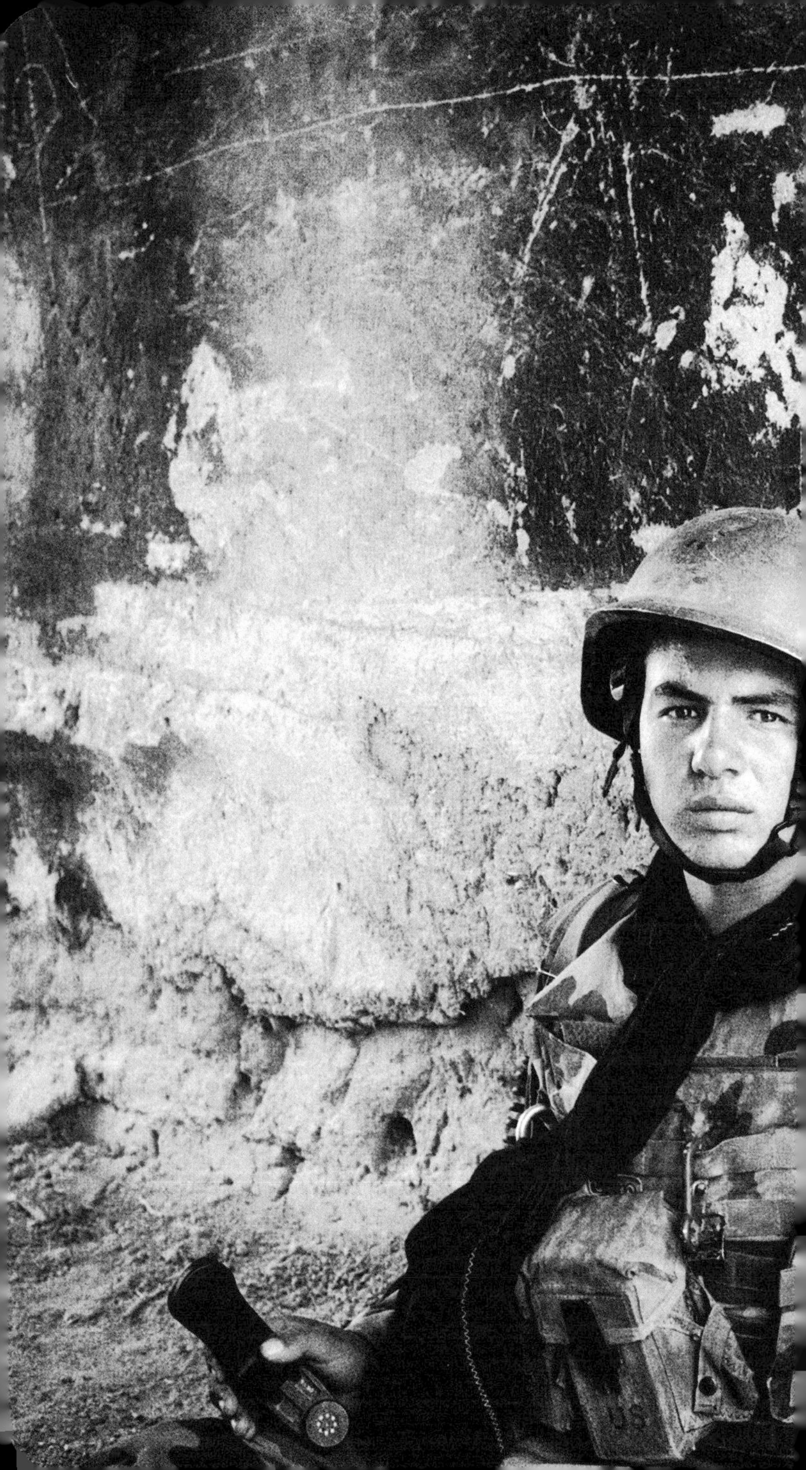

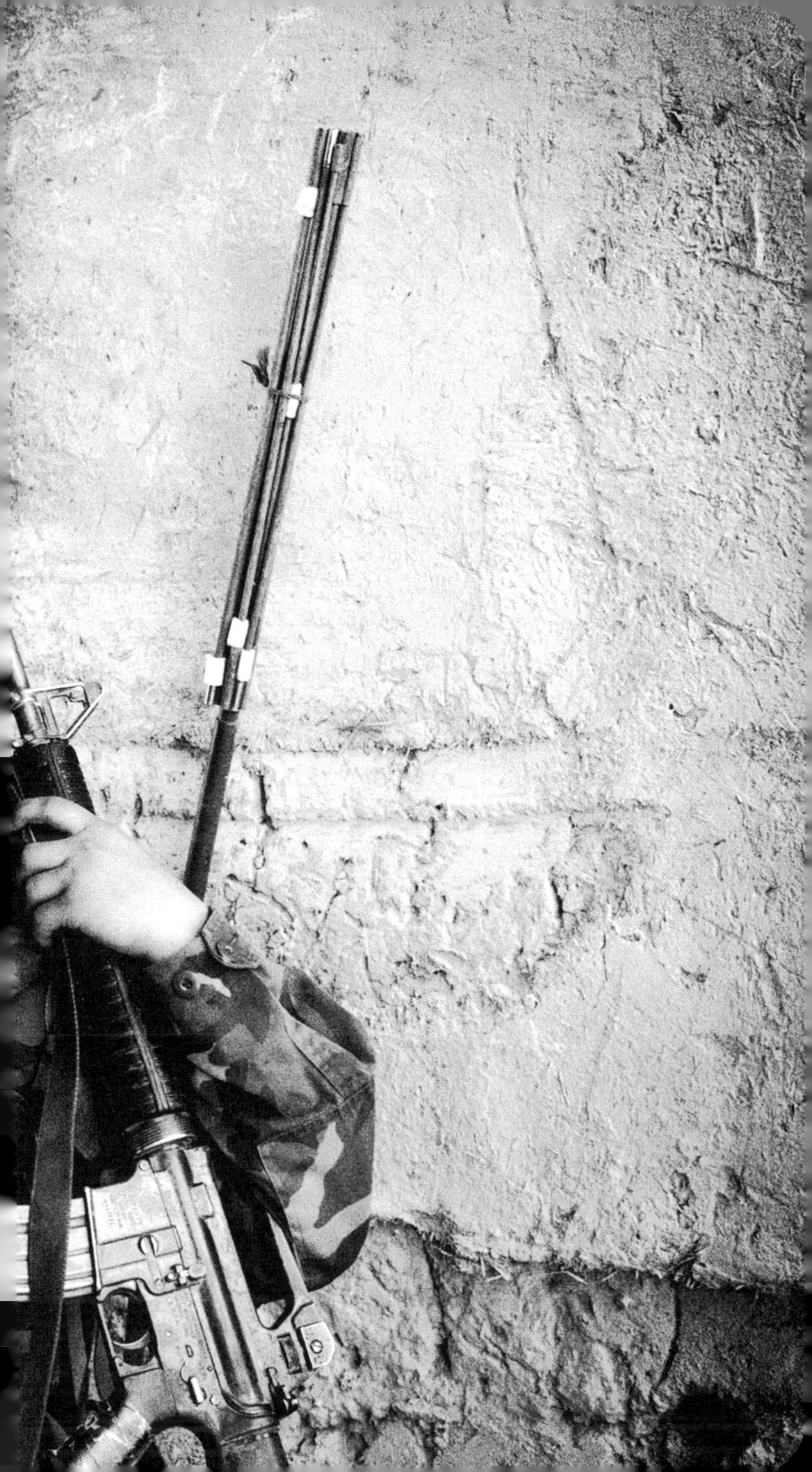

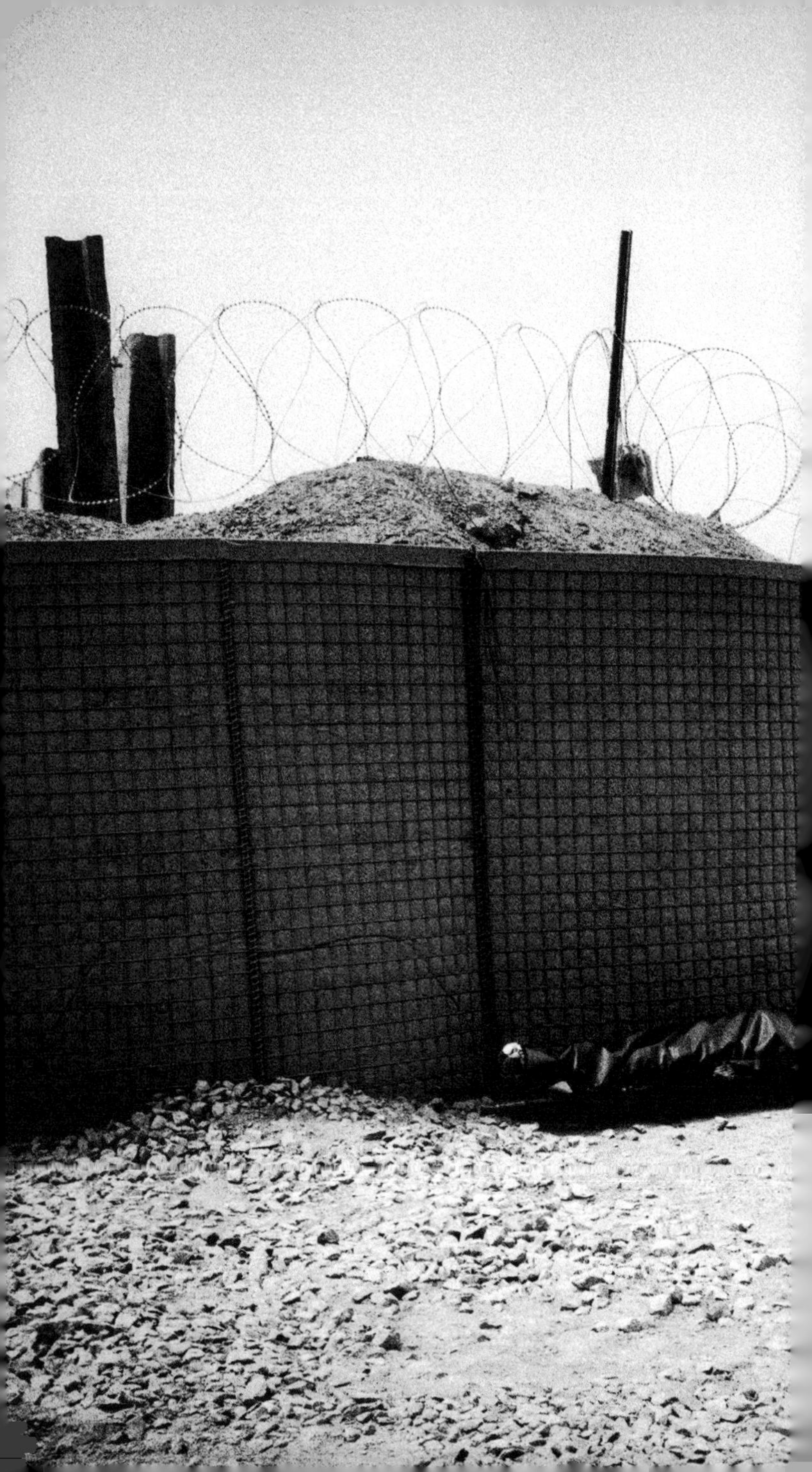

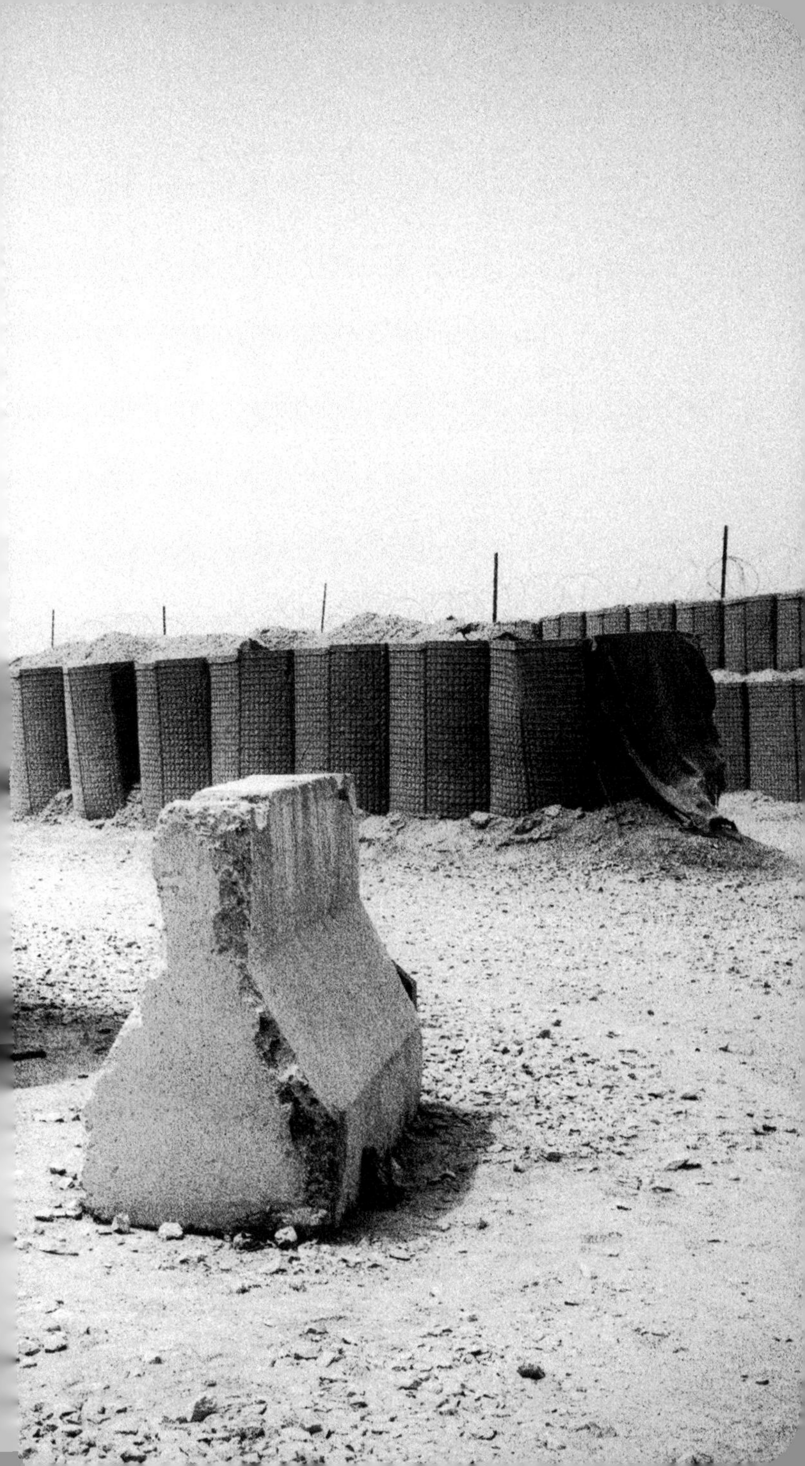

CHRIS HEDGES

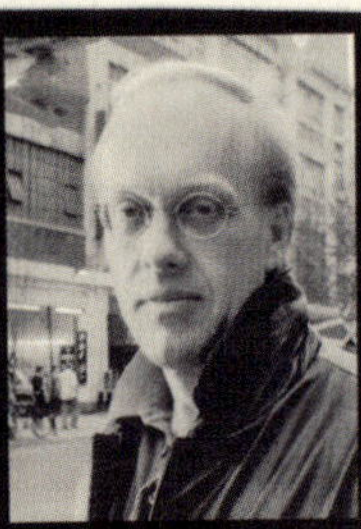

ambushes

The Myth of War

and

—The New York Times

War Is a Force That Gives Us Meaning

The rush of battle is a potent and often lethal addiction, for war is a drug, one I ingested for many years. It is peddled by mythmakers—historians, war correspondents, filmmakers, novelists, and the state—all of whom endow it with qualities it often does possess: excitement, exoticism, power, chances to rise above our small stations in life, and a bizarre and fantastic universe that has a grotesque and dark beauty.

in a brilliant, thoughtful, timely and unsettling book. . . .

War Is a Force That Gives Us Meaning

War makes the world understandable, a black and white tableau of them and us. It suspends thought, especially self-critical thought. All bow before the supreme effort. We are one. Most of us willingly accept war as long as we can fold it into a belief system that paints the ensuing suffering as necessary for a higher good, for human beings seek not only happiness but also meaning. And tragically war is sometimes the most powerful way in human society to achieve meaning.

But war is a god, as the ancient Greeks and Romans knew, and its worship demands human sacrifice. We urge young men to war, making the slaughter they are asked to carry out a rite of passage. And this rite has changed little over the centuries, centuries in which there has almost continuously been a war raging somewhere on the planet. The historian Will Durant calculated that there have only been twenty-nine years in all of human history during which a war was not underway somewhere.

The enduring attraction of war is this: Even with its destruction and carnage it can give us what we long for in life. It can give us purpose, meaning, a reason for living. Only when we are in the midst of conflict does the shallowness and vapidness of much of our lives become apparent. Trivia dominates our conversations and increasingly our airwaves. And war is an enticing elixir. It gives us resolve, a cause. It allows us to be noble. And those who have the least meaning in their lives, the impoverished refugees in Gaza, the disenfranchised North African immigrants in France, even the legions of young who live in the splendid indolence and safety of the industrialized world, are all susceptible to war's appeal.

truth

war can be exhilarating and even addictive: "It gives us purpose, meaning, a reason for living."

The myth of war rarely endures for those who experience combat. War is messy, confusing, sullied by raw brutality and an elephantine fear that grabs us like a massive bouncer who comes up from behind. Soldiers in the moments before real battles weep, vomit, and write last letters home, although these are done more as a precaution than from belief. All are nearly paralyzed with fright. There is a morbid silence that grips a battlefield in the final moments before the shooting starts, one that sets the back of my own head pounding in pain, wipes away all appetite, and makes my fingers tremble as I ready myself to go forward against logic. You do not think of home or family, for to do so is to be overcome by a wave of nostalgia and emotion that can impair your ability to survive. One thinks, so far as it is possible, of cleaning weapons, of readying for the business of killing. No one ever charges into battle for God and country.

"Just remember," a Marine Corps lieutenant colonel told me as he strapped his pistol belt under his arm before we crossed into Kuwait, "that none of these boys is fighting for home, for the flag, for all that crap the politicians feed the public. They are fighting for each other, just for each other."

Powerful human desires.

THE MYTH OF WAR

The potency of myth is that it allows us to make sense of mayhem and violent death. It gives a justification to what is often nothing more than gross human cruelty and stupidity. It allows us to believe we have achieved our place in human society because of a long chain of heroic endeavors, rather than accept the sad reality that we stumble along a dimly lit corridor of disasters. It disguises our powerlessness. It hides from view our own impotence and the ordinariness of our own leaders. By turning history into myth we transform random events into a chain of events directed by a will greater than our own, one that is determined and preordained. We are elevated above the multitude. We march toward nobility. And no society is immune.

Most national myths, at their core, are racist. They are fed by ignorance. Those individuals who understand other cultures, speak other languages, and find richness in diversity are shunted aside.

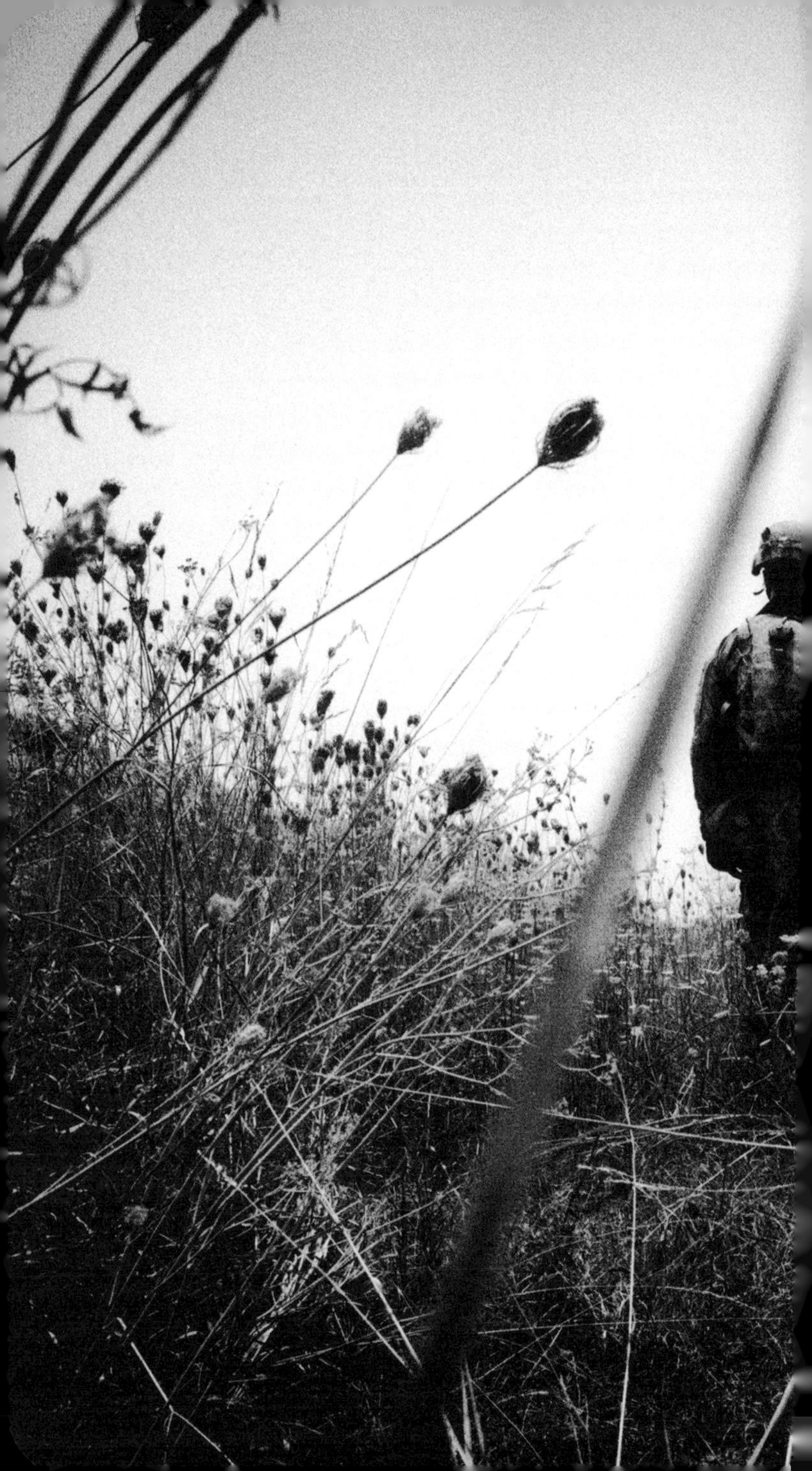

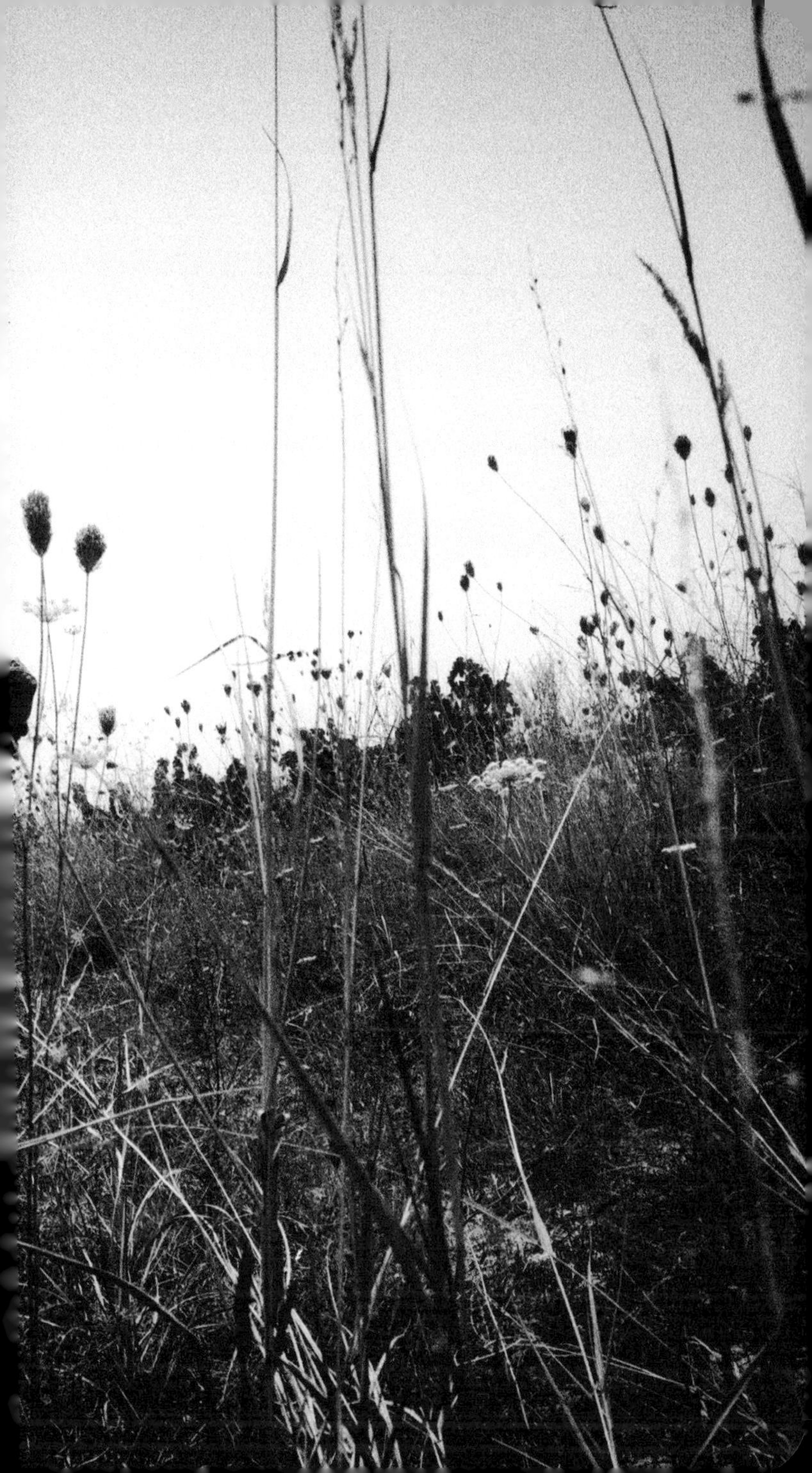

The imagined heroism, the vision of a dash to rescue a wounded comrade, the clear lines we thought were drawn in battle, the images we have of our own reaction under gunfire, usually wilt in combat. This is a sober and unsettling realization. We may not be who we thought we would be. One of the most difficult realizations of war is how deeply we betray ourselves, how far we are from the image of gallantry and courage we desire, how instinctual and primordial fear is. We do not meditate on action. Our movements are usually motivated by a numbing and overpowering desire for safety. And yet there are heroes, those who somehow rise above it all, maybe only once, to expose themselves to risk to save their comrades. I have seen such soldiers. I nearly always found them afterward to be embarrassed about what they did, unable to explain it, reticent to talk. Many are not sure they could do it again.

war correspondent,

thugs

The chance to exist

seen children murdered

identify his corpse.

The fighting was intense. As he moved down the street he heard a door swing open. He fired a burst from his AK-47 assault rifle. A twelve-year-old girl dropped dead. He saw in the body of the unknown girl lying prostrate in front of him the image of his own twelve-year-old daughter. He broke down. He had to be helped back to the city. He was lost for the rest of the war, shuttered inside his apartment, nervous, morose, and broken. This experience is far more typical of warfare than the Rambo heroics we are fed by the state and the entertainment industry. The cost of killing is all the more bitter because of the deep disillusionment that war usually brings.

It takes little in wartime to turn ordinary men into killers. Most give themselves willingly to the seduction of unlimited power to destroy and all feel the heavy weight of peer pressure. Few, once in battle, can find the strength to resist.

The German veteran of World War I Erich Maria Remarque, in *All Quiet on the Western Front,* wrote of the narcotic of war that quickly transformed men into beasts. He knew the ecstatic high of violence and the debilitating mental and physical destruction that comes with prolonged exposure to war's addiction.

"We run on," he wrote, "overwhelmed by this wave that bears us along, that fills us with ferocity, turns us into thugs, into murderers, into God knows what devils; this wave that multiplies our strength with fear and madness and greed of life, seeking and fighting for nothing but our deliverance."[2]

THE NEW YORK TIMES
has never been more necessary.

The press wanted to be used. It saw itself as part of the war effort. Most reporters sent to cover a war don't really want to go near the fighting. They do not tell this to their editors and indeed will moan and complain about restrictions. The handful who actually head out into the field have a bitter enmity with the hotel-room warriors. But even those who do go out are guilty of distortion. For we not only believe the myth of war and feed recklessly off of the drug but also embrace the cause. We may do it with more skepticism. We certainly expose more lies and misconceptions. But we believe. We all believe. When you stop believing you stop going to war.

The chief institutions that disseminate the myth are the press and the state. The press has been culpable since the telegraph made possible the modern war correspondent. And starting with the Crimean War, when the first dispatches were fed by newly minted war correspondents in real time, nearly every reporter has seen his or her mission as sustaining civilian and army morale. The advent of photography and film did little to alter the incentive to boost morale, for the lie in war is almost always the lie of omission. The blunders and senseless slaughter by our generals, the execution of prisoners and innocents, and the horror of wounds are rarely disclosed, at least during a mythic war, to the public. Only when the myth is punctured, as it eventually was in Vietnam, does the press begin to report in a sensory rather than a mythic manner. But even then it is it reacting to a public that has changed its perception of war. The press usually does not lead.

Mythic war reporting sells papers and boosts ratings. Real reporting, sensory reporting, does not.

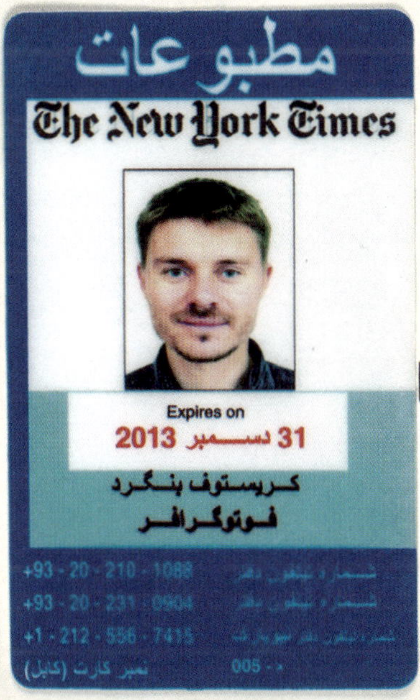

rare and frightening honesty."

And yet, despite all this, I am not a pacifist.

The poiso

that is war does not free us from the ethics of responsibilit

Force is and I suspect always will be part of the human condition. There are times when the force wielded by one immoral faction must be countered by a faction that, while never moral, is perhaps less immoral.

We in the industrialized world bear responsibility for the world's genocides because we had the power to intervene and did not. We stood by and watched the slaughter in Chechnya, Sri Lanka, Sierra Leone, Liberia, and Rwanda where a million people died. The blood of the victims of Srebrenica—a designated U.N. safe area in Bosnia—is on our hands. The generation before mine watched, with much the same passivity, the genocides of Germany, Poland, Hungary, Greece, and the Ukraine.

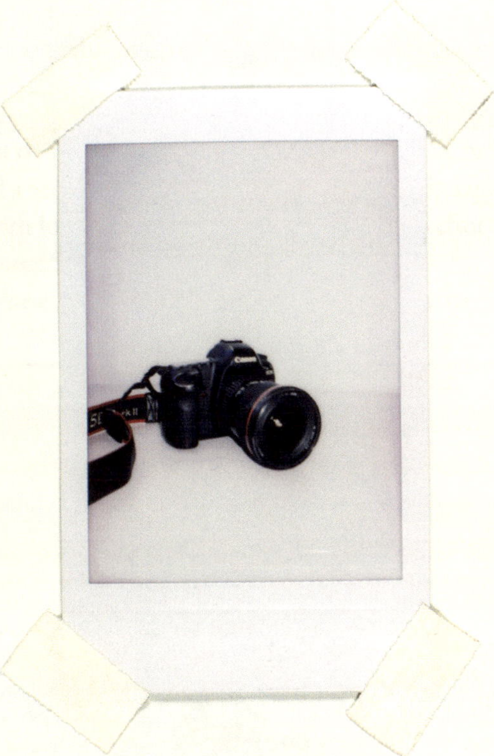

In the beginning war looks and feels like love. But unlike love it gives nothing in return but an ever-deepening dependence, like all narcotics, on the road to self-destruction. It does not affirm but places upon us greater and greater demands. It destroys the outside world until it is hard to live outside war's grip. It takes a higher and higher dose to achieve any thrill. Finally, one ingests war only to remain numb. The world outside war becomes, as Freud wrote, "uncanny." The familiar becomes strangely unfamiliar—many who have been in war find this when they return home. The world we once understood and longed to return to stands before us as alien, strange, and beyond our grasp.

We are tempted to reduce life to a simple search for happiness. Happiness, however, withers if there is no meaning. The other temptation is to disavow the search for happiness in order to be faithful to that which provides meaning. But to live only for meaning—indifferent to all happiness—makes us fanatic, self-righteous, and cold. It leaves us cut off from our own humanity and the humanity of others. We must hope for grace, for our lives to be sustained by moments of meaning and happiness, both equally worthy of human communion.

Love, when it is deep and sustained by two individuals, includes self-giving—often self-sacrifice—as well as desire. For the covenant of love is such that it recognizes both the fragility and the sanctity of the individual. It recognizes itself in the other. It alone can save us.

BEST

LOVE

intense

BOOK

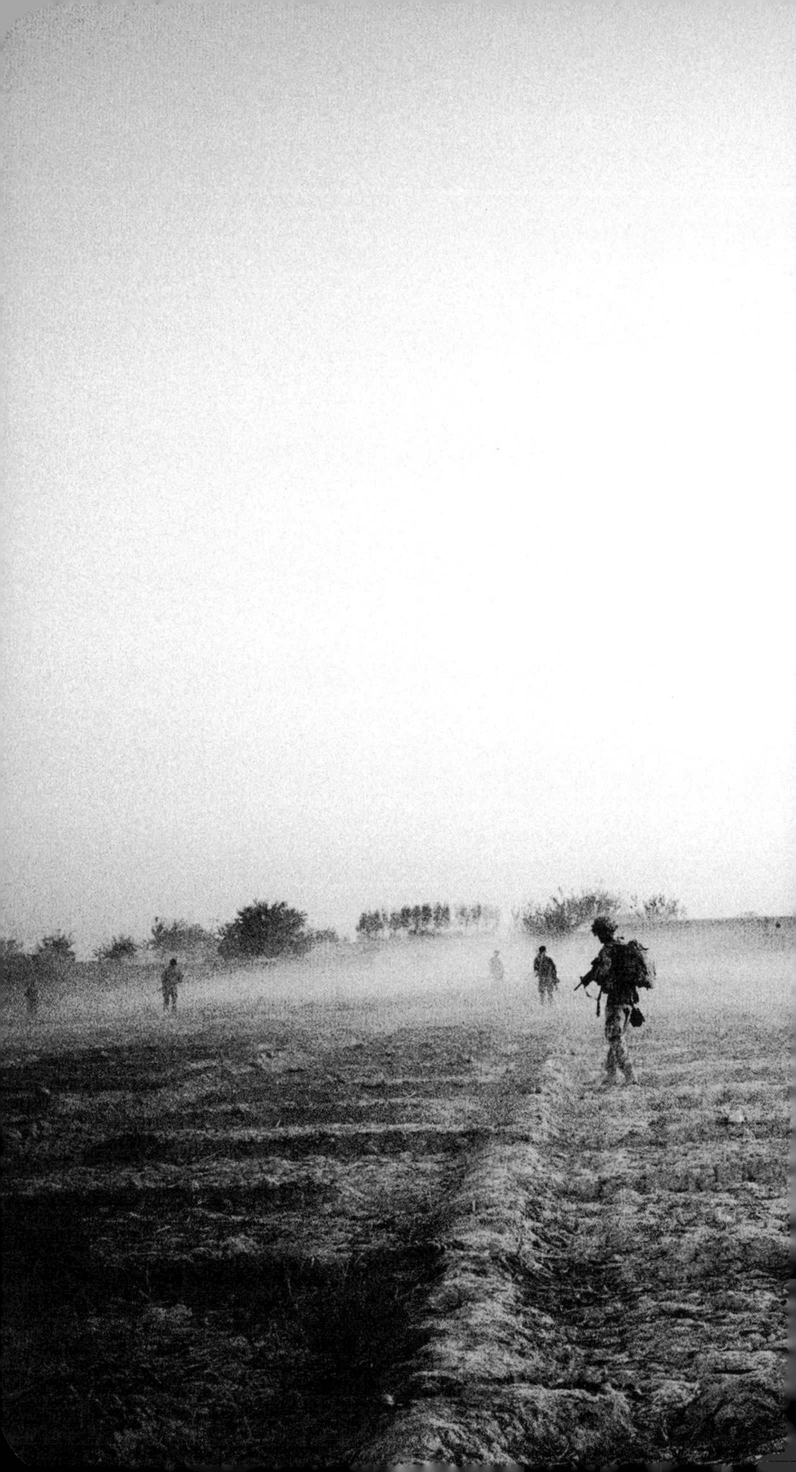

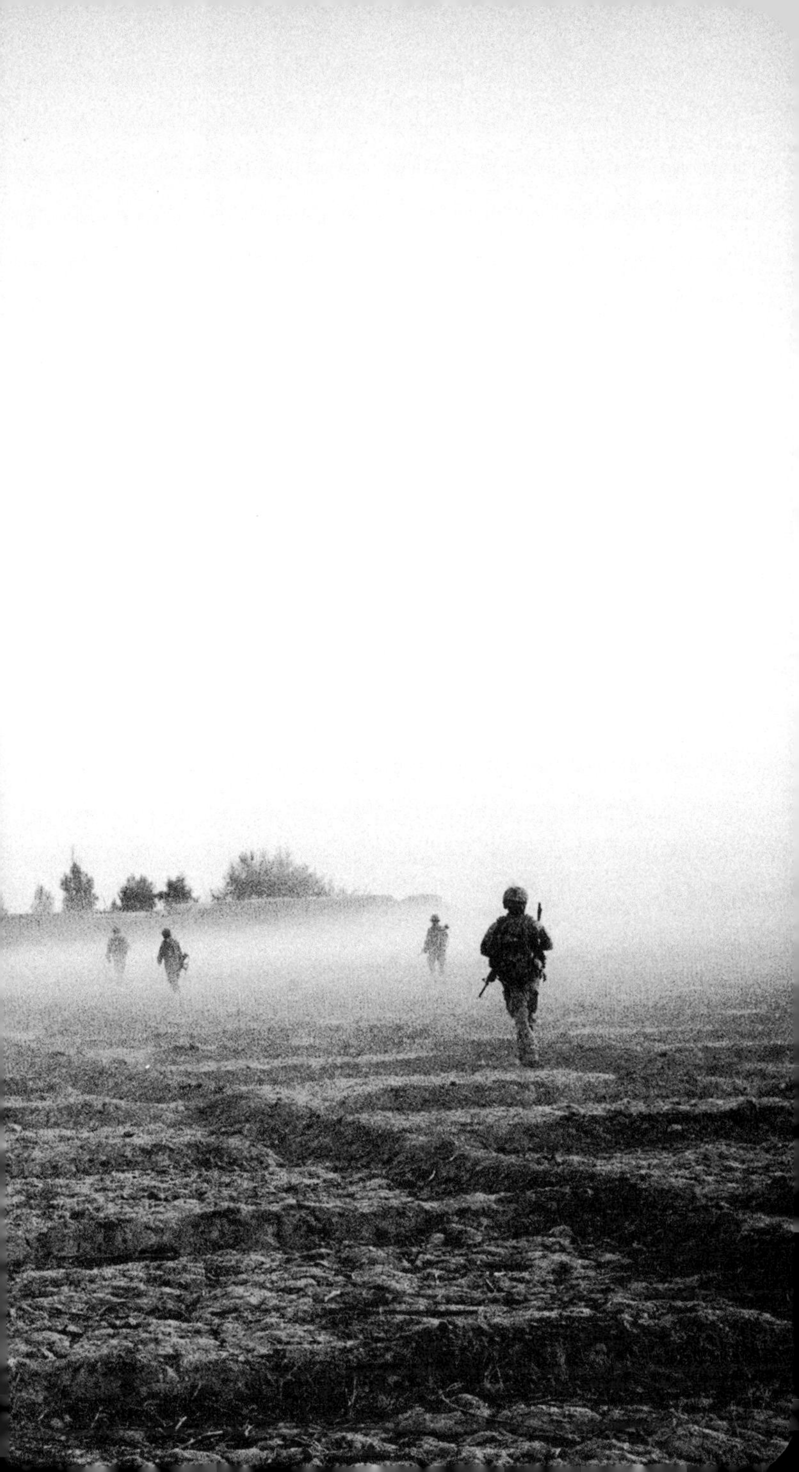

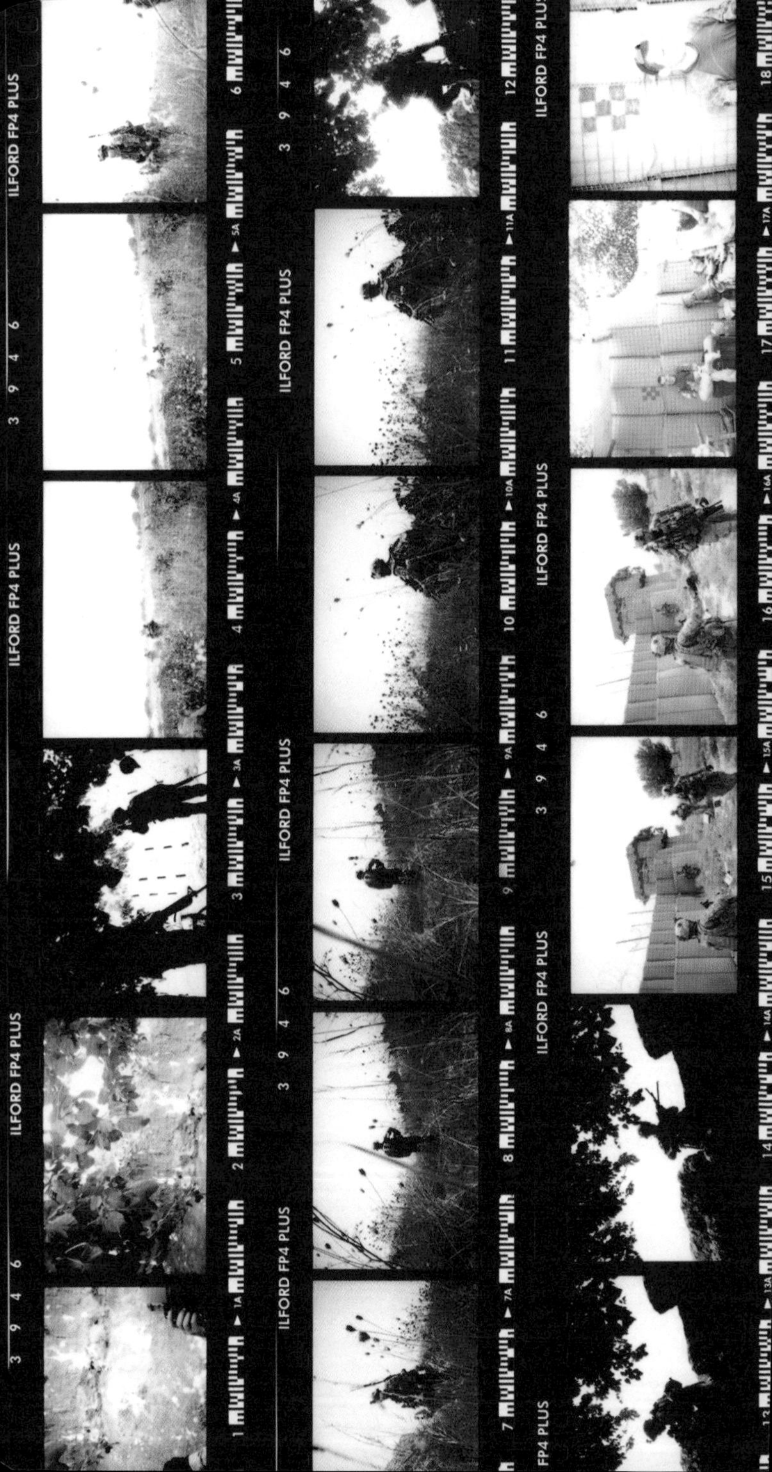
ILFORD FP4 PLUS

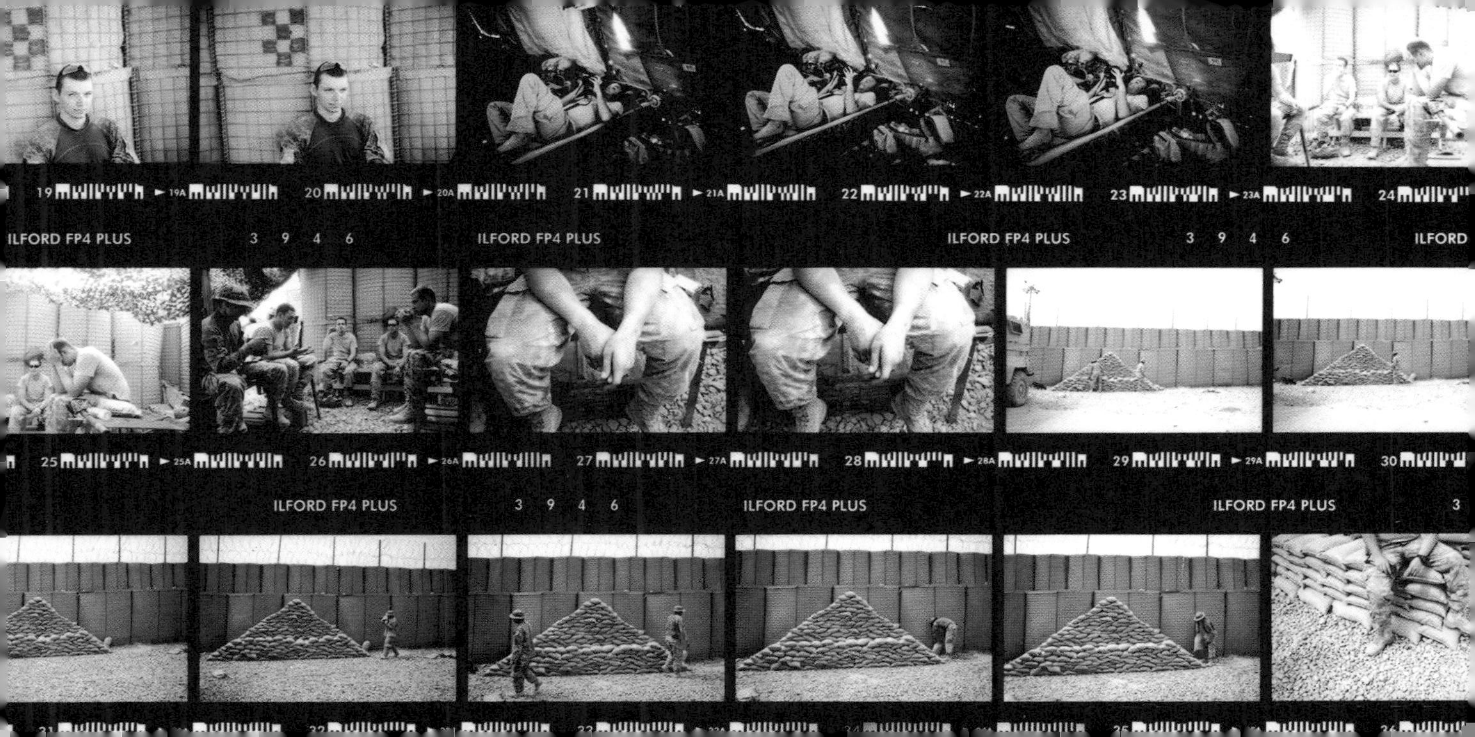
19 19A 20 20A 21 21A 22 22A 23 23A 24
ILFORD FP4 PLUS 3 9 4 6 ILFORD FP4 PLUS ILFORD FP4 PLUS 3 9 4 6 ILFORD
25 25A 26 26A 27 27A 28 28A 29 29A 30
ILFORD FP4 PLUS 3 9 4 6 ILFORD FP4 PLUS ILFORD FP4 PLUS 3

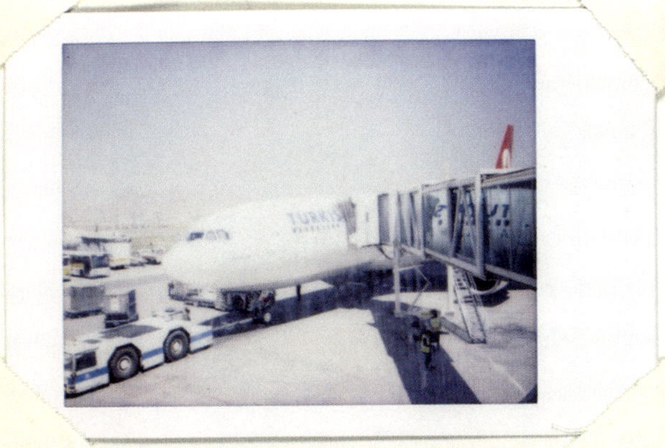

Safety

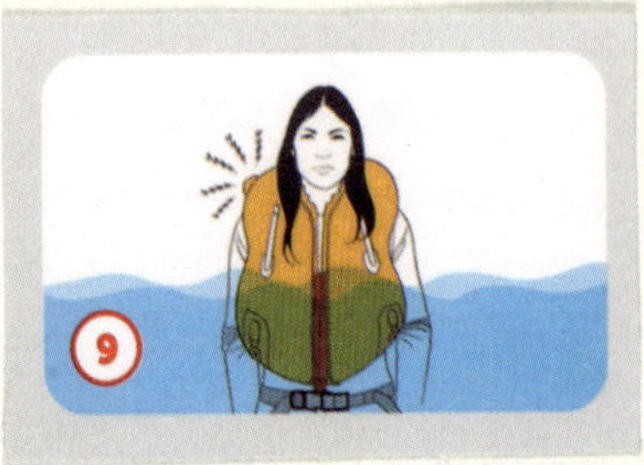

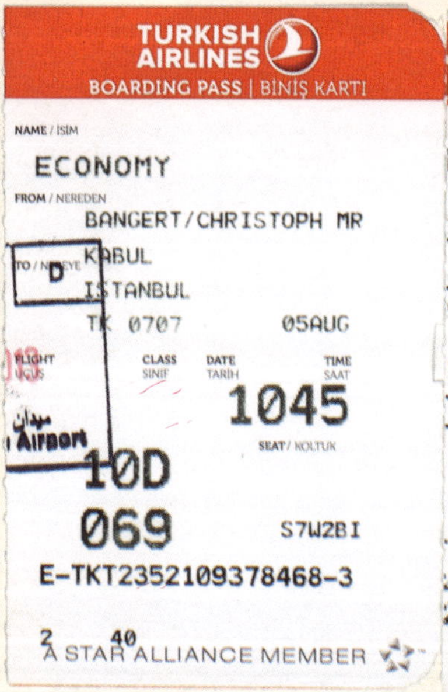

TURKISH AIRLINES
BOARDING PASS | BİNİŞ KARTI

NAME / İSİM
ECONOMY
FROM / NEREDEN
BANGERT/CHRISTOPH MR
TO / NEREYE
KABUL
ISTANBUL
TK 0707 05AUG

FLIGHT UÇUŞ | CLASS SINIF | DATE TARİH | TIME SAAT

1045

SEAT / KOLTUK
10D
069 S7W2BI
E-TKT2352109378468-3

2 40
A STAR ALLIANCE MEMBER

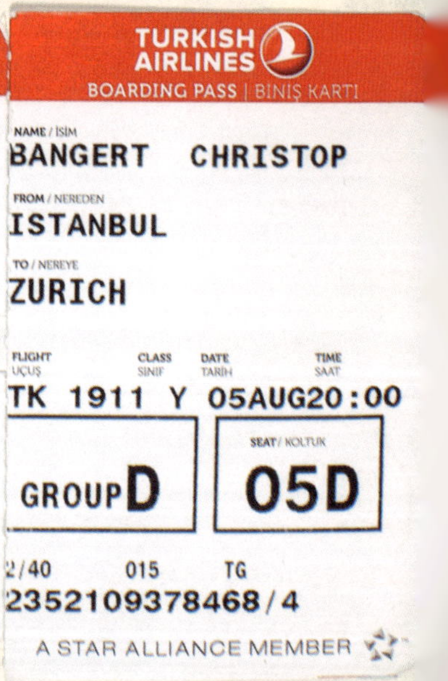

TURKISH AIRLINES
BOARDING PASS | BİNİŞ KARTI

NAME / İSİM
BANGERT CHRISTOP
FROM / NEREDEN
ISTANBUL
TO / NEREYE
ZURICH

FLIGHT UÇUŞ | CLASS SINIF | DATE TARİH | TIME SAAT

TK 1911 Y 05AUG20:00

GROUP D

SEAT / KOLTUK
05D

2/40 015 TG
2352109378468/4

A STAR ALLIANCE MEMBER

Foreijner,s Registration

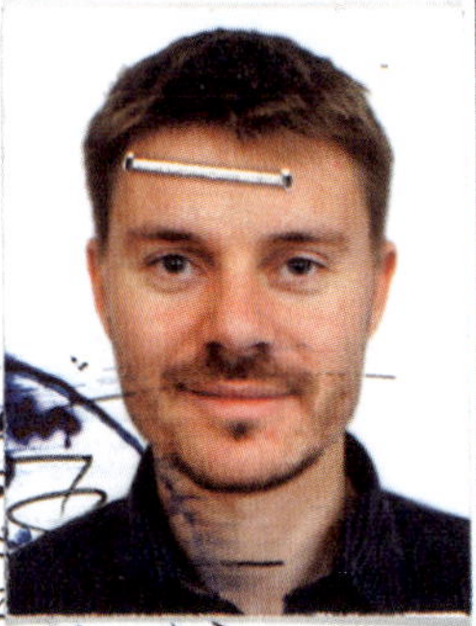

Surname: .... تخلص

Name: .... اسم

Name of country .... نام کشور

Passport number .... نمبر پاسپورت

Vise issuance date .... تاریخ صدور ویزه

Visa expiry date: .... تاریخ ختم ویزه

Lengthofstay: .... مدت اقامت

Date of entry: .... تاریخ دخول

Date of leaving country: .... تاریخ ترک کشور

NO---------

signature

war hero

Instruction

EXIT

Çıkış

Exit

Lütfen bu kartı uçaktan almayınız

Please do not remove this card from aircraft

a Case of veteran Emergency

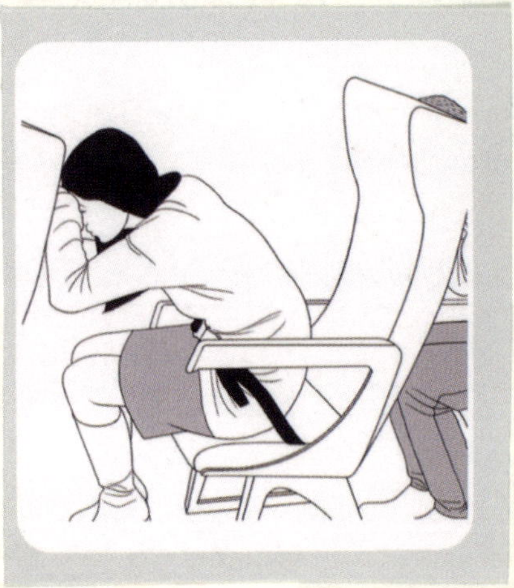

Çıkış / Exit A

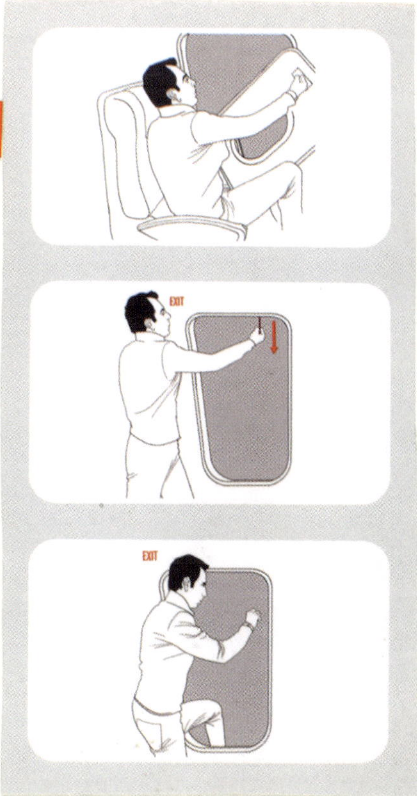

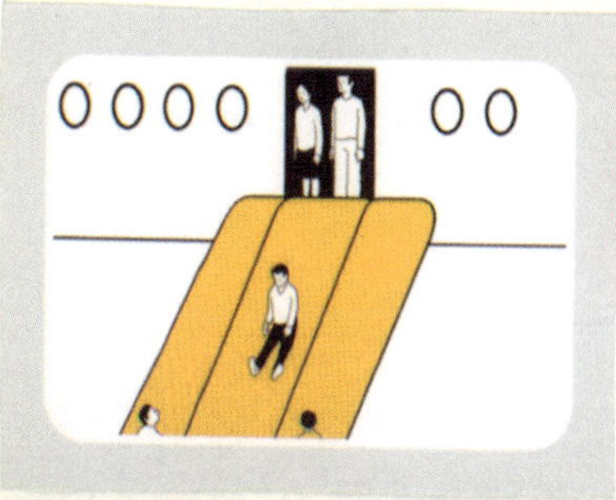

Çıkış / Exit B

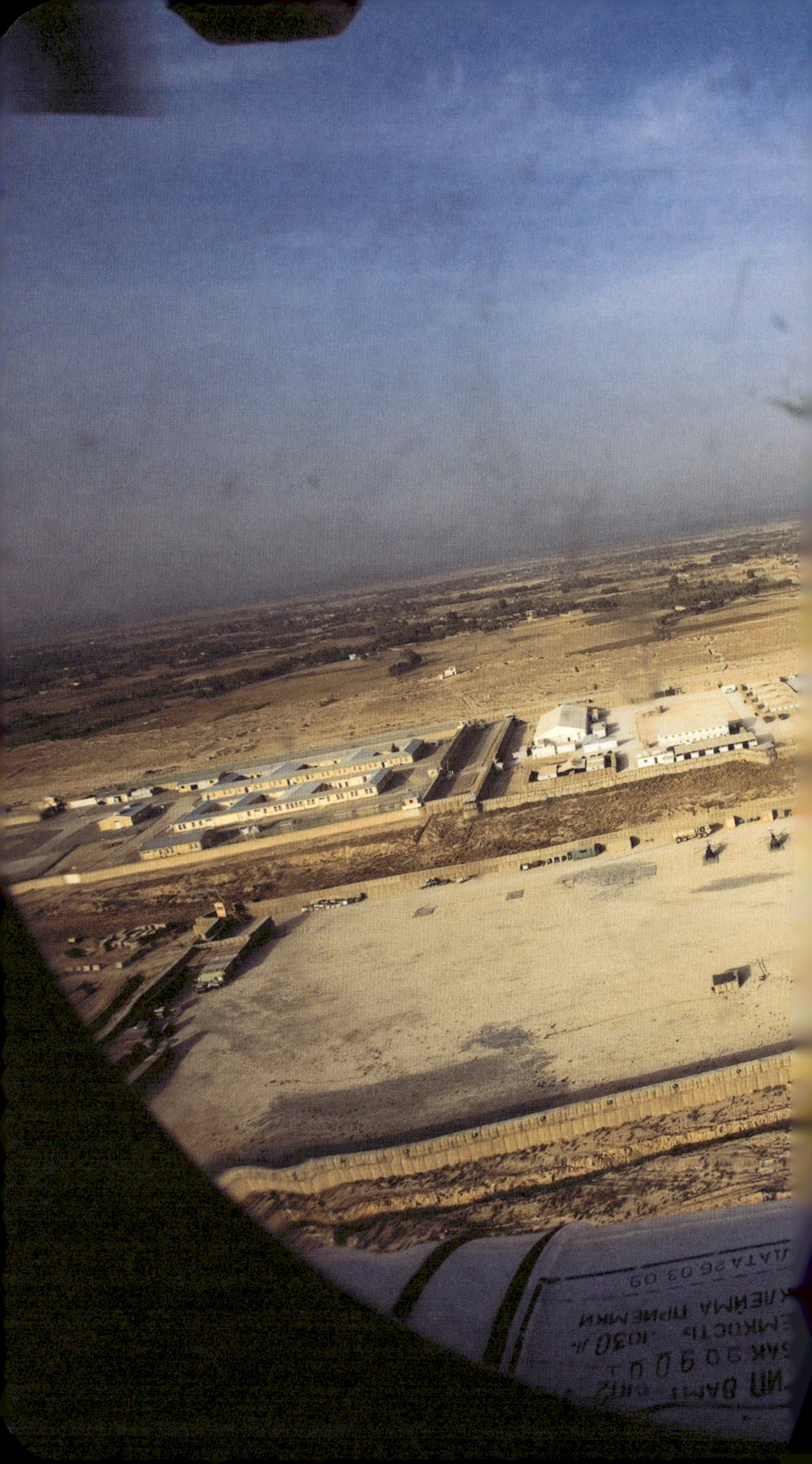

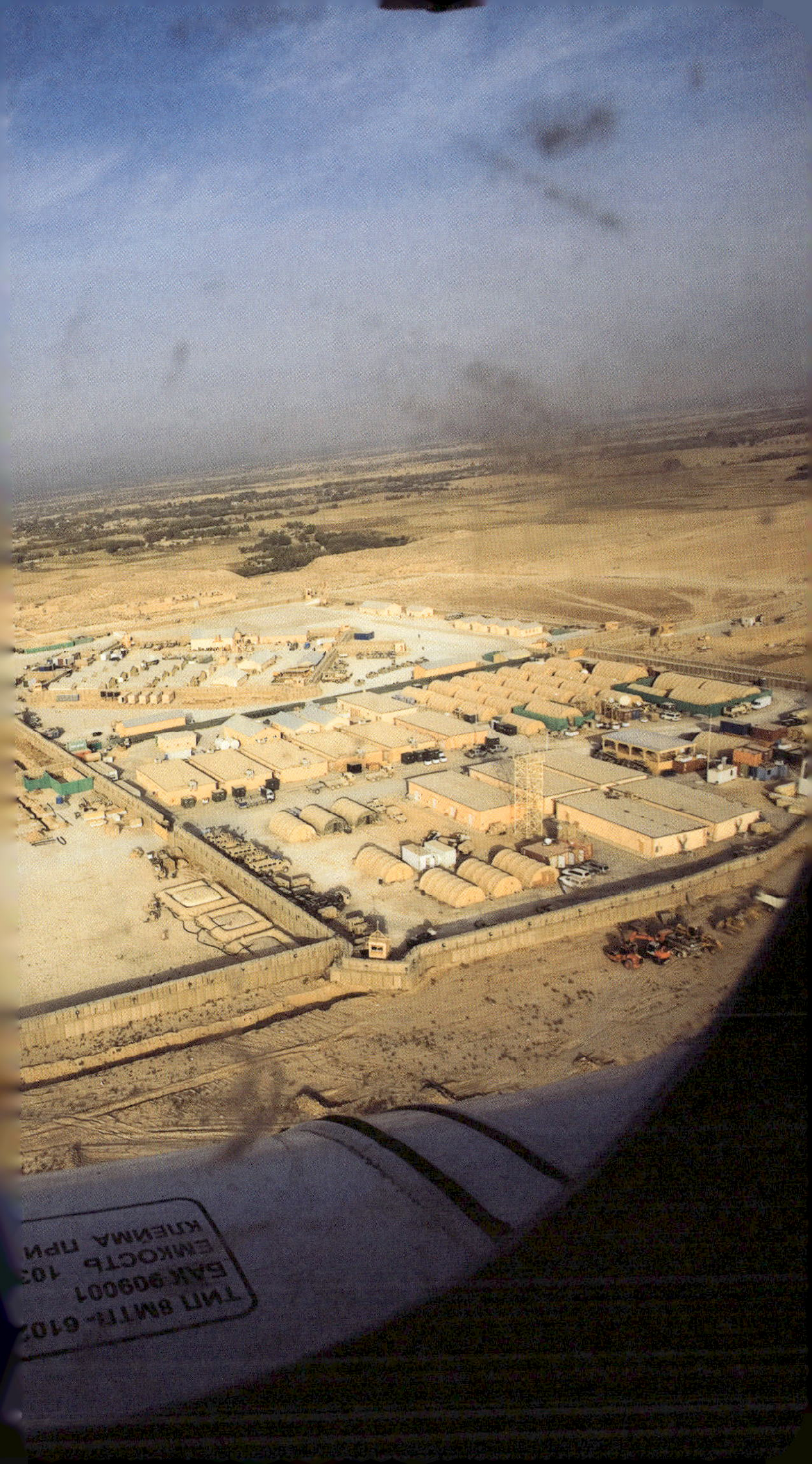

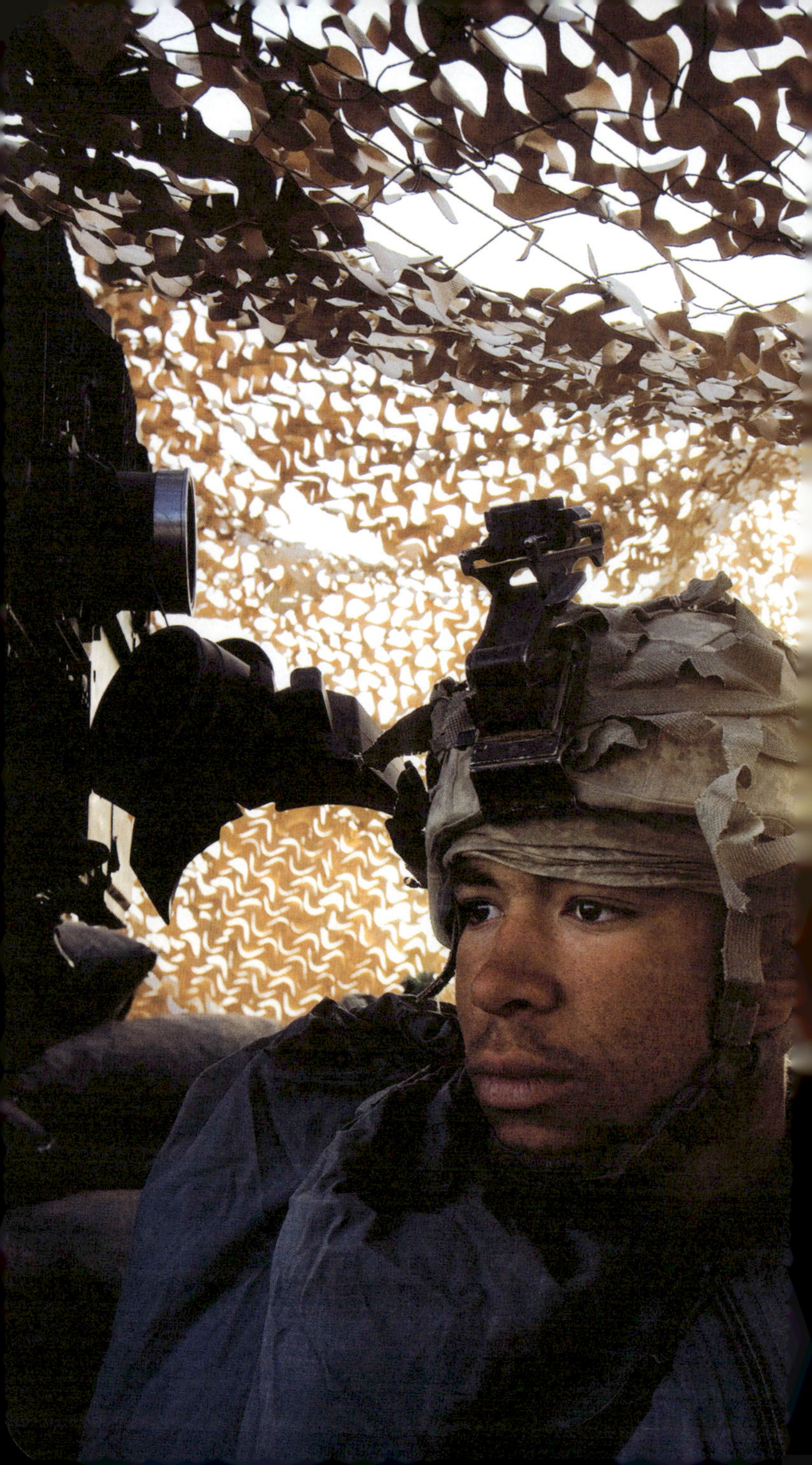

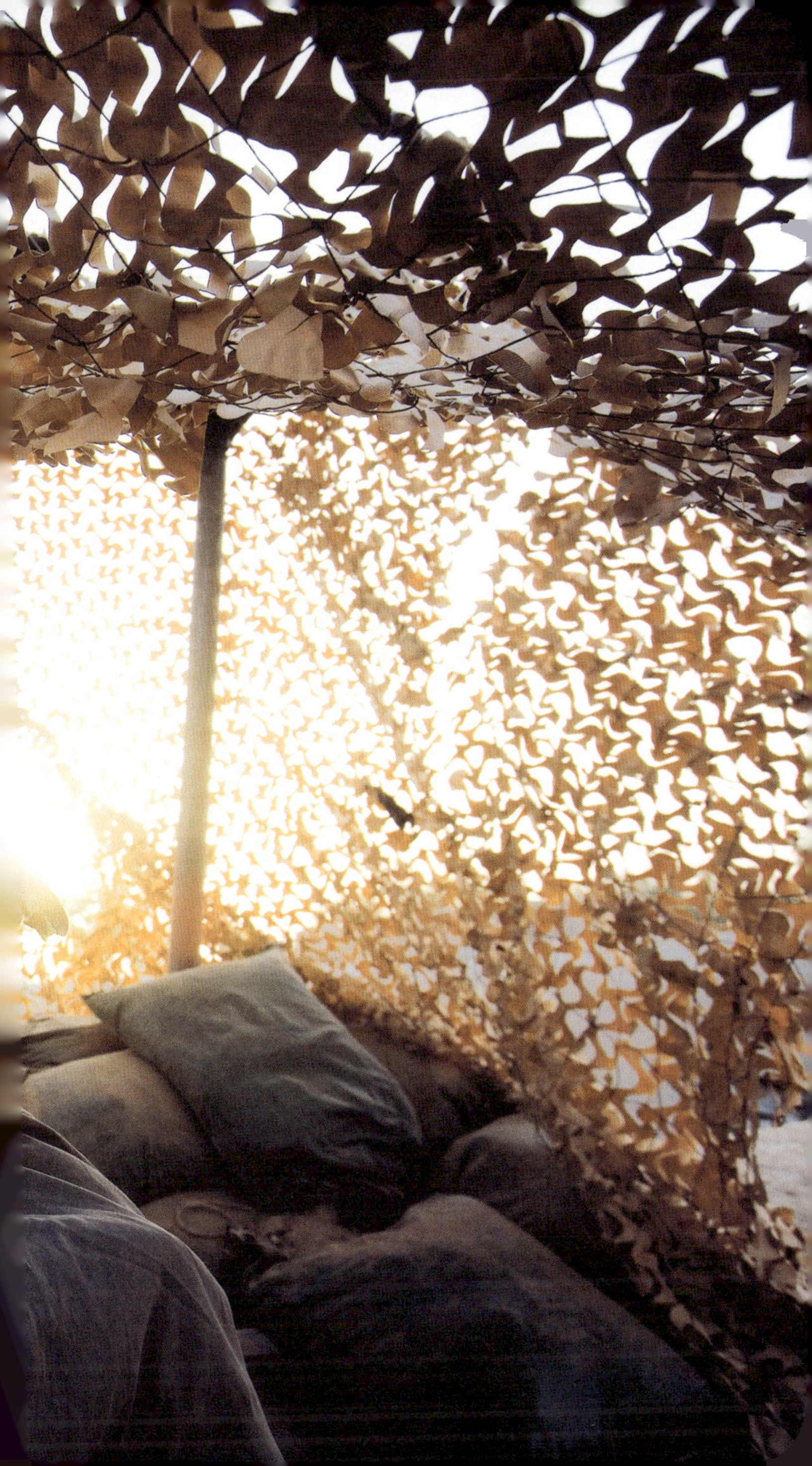

and suddenly

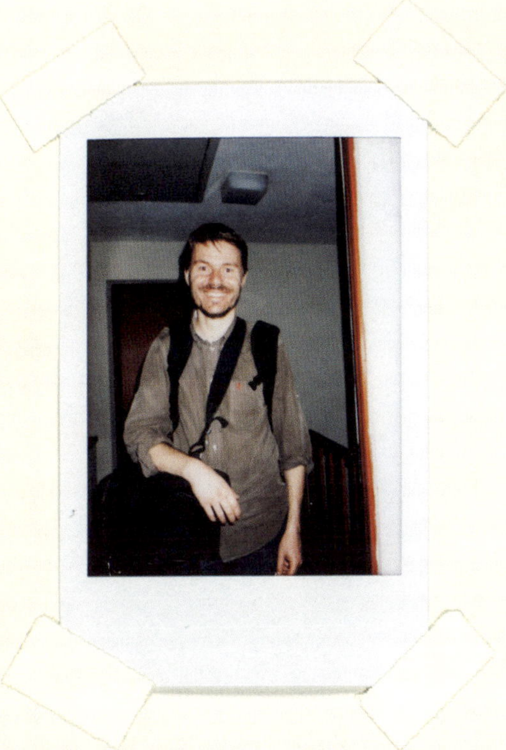

I'm home again.

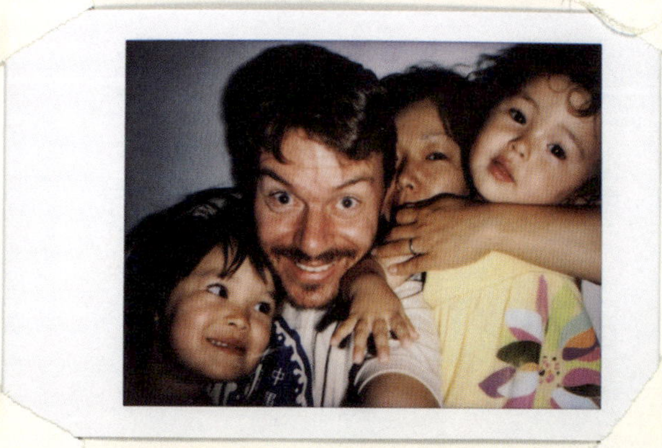

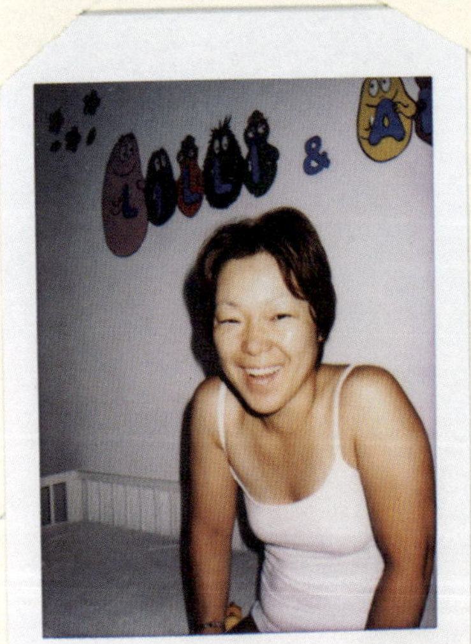

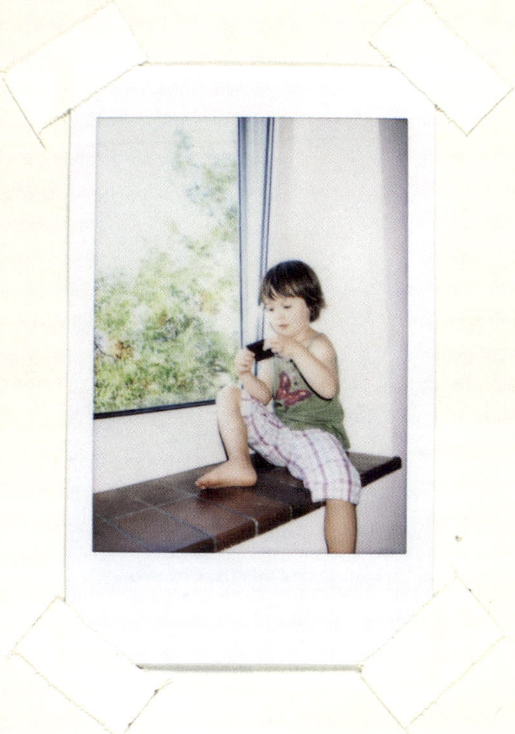

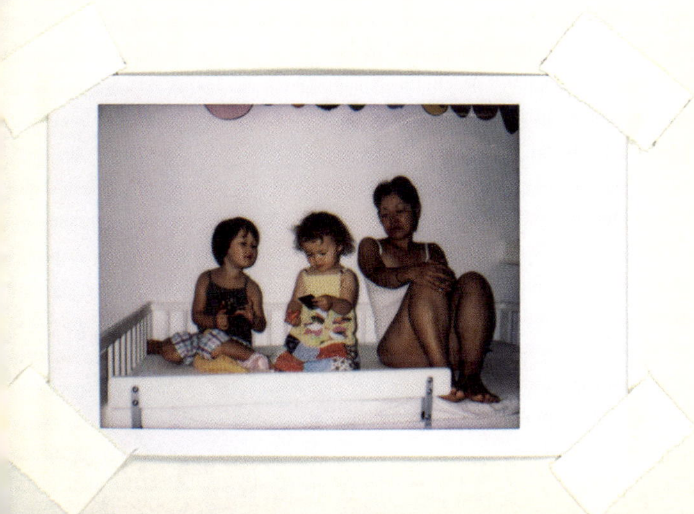

And like every recovering addict there is a part of me that remains nostalgic for war's simplicity and high, even as I cope with the scars it has left behind, mourn the deaths of those I worked with, and struggle with the bestiality I would have been better off not witnessing. There is a part of me—maybe it is a part of many of us—that decided at certain moments that I would rather die like this than go back to the routine of life.

Love may not always triumph, but it keeps us human. It offers the only chance to escape from the contagion of war. Perhaps it is the only antidote. And there are times when remaining human is the only victory possible.

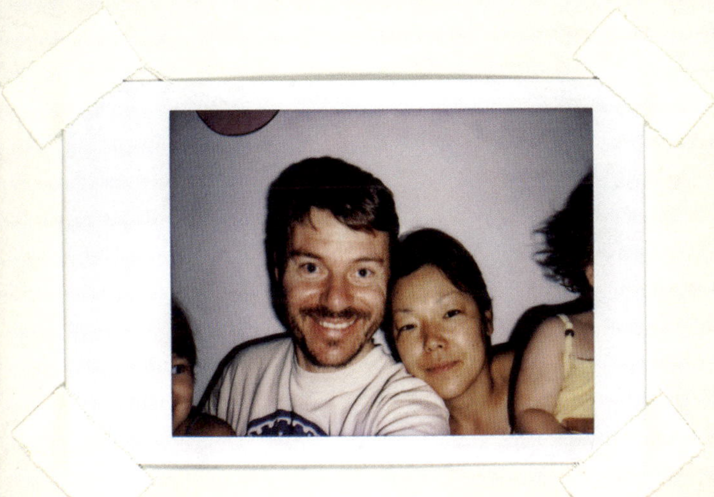

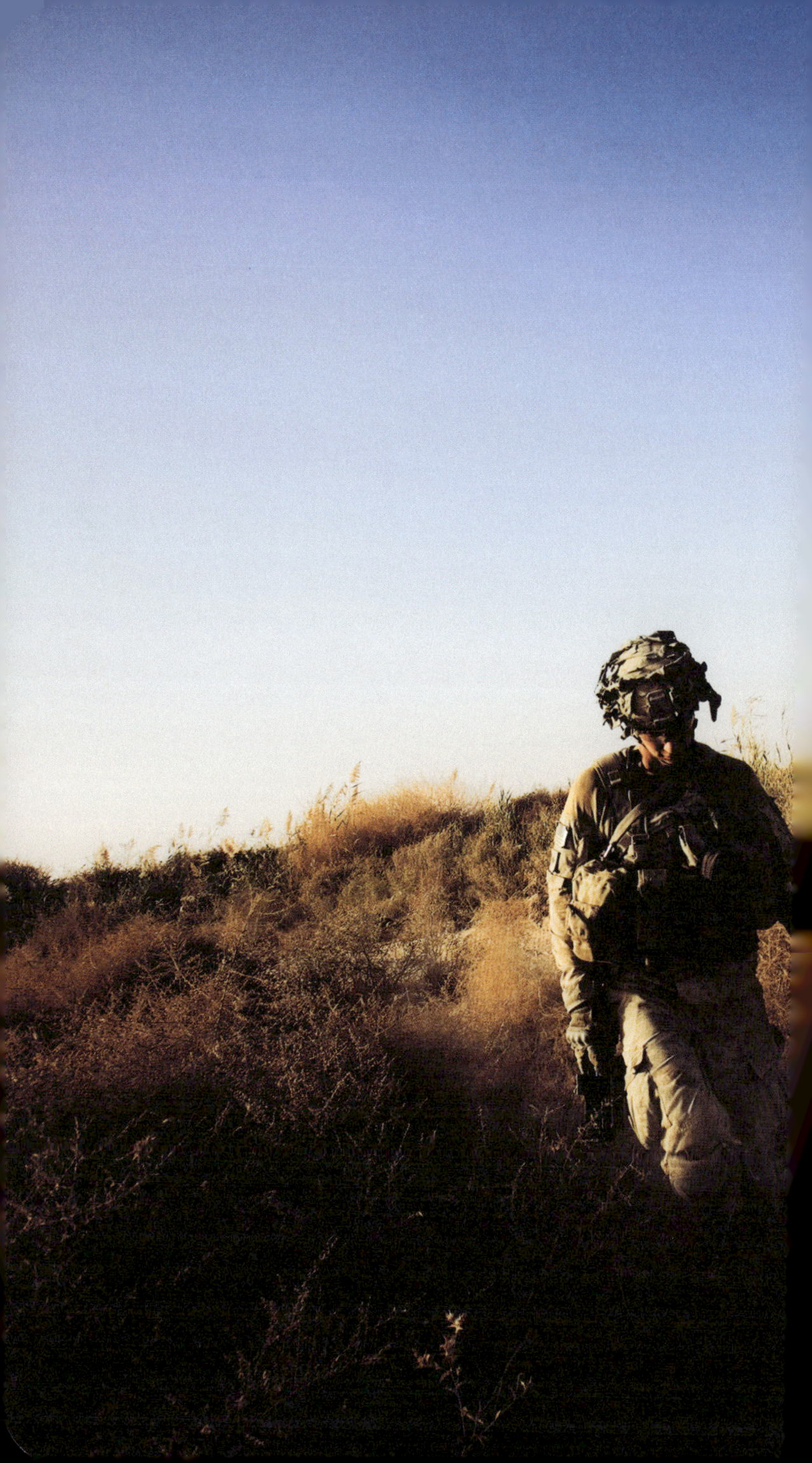

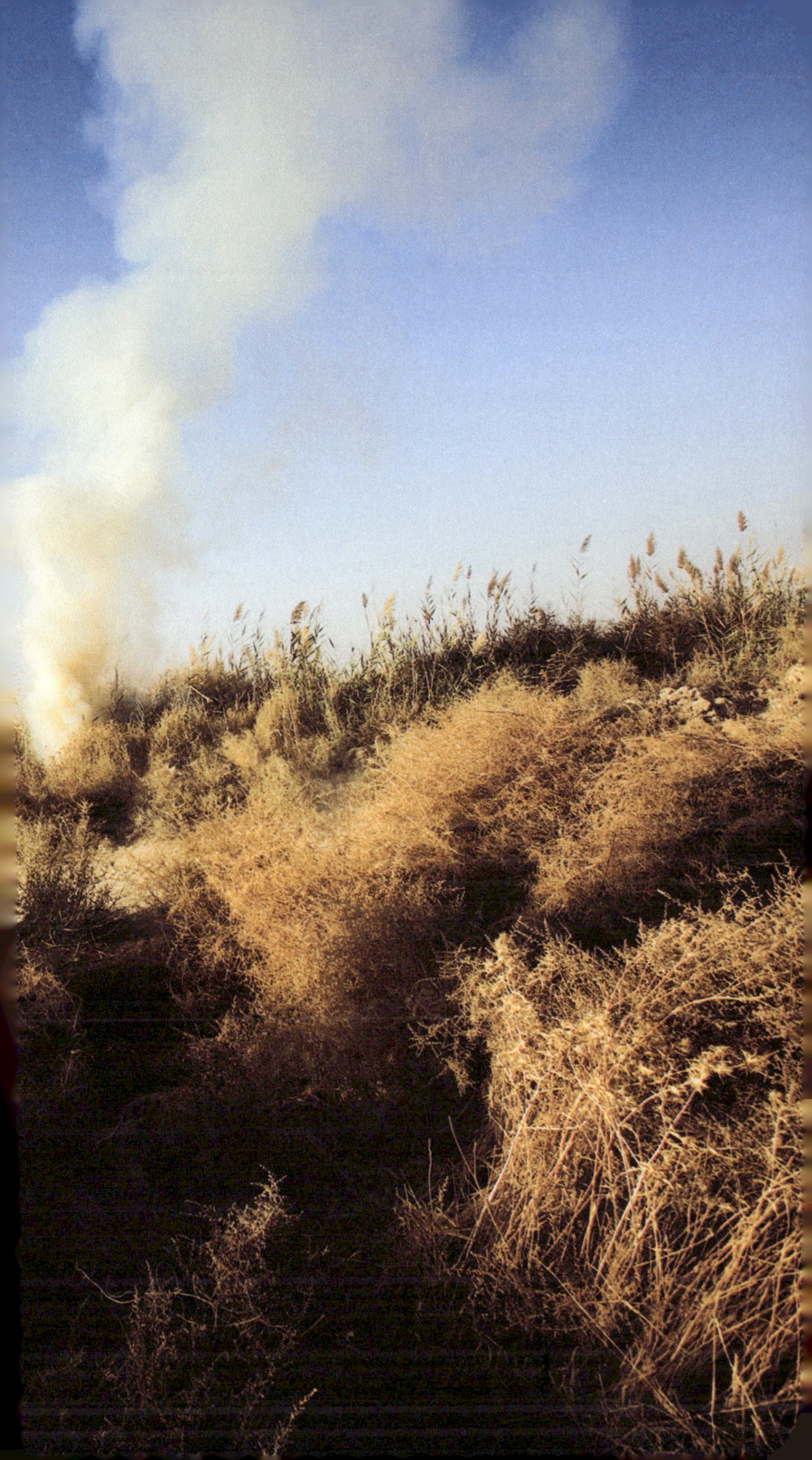

Nobody ever accomplishes anything alone. I would like to thank my wife Chiho for her love and guidance during crazy times. We have been intensively collaborating for nineteen years, and I am deeply grateful that we have each other. For their patience and unconditional love, I thank my daughters Anna and Lilli, as well as my parents Dr. Volkhard and Margot Bangert.

I am grateful to the photo editors who I had the pleasure to work with over the years, particularly Beth Flynn at *The New York Times*, who gave me my first assignment. I had the honor to work alongside incredibly dedicated local and foreign photographers, journalists and media workers in Afghanistan: Rodrigo Abd, Lynsey Addario, Azam Ahmed, Ibrahim Akbari, Max Becherer, Ben Brody, Eric Chauvistré, Warren Coleman, Dexter Filkins, Tyler Hicks, Eros Hoagland, Chris Hondros, Massoud Hossaini, Ruhullah Khapalwak, Ahmad Masood, Rod Nordland, Charlie O'Malley, Richard Oppel, Finbarr O'Reilly, Dr. Sangar Rahimi, Christoph Reuter, Matthew Rosenberg, Alissa Rubin, Sharifullah Sahak, Moises Saman, Joao Silva, Jawad Sukhanyar, James Traub, Tug Wilson, Hikmat Zahed and Habib Zohori.

I created the original journal that this book is based on between June 24 and August 5, 2013 while on assignment for *The New York Times*. It was inspired by the artistic practice of my friend and colleague Rafał Milach, who first introduced me to the instax mini camera. The images that appear in between the handwritten journal pages were taken in Afghanistan between 2010 and 2013. I would like to thank Chris Hedges for writing *War Is a Force That Gives Us Meaning* and Jeff Jacobson for being my photography teacher. This book became my greatly belated bachelor project and earned me a proper academic degree. Sabine an Huef, Kai Jünemann, Marcel René Marburger, Pamela Scorzin, Axel Wehrtmann, Cindy Gates, Roman Bezjak and Karen Fromm: Thank you for your help and encouragement in my darkest moment. To the students of the Fotobus Society: Your support during my long, hard struggle to find a permanent teaching position meant everything to me. I could never have done this alone. Thank you.

Photographs and Texts: Christoph Bangert
Project Management: Kehrer Verlag (Sylvia Ballhause)
Proofreading: Gérard A. Goodrow
Design: Chiho Bangert
Image Processing: Kehrer Design (René Henoch)
Production Management: Kehrer Design (Tom Streicher)

Bibliographic information published by the Deutsche Nationalbibliothek: The Deutsche Nationalbibliothek lists this publication in the Deutsche Nationalbibliografie; detailed bibliographic data is available on the Internet at http://dnb.dnb.de.

Printed and bound in Germany
ISBN 978-3-96900-004-5

Kehrer Heidelberg
www.kehrerverlag.com

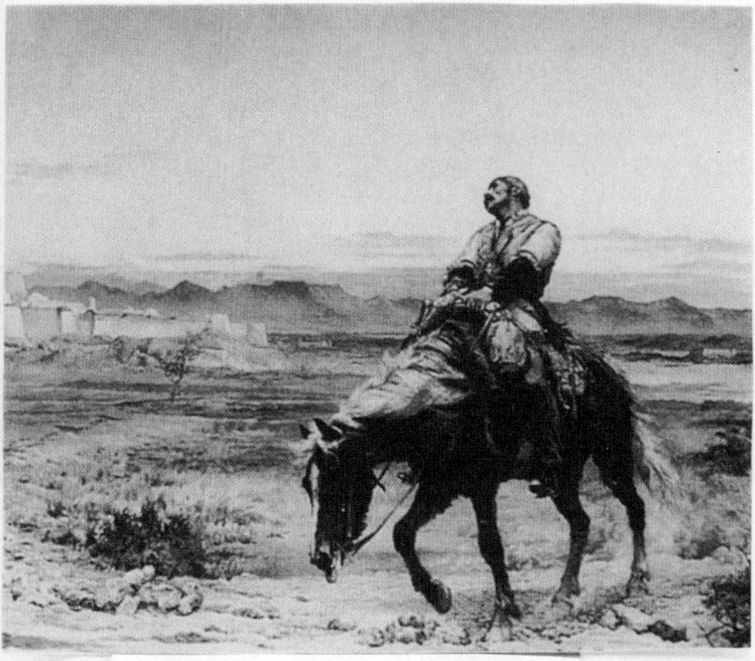

• Afghanistan, Remnant of British Army in 1842. Dr. Brydon

(WAR IS STUPID.)